Walking Rocky Ford and the Arkansas Valley

Walking Rocky Ford and the Arkansas Valley

A Tour of Rocky Ford, Colorado and Vicinity

Supplement to
Rocky Ford, Colorado—A Walk Past Local Doors
published October 2016

David J. Muth

Good Samaritan Village-Loveland Campus
Loveland, Colorado

Walking Rocky Ford and the Arkansas Valley: A Tour of Rocky Ford, Colorado and Vicinity

by David J. Muth

Published by:
Iron Gate Publishing
P.O. Box 999
Niwot, CO 80544
www.irongate.com

All rights reserved. No part of this book may be reproduced or transmitted in any form or by any means, electronic or mechanical, including photocopying, recording or any information storage and retrieval system without written permission from the author, except for the inclusion of brief quotations in a review.

The Publisher of this book makes no representation that it is absolutely accurate or complete. Errors and omissions, whether typographical, clerical or otherwise do sometimes occur and may occur anywhere within the body of this publication. The Publisher does not assume and hereby disclaims any liability to any party for loss or damage by errors or omissions in this publication, whether such errors or omissions result from negligence, accident or any other cause.

The author has used his best efforts in collecting and preparing material, including obtaining permissions for photographs for inclusion in *Walking Rocky Ford and the Arkansas Valley: A Tour of Rocky Ford, Colorado and Vicinity*, but does not warrant that the information herein is complete or accurate, and does not assume, and hereby disclaims, any liability to any person for any loss or damage caused by errors or omissions in *Walking Rocky Ford and the Arkansas Valley: A Tour of Rocky Ford, Colorado and Vicinity*, whether such errors or omissions result from negligence, accident or any other cause.

Copyright © 2022 by Iron Gate Publishing
Printed in the United States of America

ISBN 978-1-68224-180-6

For the People of Rocky Ford

A Pioneer's Introduction to Old Rocky Ford

"As we approached the settlement we came over a little hill and there beside the road was a tiny cemetery of five or six graves, mute evidence of the hardships of the pioneer community.

At a distance of about a mile there was a cluster of rough buildings in some trees along the river. Traveling along the dusty trail we first came to a large rough building with half a dozen guest rooms, a bar and dining room. We learned this rough hotel was managed by Andy Nichols.

A short distance to the east was a blacksmith shop owned by John Swift. Like the hotel it was constructed of cottonwood logs set in the ground on end, with poles laid across for a covering.

Farther north along the river was the trading post of Swink and Russell of the same construction as the other two. A lean-to shed had been added which served as a shop and storage room. North of the store a few steps was a new two room house awaiting the arrival of the Swink family.

Farther east under the bank of a little hill the Mexican family of Jesus Creo, his wife, and brother-in-law lived in a dugout.

Across the river the Barlow-Sanderson stage line had two small buildings."

Anonymous author

Published in the *Enterprise,* December 27, 1888

Notes: The *'tiny cemetery'* was likely approached from the east as the Pioneer trailed on the south river bank. Known well-traveled trails were on the river's north bank but description indicates site of the ford buildings were about a mile distant continuing on the same *'dusty trail.'* This would place the traveler near midway between the settlement at the ford and site of Dye Reservoir north of the river. A reservoir or lake may not have been in existence at his passing since such a large body was not mentioned. A lake would not have been detected from the south side of the river because of lower elevation of the south bank.

Biblical description *'Dust to dust'* and future floods likely completely obliterated the cemetery and its graves since it is not known or spoken of by later pioneers and settlers.

The Swink and Russell log stockade store was later replaced by an adobe structure.

In Appreciation
Of the *ENTERPRISE* Chroniclers of Rocky Ford.

Acknowledgments

Editors:
Harry V. Alexander, 1887
    David W. Barkley, 1890
        Richard C. Herrick, 1890
            Charles S. Linn, 1891
                David W. Barkley, 1893
                    Will R. Monkman, 1907
                        James B. Woody, 1944
                          [merged with Rocky Ford *Tribune*, 1947]
                          James W. Martin, 1949
                              Miles F. Porter, III, 1950
                                [merged out *Enterprise*]

Of all vintage Rocky Ford newspapers *Enterprise was* the chronicler most consistently published the longer period of time. Publishing began June 1, 1887 with consolidated *Ordway News* September 3, 1896 to May 20, 1897, ceasing publication Mar. 17, 1950; began as *Rocky Ford Daily Gazette-Topic and Enterprise* Mar. 17, 1950, and was renamed *Rocky Ford Daily Gazette* Aug. 16, 1954.

A First for George Washington Swink

Certificate facsimile from *Rocky Ford As the School Children See It*

Timber Culture Certificate No. 1, granted November 13, 1887 by president Grover Cleveland. Trees planted were the first near Rocky Ford, once a treeless area except for large arroyos and river and stream bottoms. Town incorporation papers filed just prior in Bent County Court, Las Animas, August 10, recorded August 19, 1887 in Denver.

Three thousand cottonwood trees were planted in town by city council in 1888 in a separate action after the G.W. Swink Claim.

A Letter by a First Resident

"Perhaps the most important feature in Mr. Swink's undertaking in founding a town was his highly commendable outlay of time and expense in the matter of planting the large number of cottonwood trees now grown to large size, and the subject of much appreciation to every citizen and visitor".

William A. Matthews

Published in the *Enterprise,* December 27, 1888

Note: William A. Matthews came to the Old Ford from Illinois in 1872 where he had known the Swink family.

Swink and Russell 1871 Store

The first store after the trading post at Old Rocky Ford near the *ford* of the Arkansas River was visited by many traveling west and south. The nearby ford was traversed easily in normal river flow but both the store and ford disappeared during a devastating 1921 flood.

Photos courtesy *Rocky Ford Public Museum*.

Note: The first trading post was of stockade construction with poles supporting brush for a roof.

Contents

PREFACE	xiii
INTRODUCTION	1
PART 1: A Walk In The City Citizen Pursuits	3
PART 2: A Walk In The Country Significant Events	77
PART 3: A Random Walk Different Directions	131
Postscript People Who Influenced	167
Afterword The Author Experience	177
Notes Of Interest	179
Sources	183
Indices 　Name 　Place and Subject	 185 189
Addendum	197

A Place of Industry

American Beet Sugar Company was in the production campaign of 1905, five years from its beginning in 1900. The economies of Rocky Ford and the Arkansas Valley were enhanced significantly by the beet sugar industry.

ebay.com

N.W. Terry's brick yard at east end of Maple Avenue supplied the first one million bricks for the factory building with more to come later for smaller buildings and large warehouses. Rocky Ford was growing, now eighteen years from incorporation and town charter. At opening sugar campaign in 1900 the population of town and environs was 2,018. By 1910 it was 3,230.

Preface

Events that were not fully reported in the news are part of this narrative. Not everything about a story is printed, often missing is the ending. Readers, for example, are left uninformed of the fate of the young woman seen possibly contemplating suicide at a local lake. Conjecture enters.

Commitment of column space affects newspaper economy. Therefore, in the absence of more news, searching for facts or details of a person's activities may foster reader speculation. Even with *Ockham's razor* applied, that may not allow discovery of truth.

My goal was to present several short articles and at the same time offer my speculation on the subjects. To do so I have included many clips from the news, the *Enterprise* and other Valley papers, hopefully to spare *razor* use. Readers will find the subjects change nearly every page.

Rocky Ford, Colorado–A Walk Past Local Doors, published October, 2018, is about the town's history in photos of businesses and some residences. References to that volume are included in this narrative to reduce duplication of subject or theme matter.

Reading historical news accounts for this narrative has brought out many events around town, the countryside and in the Arkansas Valley. Topics are not taken chronologically but randomly from newspaper pages, principally, the Rocky Ford *Enterprise*. Many subjects were omitted because information was lacking a name, title, or brief reference. In summary, this narrative is a random collection of former news items of the City and the Valley.

Editions of the *Enterprise* digitized and placed online begin August 31, 1893 inclusive to December 29, 1916. Years not included were 1887 through 1892 and 1917 through 1950 of the total publication life of the *Enterprise*. Those issue years are not found in libraries today. Sanborn Maps have also been useful in several illustrations, aiding understanding of a topic visually.

I have much interest in events of the first and formative years of Rocky Ford, 1887 through 1892. Unfortunately, many of those details are no longer available. My hope is that the reader finds interest among those items that are included here as a series of brief essays in

Walking Rocky Ford and the Arkansas Valley

Sanborn Map Company

Sanborn Fire Insurance maps are detailed city plans, usually at scales of 50 or 100 feet to an inch. They show individual building footprints, complete with construction details such as building material, number of stories, building use, and more. The maps were originally produced for insurance underwriters, but today are used by researchers in history, urban geography, architectural history, and other fields. They are commonly referred to as Sanborn maps because the Sanborn company was the largest national producer, covering the United States, Mexico, and Canada.

Sanborn map collection for Rocky Ford consists of a series of large-scale maps, dating from 1895. Maps in general depict the commercial, industrial, and residential sections of about twelve thousand cities and towns in the United States, Canada, and Mexico. Information of building construction was detailed for each map set with the fire insurance industry in mind. Information was used by the industry to set coverage rates.

A series of maps for Rocky Ford was developed beginning 1895 through May 1936. A complete collection includes maps from 1895, 1901, 1906, 1911, 1919, and September 1929 thru May 1936. Map keys detailed building materials, size, number of stories, and often, use of the structure.

Sanborn Company discontinued this type of map-making service, published its last catalogue and downsized operations to continue in other than city and town mapping types of business. Several Sanborn Map sections of Rocky Ford are included in this text.

Ockham's (Occam's, Ocham's) **Razor** is a rule in philosophy and science that assumptions made to explain something must not be multiplied beyond what is necessary. *Ockham's Razor* is attributed to English Franciscan friar William of Ockham, c. 1287–1347, a scholar in theology and a philosopher who favored simplicity to defend the idea of divine miracles. His figurative razor is used to remove contending ideas about something until one remains which requires the fewest assumptions. Also called *Law of Parsimony* (thrift), a rule that the simplest of several possible explanations is usually the best one.

Introduction

The Arkansas River Valley, lying among our part of the Great Plains, did not attract great attention of those coming from the East. It seems that most, taking a first look at the treeless place, decided to go farther West, or South, or North, or even back, but many stayed.

The mountains were in view when pioneers left western Kansas Territory and entered what would become Colorado Territory in 1861. The impulse was to continue westward which seemed far more inviting, promising a more fascinating and productive future. After all, gold was discovered there and that meant possibility of wealth. They didn't fully realize that another type of wealth was flowing in the rivers they traveled near.

Those who stayed on the Plains learned of their resources, and promise, especially when water was applied. Moving off traveled routes they discovered beauty in the canyons and river courses, a fertile plain right under their feet when it was cultivated. Insightful individuals saw the possibilities when the first crops rewarded them with variety and abundance.

Mankind, in this century and the last, have lived enough of history to have experienced much of the development in the Arkansas River Valley, how it has flourished to now. But writing about these things I have encountered limited written historical and photographic record, especially the latter, of times and events that made our town. Few originals survive in photographic record.

Among the earliest photos were the adobe store of Asa Russell and George Washington Swink and the original ford in 1871. There appears no name of the photographer. The scenes were depicted as of the date given, obviously some time after construction of the store. Photos may have been the work of an itinerant photographer traveling and paying his way by sale of his work.

In contrast, reams of printed history, along with an abundant photographic record, are found everywhere in state archives of even the most rudimentary town or settlement in the mountains. It is evident photographers of the times did not find interest here on the plains. So, it has been a bit limiting to produce a narrative based generally upon words to describe adequately the abundant, silent but eloquent detail of a photograph. Even so, we will make do.

Eighth Street Crossing Proposal

Enterprise Editor issued a reminder, at least a year after the first interest was expressed by citizens, regarding an Eighth Street Crossing.

Considerable expense would be attached to the project, if ever taken up by town council and the Santa Fe.

Sanborn map of 1906 shows the tool house near the rails and at least three other locations where businesses would site in the future.

Enterprise, July 13, 1899

> —A year or more ago a movement was started to open Eighth street between Elm and Walnut streets. This opening would require the building of a bridge across the Rocky Ford ditch and the removal of the Santa Fe tool house. To aid in paying the expenses over $50 was subscribed by interested citizens. For almost a year the mattter has been quiet. Interest in the opening of this street should be revived and the work pushed to completion as the change is demanded by the interests of adjacent property holders and the town at large.

During the years of extension of streets and Avenues, thought of rail crossings were tempered by needs of safety and cost. Eventually, seven rail crossings were allowed; 2nd, 5th, 7th, 9th, Main, 10th and 12th streets, but not Eighth Street.

Godding House (banker) eventually to be Ustick Funeral Home.

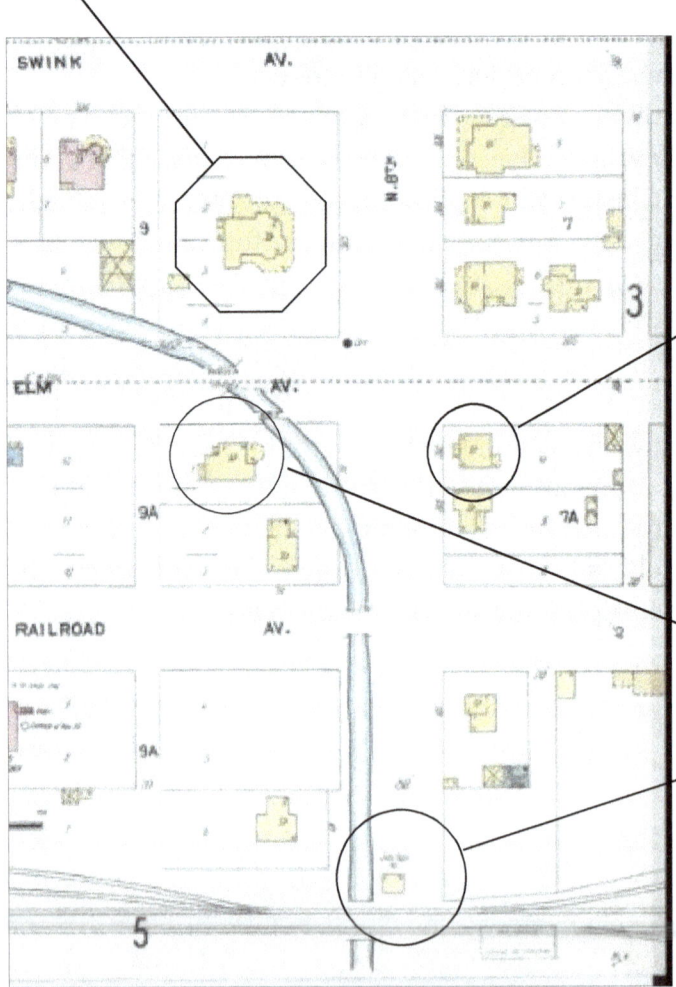

Sanborn Map section, September, 1906
Walnut Avenue at map bottom.

Auto Clinic site in later years

An Eighth Street crossing was once considered an important ingress and egress route to the town's business district. Citizens who offered fifty dollars to get things started never saw progress to it.

Rocky Ford Co-op Creamery

Santa Fe tool shed similar to one depicted in *Rocky Ford, Colorado-A Walk Past Local Doors*, p. 273.
Rocky Ford Canal adjacent rails.

Though the tool shed remained an obstacle in 1898-1899 it was later removed and the city conformed to the decision for no crossing. Impetus had also waned.

Part 1: A Walk in the City

Citizen Pursuits

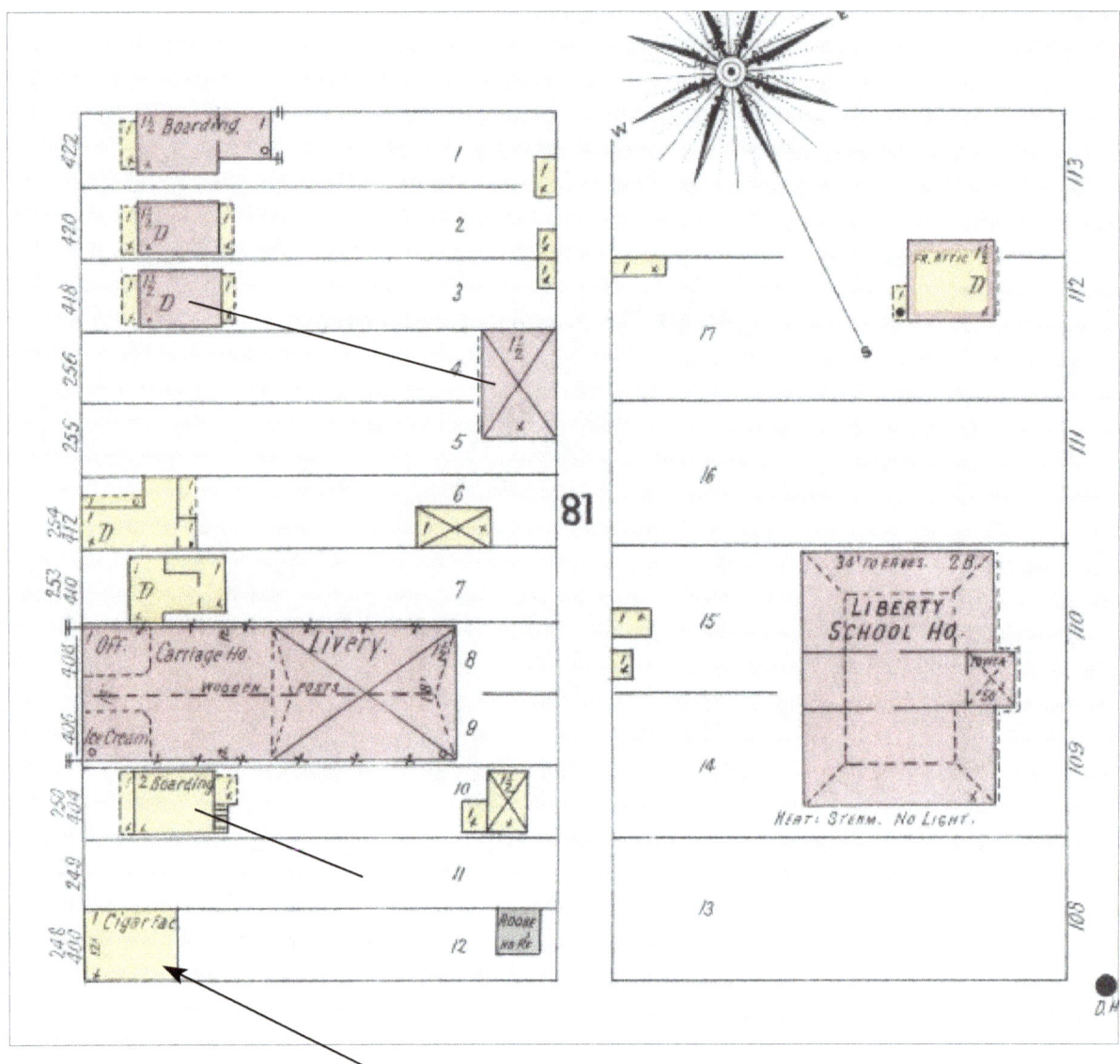

Swink Avenue at bottom, Chestnut Avenue at top. Main Str. at left and Tenth Street at right, an alleyway at center.

George Higgin's 1900 Livery was incorrectly sited in *Rocky Ford, Colorado-A Walk Past Local Doors. It* was built at 406-408-*left column*, *above*, as on this Sanborn Map of 1901. Livery was a large carriage house with office in the front, now extant as B & AIE Center. An ice cream parlor was in the south store front. Livery was occupied by three successive automobile companies after Higgins' retirement. Effie Hall's boarding house-*marker*-at 404 N Main was razed.

North Main at 400 in 1895 to c. 1900 was site of a small cigar factory-*arrow*-shown on this 1901 map where directories for 1911, 1914 and 1915 list *W.H. Russell, manufacturer of cigars*. Retail outlets were Funk's Confectionery at 307, 312, or 315 N Main Street. Swink & Swink Cigars was also an outlet, business probably also known as *Swink Recreation Parlor*, site not clear.

Sanborn maps for Rocky Ford were published in 1895, 1901, 1906, 1911, 1919, and September 1929 thru May 1936. There is a delay of map distribution thereby not showing some building changes. Map series discontinued for the US in 1977 when insurance companies ended their use for fire underwriting.

North Main Street at 400

Building extant at 400 N Main was originally a garage with a diagonal drive-under front corner at Main and Swink. Building construction began December 1915, continuing into 1916. Garage had a gas pump on the corner, cavernous interior with high, open rafters, concrete floor with maintenance pit, large depressed floor drain, large exterior doors to the rear at the alleyway and on Swink Avenue to accommodate large vehicles.

The large brick building center of left column-*map on previous page*- with diagonals indicating a stable was Higgins Livery. A small house at 402 North Main was vacant in 1901, razed later for the large building extant at 400. North Main at 404 -*line marker*-was the home of Mrs. Effie Hall who rented five rooms to individuals.

Buildings north of the Higgins livery were homes, two were frame-*yellow*-and three of brick-*red*. One brick building was site of veterinary surgeon Paul Keck at 418 N Main, and his small brick livery-*connected by marker*-at the alleyway on rear of lots at 414-416. This apparently his location before his move to the larger Grand Valley Livery.

Far right brick building was Liberty School at 401 North Tenth Street. Position of Higgins Livery in relation to Liberty School is also given page 51 in John Doll," . . . *west of the new school on Main Street* . . . " or, directly across the alleyway. Two small frame structures on the alleyway were outhouses replaced eventually by outdoor water closets, indicated on the 1911 Sanford map.

Sanborn map of 1895 showed a small frame building labeled *GAR* [Grand Army of the Republic] a fraternal order of Union veterans of the Civil War, where Liberty School was built. Activities of the organization were noted in several early council proceedings.

A metal-clad frame building appeared later north of the school. At this time in Rocky Ford several buildings, large and small, were clad with corrugated sheet iron. An example of such a building was the business of Frank H. Boraker at the intersection of Railroad Avenue-100 block of N Main Street-page 16 of *Rocky Ford, Colorado-A Walk Past Local Doors*.

Fenton's Drug Store, 202-204 North Main Street stocked several non-drug items, such as oils and oil-based paints stored in the rear of the store. Fire started there September 8, 1898 among the paints that involved the entire 200 block east side of North Main Street. Firefighters soon arrived but were hampered by low water pressure and the corrugated iron covering of the building preventing much water reaching the fire. Use of sheet metal clad for buildings came under disfavor as a result of this experience.

Note: City administration requested reservoir water be used for irrigation odd-numbered days when mains were filled from Catlin Canal. No irrigation was allowed when mains received well water. Citizens were asked to refrain using water from mains when the fire signal sounded until a pumping station was installed in 1907 to provide additional pressure for fire hoses.

Little White Schoolhouse, built in 1877, was removed c. 1897-1898 to 407 North Twelfth Street prior construction of Liberty School. It was until recently the annex to *La Clinica del Valle'*. A small cemetery was also moved which involved at least two grave sites established the year of the school. Mr. Ben Vroman and a twelve year old daughter of James Lowe were on horseback to Rocky Ford in July when struck by lightning. They were interred on the grounds near the school. Removal of the graves to the southeast corner of Hillcrest Cemetery took place in 1887, re-interred among a number of Rocky Ford pioneer family names.

Ford Company Garage

Businesses at the intersection of Swink Avenue and Main Street have changed few times over many years. First at this intersection was the two-story adobe saloon of John Mitch and James K. Dye. *Enterprise* edition December 15, 1887 describes it being built at "Swink Road and Main Street." Saloon existed no more than eight years when Sanford map of 1895 shows a cigar factory at the location.

Location is unclear in the news in establishing the *street number* of the new Ford Garage built in 1916. The quadrant was not specified but possibly was the N E corner formerly occupied by the adobe saloon and later by the Russell cigar factory. That 12' x 18' frame structure shown on the 1895 Sanford map would have been easily moved by 1915 when the Ford company began construction of their new garage in December.

The cigar factory was reported active in the City Directory for 1911, 1914, and 1915 but address not given. Sanborn map of 1919 described an automobile agency with capacity for 30 cars at 400 North Main Street, following Mr. Russell's cigar business-see p. 22.

Raised brick pattern in the construction indicated in the small article was visible as a design pattern to be exposed after stucco was applied. Appearance was of protruding squares, lines and circles.

> The Ford Company has commenced the building of a pretentious brick garage on the corner of Swink avenue and Main street.
>
> *Enterprise,* December 1, 1916

Knights of Pythias chartered in 1896, opened in 1902 on the N W quadrant of Swink Avenue and Main Street, remains at 401 North Main Street. Building preceded the garage at 400 N Main aross the street by at least 14 years.

North Main Street at 313-315 on the S W quadrant was occupied by Funk's Soda Fountain in 1914, preceding the Ford Garage at least two years. The SE quadrant was site of Bruse's Variety Store at 312 North Main Street, dates of existence not known. The site has long been vacant; demise of Bruse's brick building not known. In the 1940s that site, 312 North Main Street, was parking space for the first Rocky Ford Safeway Store next door at 310 North Main Street.

Occupied corner addresses at the Swink and Main Street intersection secures the location of the new Ford Garage at the NE quadrant, or 400 North Main Street.

Building was previously known in the *Enterprise* as a garage, lacking identifying ownership, construction date and street number. It had a diagonal drive-under front corner at Main and Swink. Garage had a gas pump on the corner, high ceiling with exposed heavy wooden rafters, concrete floor and maintenance pit, large grated floor drain, double exterior doors to the rear at the alleyway and a sliding door on Swink Avenue to accommodate large vehicles.

Note: In 1916, except for minor changes, Ford Model T was an extension of the 1915 model. The 1916 Model T was offered as a touring car, runabout, town car, sedan, coupe and military ambulance.

Ford 1916
Model T Touring Car

Keck Veterinary Hospital

Buildings on the east side of 400 block North Main Street in 1901 were homes, two were frame and three of brick. A brick building was another site of veterinary surgeon Paul Keck at 418 N. Main, with a small brick livery at the alleyway on rear of lots at 414-416.

Dr. Keck moved to this building on Walnut Avenue in 1907, an adobe built before 1901, weathered several years at time of photo.

It was sited near the Rocky Ford ditch, south side of Walnut Avenue at 900-904.

Building was George Higgins' first livery beginning June 29, 1899. He moved to 406-408 North Main in 1900 and built with brick. That building-modified-is now the B & AIE Center.

Enterprise inset below from September 27, 1907

Building in these photos housed Eclipse Livery in 1901. After another name change to Grand Valley Livery, became the office of Dr. Paul P. Keck - *inset*.

Livery fronts on Walnut Avenue, side view at right faced Ninth Street. *Brick here* describes adobe rather than kiln-fired.

Note: 400 North Main is incorrectly identified built by George Higgins in *Rocky Ford, Colorado-A Walk Past Local Doors*. Sanborn Company Maps place location of his livery at 406-408 N Main.

Dr. P. P. Keck, veterinarian, arrived Tuesday from Stratton, Colo., and has opened an office in the Grand Valley Livery Barn. Dr. Keck is a student of the South Dakota Agricultural College and for the past five years has practiced his profession with marked success. He bears excellent recommendations and should soon build up a splendid practice here.

Photos courtesy: Archives and Special Collections, Colorado State University Libraries, Colorado State University.

Dickenson & Davis Groceries & Provisions and Central Market

Photo courtesy of Rocky Ford Public Museum

Albert Lee in doorway stands with Mr. Dickenson, (R). Mr. Davis is not identified but may be the poser behind the Central Market delivery rig, possibly serving both businesses. Dates of business startup given for the neighbors are August 2, 1907 for Dickenson & Davis, 977 RR Avenue, who closed December 26, 1907 and June 21, 1907, for Central Meat Market, at 975 Railroad Avenue. Location of these businesses with odd numbered addresses placed them between North Main Street on the north side of Railroad Avenue toward Tenth Street.

Central Market advertised as a meat market by A. Lee, proprietor. Dickenson & Davis market advertised groceries and provisions next door. Fire destroyed eight businesses of Martin Block April 5, 1912 all located on Railroad Avenue beginning rear of Maxwell Building at 200 North Main Street east to Tenth Street. None were ever known to rebuild.

Leroy's Market
Built in 1905 at 723 South Eighth Street, this building, was the Leroy Saulmon market that served a growing neighborhood for many years south of the 1915-1916 Lincoln School. The School eventually was a casualty of downsizing and District reorganization and the building at 601 South Eighth Street would become the School District R-2 Administration Office.

propertyrecord.com

Beek's Grocery
The location at 1100 Pine Avenue is the junction with Eleventh Street where it angles southward to meet Twelfth Street-State Highway 71 near Pioneer Nursing Home.

Bertram and Maude Beeks operated their business for many years before retirement and return to their former home in Missouri. Their offer of credit to patrons during the lean WW II years was often the way many families were able to provide the basics for their families. Gasoline and kerosene were pumped near the column.

realtor.com

White's Grocery

Located at 611 Chestnut, the building is extant though long ago closed as a grocery. The proprietor catered primarily to the Hispanic population in packaged dry foods, some canned and shelf products.

The building today presents a stepped facade front, a door and a steel plate above, anchoring a crack in the facade. Years of memories for many patrons are now sealed behind its windows and covered with a heavy coat of white paint.

Engle Grocery

Property once owned by town pioneers at 300 South Third Street, extant. South of the brick home, later the property of the Engle family, was a small building-*arrow*-at 303 South Third with a peaked roof [*now behind the present-day Quonset*]. Building once was Maude Engle's single-room grocery.

As for other small Mom and Pops, inventory was limited to basic foods, breads, canned goods, packaged food and little or no refrigeration.

Charles J. Engle, Maude's son, with the author brewed beer in the late 1950s in the former grocery while students and room-mates at Otero Junior College. Product, not intended for public consumption, was dispensed, bottled and consumed entirely in quality control tests.

Photos, *Zillow.com*

Bailey's Grocery (no photo)

Bailey's was a small, narrow house at 608 Chestnut Avenue across the street from White's. It was de-constructed several years ago, the site now the back lawn of a neighboring property. Partially visible between the curb and sidewalk on Chestnut Avenue nearest that property are remnants of the concrete pad once before the store entrance.

Entrance off the pad of the two story house was through a curved recessed set-back before the door, all under a protective canopy with large windows each side of the door. The proprietor lived on the upper floor and was open for many years west of the former Rocky Ford High School. Located between Sixth and Seventh Streets the store was a popular drop-in for many students but was primarily a convenient neighborhood source for basic groceries.

Keenan Cash Produce Company, 1916

Courtesy of Rocky Ford Public Museum

Photo Zillow.com

Original building extant at 966 Front Street, most recently site of **Aragon Tavern**.

Main Street Crossing

This view is to the east of two engines pulling to the west. Shadows from trees of Central or Railroad Park on the right (to the south) show late morning or early afternoon hour.

Tracks are crossing Main Street in Rocky Ford. Absence of crossing signs or signals may imply they are present but out of photo frame. Motorized traffic was to come with wig-wag signals, yet to be installed on Main Street in 1921. Absence of automobile service signs at Bryant and Johnston Co. may indicate service only for hoofed stock.

North Main at 100-108 at left is site of Rocky Ford Trading Company, later to be Bish Hardware, Lumber, Feed and Furniture enterprises.

Man near kiosk at left center is observing first engine no. 11. B.R. Buis, signalman in 1940s-1950s when ACS Company switch engines were active, stood in the same area during sugar campaigns. He was stationed in a similar kiosk.

Postal card photo courtesy Steven E. Carlile.

Site of the original small sand-painted depot would have been east of the kiosk between Main and Tenth Streets. The 1887 wooden depot at 105 South Main Street replaced it.

Stoop and Green Lumber Co. is behind Swink Milling and Grain Co. circa 1906–left of the engines. George Bryant and Fred Johnston Co. were in coal and feed business in Rocky Ford–center right, also providing artesian water. Their building site at 102 South Main would later be occupied by Bish Lumber and Feed; later Bish Building Materials–page 232 bottom, *Rocky Ford, Colorado-A Walk Past Local Doors.*

Sanborn maps of 1895, 1901, 1906, 1911, and 1919 do not show exact configuration of buildings as in the photo, indicating building site changes between map years.

Photo year c. 1910, indicated in interview of early residents during Rocky Ford's 75th anniversary in 1962 when Bryant and Johnston were specifically noted among other businesses.

A Walk in the City

Cover Photo, South Main Street, 100-200 Block

Courtesy, facebook.com

South Main Street was photographed in 1920 from near the railroad tracks. Two buildings are recognizable, IOOF Building, 200 South Main at left and the 1897 Recker's Hall right at 201-209. The latter building, demolished in the 1960s, provided the space for the current administration building at 203 South Main.

Recker's Hall is recognizable as the cover photo of *Rocky Ford, Colorado–A Walk Past Local Doors.* Though the photo above was produced about 14 years after that cover photo, little change has occurred to the building exterior though some original merchant occupants have.

Noticcable in this photo are new tri-globed street lights. A few more trees have been removed and pavement would not be seen until 1925 and after. Cement sidewalks have been replacing boardwalks to the delight of those who in the past complained of nail heads working loose and popping up.

Transportation was changing, demonstrated in this photo by the presence of horse-drawn wagons and at least one of those *'scorching automobiles,'* (page 63).

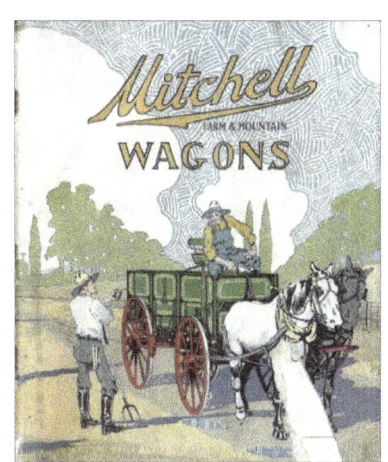

B.U. Dye advertised and sold Mitchell Wagons from his business on the original Main Street (Railroad Avenue), (*page 198*). The type of low-sided dray in the photo at left and right corners may have been those from Dye's business.

Mitchell wagons offered several styles and sizes designed for different uses, advertised in this 1913 catalog.

https://mitchellcarcollection.com/vehicles/wagons/

Santa Fe Depot at Rocky Ford

A station existed before the 1887 first wooden depot. See page 130 *Rocky Ford, Colorado-A Walk Past Local Doors* for a photo of the 1887 depot.

D.K. Spencer, in *The History of the Rocky Ford, Colorado Depot*, began his chronicle with the 1887 combination passenger and freight building then at the site of the present 1906 brick depot. He offered only brief description of a station in use before the 1887 depot was built.

The station history begins in 1876 at the completion of tracks to town and onward to Pueblo. This was the work of the Pueblo and Arkansas Valley Railroad, to be eventually absorbed by the parent company, Santa Fe. G.W. Swink served as Station Agent based at his rail-side store east of the station until Santa Fe appointed an Agent to take charge of the small station near Main Street.

Eleven years passed before the 1876 small station and construction of the 1887 combination passenger and freight depot. Rocky Ford was served by the *'little frame box'* described by Rocky Ford school children in their 1925 book, *Rocky Ford As the School Children See It.*

This first station, *Little Frame Box of* Rocky Ford school children, was also described as *Small, Red, Sand-painted Building* by pioneer LeRoy Elser in his 1955 interview and recall of 1889, *Sand-colored Building* by John Doll in 1987, and *Small, Red, Sand-painted Frame Depot* by Santa Fe historian D.K. Spencer in 1987.

This 'box' was a temporary station serving as depot until the 1887 board-battened combination passenger and freight depot was built on the present site of the 1906-1907 brick depot. The 'box' served the railroad and community until c. 1887 when it was moved to Hoehne, Colorado. In 1916 it burned and was replaced in 1917 by the Santa Fe designated *1910 Standard No. 1 Depot for Branch Lines*, a design introduced November 1910.

To this time no photo of the *little frame box* is known but it may have appeared as in the station in the photo on page 17. *Enterprise* editor speculated the town of Swink would receive the 1887 depot removed to Ninth Street for the building of the current 1907 brick replacement.

Residents of Swink, Colorado might have been expecting the Rocky Ford 1887 depot to be moved to their town.
Enterprise, February 28, 1906.

> The town of Swink has nothing but a box car to serve as a depot at present, and it is probable that the old depot at Rocky Ford will be removed to the new town which is now the scene of so much activity.

In fact, Santa Fe built a new depot for Swink and the 1887 Rocky Ford depot, converted to a freight station, was de-constructed in 1942 at its location on Ninth Street. About the same time the large loading dock near the freight depot was dismantled because of rotting timbers. The need for the dock was also diminishing with the growing trucking industry whose freight was mostly from the factory door delivered directly to point of use.

Hoehne

The *Delta Independent* published a small note April 26, 1887 two weeks after Rocky Ford was platted for the second time on April 12.

Hoehne was founded by German immigrant William Hoehne in 1859. He founded the Hoehne Ditch Company and introduced the first mill and threshing machine into the area.

> The point where the Denver, Texas & Gulf will cross the Atchison, Topeka & Santa Fe railroad is twelve miles northeast of Trinidad. A town is soon to be started there called Hoehne.

William Hoehne farmed 1,000 acres, predominantly fruit; strawberries, apples, and cherries. The town is yet in farming community but with emphasis now on alfalfa and grass hay. The population today is about 100 people.

The Santa Fe had already laid tracks thru Rocky Ford all the way to Pueblo providing freight and passenger service along the way before the printing of the *Independent* article. A station for passenger and freight business was in place in 1876 in Rocky Ford, referred to as *a small, red, sandpainted (sic) building* by pioneer LeRoy Elser.

Hoehne, the town yet-to-be, would in the future be recipient of this small red building then in Rocky Ford. That building would burn in 1916 and be replaced by the depot in the photos. This depot would be retired in 1967 and moved to Texas Creek, Colorado-*see page 18*.

Hoehne Depot

Rear quarter view
May 27, 1992.

Building was on a vacant lot, idle for some time before being moved.

Front quarter view May 27, 1992.

Size of this depot was 16' x 40', a *standard* provided for branch lines, as the Santa Fe referred to them.

Photos courtesy of Evan Werkema

Little Frame Box
Students of Freshman Class 1923, Rocky Ford High School wrote an opening chapter of six pages, Rocky Ford of Pioneer Times, under their mentor Miss Lytle. Their chapter appeared in *Rocky Ford As the School Children See It*, published 1925.

One of their subjects was the railroad and how it influenced the early development of town. Settlers built the first businesses and homes determining their position and location according to the railroad right-of-way and pre-existing government claims.

First settlers determined that Kit Carson Road-now Tenth Street-would become the Main Street and the center of town to be the intersection of Tenth Street with Railroad Avenue. This was a practical change since location of the Swink store was just off Tenth Street with a railroad track siding. Handling merchandise was convenient to the store which had large doors on the track side opening to the boxcars. Other businesses took sites along the north side, paralleling the tracks on Railroad Avenue.

The Swink store was a few yards east of the first station, *little frame box c.* 1876 when the rails reached town. The 'box' was between the tracks near Main Street with Horace Amos as first night telegrapher. Not stated but likely, a day operator would have been at the same depot. Although Mr. Swink had been the first station agent at his store in 1876, nothing is revealed of his telegraphic abilities. Mr. Amos might have served in daytime except for work three miles from town proving up on his land claim. Miss Lytle's students wrote:

> *"Just down from Mr. Swink's store on the edge of the track was a little frame box of a building which served as a station. Later when the old station (now the freight station) was built, this little structure was moved from here and may now be seen at Hoehnes* [sic] *Colorado, where it still serves the traveling public in its old,* [former] *capacity."*

An online search was made of Hoehne buildings, especially those track-side. Students noted the little station was "... *now the freight station* ..." after building the 1887 wood-battened depot in Rocky Ford. Many communities preserved at least some of their past as did Rocky Ford and Santa Fe officials by moving the 1887 depot across Ninth Street and making it a freight station when the 1906 depot was built. The *little frame box*, then freight station, was moved to Hoehne, c. 1887.

Hoehne residents kept their *box* depot until fire destroyed it in 1916. Its replacement was a more permanent one, Santa Fe designate, *Frame Depot No. 1 for Branch Lines*, built on site in 1917.

During its heyday as a fruit and vegetable producing area, Hoehne boasted a hotel, the depot-residents called "Hoehnes,," a blacksmith, Catholic church, and several stores.

Their depot was retired in 1967 and moved twice, first to a nearby lot within Hoehne, vacant until the move to Texas Creek on Colorado US 50. From there it was moved 10 miles south on SH 69 to private property where it was restored to original appearance.

Little frame box served Rocky Ford from 1876 to 1887 when a new wooden depot was built at 105 South Main Street. Existing in 1876, moved c. 1887 to Hoehne, the *little frame box* was in service 11 years. When it burned at Hoehne in 1916 it had served that community 29 more years before the new depot built there in 1917.

Little Frame *Box*

The *little frame box*, named by Rocky Ford school children, might have appeared as this one at Oldham, Texas. The Rocky Ford structure, also known as the *small, red, sand-painted building* has no known photograph. Modest in printed description and as in this photo, offered portability and shelter on a small base in an area between tracks as described by pioneer LeRoy Elser-see *Note*.

Minimal amenities, speculating, might have included a short bench, water cooler, outbuilding, small stove and lantern light. A small desk would provide space for the station master's freight and ticket paperwork while seated on a chair or stool. Telegraph lines were wired in and the telegrapher was also Station Master.

Practical use of a small sturdy frame building such as this 'box' afforded ease of movement, low maintenance, and light freight weight. A rail crane could lift and place the station on a flat car to carry it to another location. In another use this structure could be recycled as a tool shed.

MKT Line (Missouri-Kansas-Texas) Railroad, 1962

Small communities like early Rocky Ford did not have much passenger business. There were 47 people in and around town in the 1880 census. Freight was more likely to occupy the railroad but eventually, as business grew, there would have to be a larger depot, the one built in 1887.

Santa Fe officials retired and moved the *'little frame box'* depot in 1887 to Hoehne, Colorado, an unincorporated community northeast of Trinidad. It served there for about 29 years before it was destroyed by fire in 1916. A new 16' x 40' depot was built in 1917.

Note: *"The railroad station was a small, red, sand-painted building north of the tracks some distance east of Main Street. A wide strip of cinders held in place by large timbers extended along each side of the railroad."*
Interview August 26, 1955 in *Rocky Ford Daily Gazette*. LeRoy Elser's family arrived in Rocky Ford March 2, 1889.

Frame Depot No. 1 for Branch Lines

Rocky Ford was home to 47 individuals in 1880. G.W. Swink was Station Agent at his store four years since arrival of tracks in 1876 and until Horace Amos was appointed Agent. *Little frame box* was eventually moved to Hoehne, Colorado. The Frame Depot No. 1 for Branch Lines, depicted in these photos, was built on site in Hoehne, Colorado in 1917. *Little Frame Box* from Rocky Ford had burned in 1916 before the depot above was built.

Top photo May 27, 1992, courtesy of Evan Werkema. Bottom, May 2000, courtesy of Mark Roper.

The depot was retired in 1967 and moved to Texas Creek, Colorado where it was idle for some time. It is now part of a private railroad memorabilia park south of Texas Creek on state Hwy 69.

St. James Hotel

Rocky Ford businessman and historian John Doll wrote about Swink Hotel in his 1987 book *The Story of Early Rocky Ford:*

"In 1888, Mr. Swink and some other businessmen built a large two-story brick hotel on the southeast corner of Walnut Avenue and Main Street." It was first named the West Hotel after one of the investors. *"It had two store rooms below and the hotel apartments above."* He also related *"... an unusual feature of the hotel was a two-story privy on the alley with an elevated walkway between the two buildings."*

The two-story privy is described on other pages of this narrative. Several changes in management followed the hotel opening that prompted G.W. Swink to act in the investors' behalf. Apparently apprehension was growing among owner-investors about stability of their enterprise that prompted him to take over the hotel ownership.

West Hotel became Swink Hotel after Mr. Swink's purchase and it remained so until leased to a Colorado Springs man in 1892 who apparently removed the privy and made other changes. Whether the new owner was one of two previously interested Colorado Springs investors is not known but the hotel was again sold September 27, 1894 to Colorado Springs investors J. P. Salls and Charles Chandler. They re-named the hotel St. James. After brief ownership the hotel was sold again to J. S. Seeley January 3, 1895.

Mr. Seeley installed W.P. Noe as new proprietor [or sold to Mr. Noe] the former West Hotel because the Swink Hotel ad appeared the same day as the sale was announced.

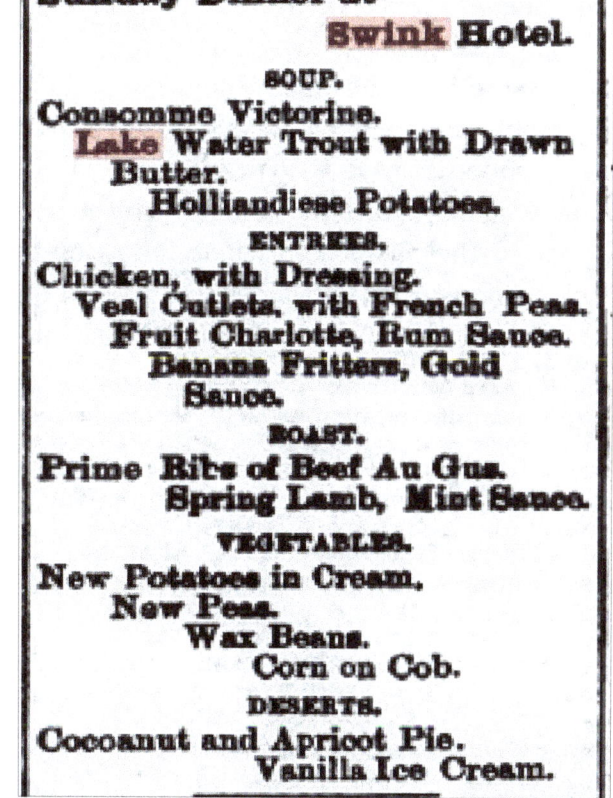

Note: J. S. Seeley bought Hotel Welcome Home from Andy Nichols, eventually to raze it and build the De Seeley on the same site. It is not known if he had sold it before buying the St. James. After other changes in ownership and several in management the hotel operated until c. 1942 housing a succession of businesses on the ground floor store fronts. In 1952 St. James at 300 South Main Street was razed for parking at Rhoades Food Center.

A Sunday dinner at Swink Hotel

While Mr. Swink owned the hotel he established a kitchen and staff that provided a varied and excellent series of menus for hotel guests and the public. His frequent advertising in the *Enterprise* gave notice of menu changes.

Although many Swink menus were printed, one example of the cuisine is duplicated here, published for a Sunday, July 12, 1896 dinner.

Enterprise, July 9, 1896.

St. James Water Closet

Possibly the first appearance of indoor plumbing or of a water closet in Rocky Ford was at the St. James. Toilets did not generally surface as newsworthy unless concerning sanitation involving the ubiquitous outhouse. The English are credited with one of the first devices named for indoor placement and use, *the necessary*:

> *"There was a noble origin to the water closet in its earliest days. Sir John Harington, godson to Queen Elizabeth, set about making a 'necessary' for his godmother and himself in 1596. A rather accomplished inventor, Harington ended his career with this invention, for he was ridiculed by his peers for this absurd device. He never built another one, though he and his godmother both used theirs."*
>
> Wiktionary

General availability and use of indoor plumbing in the United States was common by mid-1850s. Platting of Rocky Ford in 1887 included bare essentials; no water for indoor plumbing was available until the first well was completed in 1895 and piped into a street system in 1896. The advent of indoor plumbing came with accompanying sewerage, providing for raw outflow, to the river in the early development of the town. First framed or bricked homes and larger buildings were being supplied with plumbing after 1895. Until then, many small framed outhouses stood on business and homeowners' lots.

Sanborn maps did identify homes or buildings supplied with water-using devices. When water was mentioned in map details it was in association with firefighting, pipe size and direction of underground service to dedicated fire hydrants. Santa Fe water towers and city reservoirs were mapped along with canals and rivers and sometimes wet areas. So, it is significant that in the drawing of the 1901 Sanborn map-following-the first water closet identified in town is in the two-story outhouse of the St. James Hotel. It was an addition to the original 1888 structure shown on the 1895 map but apparently added 8 years later when plumbing was new in town.

This facility could not have been the only such in Rocky Ford then. The Santa Fe Depot of 1907-*extant*-exhibits today the type water closet likely common in town and maybe, at the the St. James. So also the public schools though they are shown on early Sanborn maps with outhouses. The map of 1911 shows gender-separate outdoor water closets at the alley on the Liberty School grounds.

Washington School early in its existence maintained an outbuilding near the intersection of Washington Road and Twelfth Street. It was described only as an 'outbuilding' likely a privy until the main building was enlarged and water was added. This outbuilding burned July 27, 1904 but extent of damage is not noted among council notes. Pranks were suspected

When the addition was finished in 1902 for the 1889 Washington School, several upgrades were incorporated; iron rails at each ground floor window well for protection against falls; fire escape ladders added to both sides of the building for upper story exit, and an outdoor uncovered drinking fountain placed under a large tree that was left running in summer.

Apart from additional classroom and office space, plumbing was designed into the ground floor. Metal urinal troughs for the boys along with porcelain floor commodes in stalls for separate boys' and girls' toilets. Many children in Rocky Ford first encountered, at school, the lavatories and semi-private stalls designed for the individual while at their homes the outhouse was the standard.

Something new added.

Hotel St. James and patrons experienced several ownership changes and managers, the latter all living on premises. During personnel changes in 1895 water from the first artesian well was found at 790 feet, just a little over a block away in the north part of the future Railroad Park. Artesian water was piped to reservoirs on former Cullings Hill, now Reservoir Hill, location of two open city reservoirs built of concrete.

Soon, pipe delivery by gravity was bringing water to businesses and residences. Service to the St James followed and both the elevated walkway and out house on the alley were *supposedly* removed. The year 1896 has been suggested, but not confirmed-*see Note*.

The addition of plumbing would have been less than a year after the first well water was piped into the city system September 2, 1895. Details are similarly lacking but plumbing apparently had been incorporated into the hotel during the updating of furnishings introduced by new proprietor W. P. Noe. Something new had been added.

Bath Rooms Attached.

Though added to the ad almost as an afterthought-*in fine print*-this change for the hotel must have been a welcome innovation and a source of pride for both the owners and patrons. But how the baths were attached leads to speculation as to whether each room had a bath, plural as in the ad, or that a common bath or baths were built to accommodate all.

Questions also arise about the 1895 understanding of *bath rooms*. Language today communicates to most people that 'bath room' is where bathing tubs, showers, and lavatories are along with a toilet, urinal, and maybe a bidet. Language in 1895 may have strictly indicated only a bath tub, not necessarily piped. If so, an outdoor privy would remain a necessity.

Some time between 1895 and 1901 a change was made to the outdoor facility. The Sanborn map of 1901 shows the addition of a water closet to the privy, not present in 1895. The removal of the privy walkway, c. 1896, may not have been time enough to eliminate the illustration from the 1901 Sanborn map since map preparation required time for a publication and distribution.

Enterprise January 3, 1895

Note:
A discrepancy exists between the printed record in several publications that the 1888 elevated walkway to the privy was removed c. 1896. However, the walkway is present on maps at least through 1920. The water closet that first appeared on the 1901 map was not on 1906 or later maps.

SWINK HOTEL,
(Formerly West Hotel.)
W. P. Noe, - Prop.
Has just been thoroughly refitted, refurnished and put in the best possible condition from kitchen to parlor and will compare with the best hotels in the west outside the large cities.

The House will be run in first-class manner and will fully meet the demands of those desiring the very best of accommodations.

A Share of the Public Patronage is Solicited.

Superior Sample Rooms
For Commercial Travelers.
☞ Bath Rooms Attached.

Sanborn map of 1895

The first map of the Sanborn series for Rocky Ford located a 12' x 18' one-story wooden frame building at Swink and Main that today is 400 N Main. It was site of W.H. Russell's cigar manufacturing business. It survived the years to be listed in directories for 1911, 1914, and 1915.

Sanborn map of 1919 describes an automobile agency with capacity for 30 cars at 400 N Main apparently following Mr. Russell's cigar business. There is indication that someone, perhaps Mr. Russell continued making cigars in the north store front of a frame building at 208 S Main. This would be the future site of Bill and Bob's Super Service many years later.

Framed wooden buildings owned by Charles Recker housed another cigar factory on a second floor store room in 1898. These buildings were along Ninth Street west of the new 1897 Recker's Hall on Main Street. The *Enterprise* wrote that Mr. White was engaged in *"... one of Rocky Ford's growing industries... having put in two new workmen last week."*   Enterprise April 7, 1898.

An article in the *La Junta Tribune* March 2, 1899 informed of F.L. Barney who established a cigar factory in town employing several men. No space was given to location or other details.

Information about women shop owners in the business in Rocky Ford wasn't publicized. Some occupations and activities, perhaps were not viewed as appropriate for involvement of ladies following the mores of the Victorian era.

Tobacco industry as a growing commercial enterprise prompted the scientific community to test the ability of Colorado soils for production of various plant varieties (*note article misspelling*).

Colorado State Agricultural College- now Colorado State University-with its particular interest in agriculture, was involved in determining the best plants for cultivation in the environment of the Rocky Mountain Region and soils of the state.

The number of plant varieties, very recognizable to southern and southeastern US farmers, offered a new array of choices to Colorado farmers should the industry take hold in the state. History revealed that it would not.

> **Collorado Tobacco.**
>
> A report made by Professor Cassidy, of Colorado State Agricultural College, Fort Collins, on tobacco growing in this state is important. Tests have been made for two years, giving most satisfactory results. Eighteen varieties were grown that season, and all ripened before the end of August. The varieties were the Isabella, Cuboni, General Grant, Cienfuegos, Flanagan, White Stem, Orinoco, Vuelta Abajo, Elkerson's Yellow Havana, Saqua Grand, One Sucker, Virginia improved Havana, Missouri broad leaf, Yara golden leaf, White Barley, Connecticut seed leaf, Wilson's prolific, Fiji and Orinoco. Both manured and unmanured land were planted. The professor says the yield was phenomenal, and concludes that tobacco of any variety may be grown here, and of superior excellence.—La Junta Tribune.

Bent County Register, March 17, 1888 reprint of a *La Junta Tribune* article.

Mr. Swink sold tobacco at his store. He purchase it by the *butt,* one in a series of English wine cask units, being half of a tun or (252/2)=126 gallons. Rail shipping in barrels was preferred for protection of coarse cut, loose and leaf tobacco ready for pipe, cigar or cigarette rolling.

Note: Some nefarious cigar rollers included sawdust, straw, paper, or broom fibers to extend their tobacco supply. For want of such stretching, those cigar men chanced alienation of their cigar-smoking clientele.

St. James Bridge

This map reveals a water line-*dashed*-and dedicated fire hydrant-D.H. in 1901.

The *Bridge* from the rear of the hotel second floor leads to the W C above and away from the ground floor kitchen and dining rooms. Bridge is forty feet long by scale. Height is not given nor length of the ladder reaching it. Ladder was a convenience for ground-floor patrons and workers but as likely also served as a fire escape for the second floor.

Double hash marks indicate second floor windows, single marked hash marks for ground floor windows.

Brick building nearest the ladder was divided by frame partition and had a framed cornice, and likely was used for storage. Small framed building at bottom center was a one-story on the alley, use unknown.

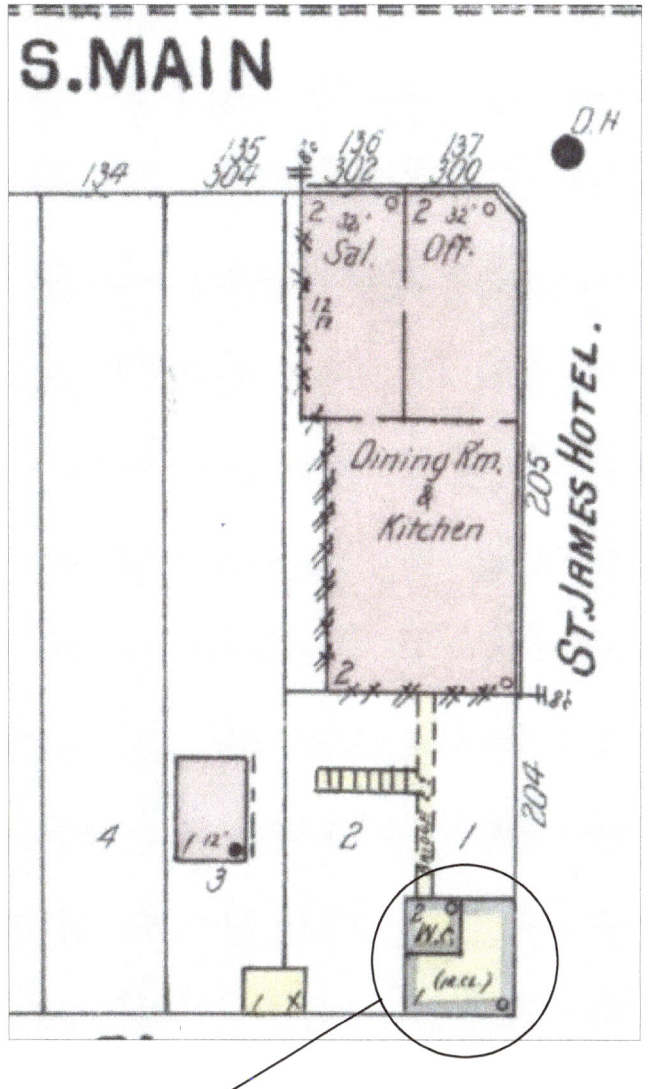

Walnut Avenue is at right, alleyway between Main and Tenth Streets at bottom. Red indicates brick construction, yellow, wooden framed, and gray, iron clad. A saloon was in the south store front in 1901. A succession of businesses, among them the *Enterprise*, occupied the north store front at other times.

Facility identified as water closet (WC) was set in a 10' square structure atop a 25' square lower level enclosure, possibly a vault enclosure for the former privy. Lower structure and WC do not appear on earlier maps. Both structures were iron clad (IR. CL.) and sat near the alleyway.

Among several published articles about the 1888 elevated walkway one suggests the privy was removed c. 1896. However, the walkway is present on Sanborn maps at least through 1920. The water closet first appeared on this 1901 map but not on the 1906 or later maps. [*Speculation suggests the W. C .s were moved indoors*].

An outdoor WC is also identified on the alley at 211 N 12th on the 1919 map and two on the Liberty School grounds, also outdoors. In future construction, indoor plumbing was becoming a desired improvement to the standard of living.

Author's note: My home, c. 1900, was equipped with a water closet-possibly retrofitted-iron piping and leaden drains. Hot water was supplied to the kitchen and bath when new plumbing was added later. The oak-covered WC tank overhead near the ceiling presented certain fears during my visits under it. Pulling the water release chain on the tank was an action certain to bring it down on my head.

Swink's Artificial Lake-*Plausible Location*

Satellite View of Northeastern Garden Place

○ Area of Stauffer's Packing Plant.

▢ Original Main Street entrance with the obelisks marked the beginning of eastern Railroad Avenue at the curvature of Elm Avenue.

Elongated dotted-line enclosure is described in *Satellite View* page 25. Information of G.W. Swink's Lake continues page 103.

Garden Place and Swink's Artificial Lake.

Open space east of Fourteenth Street and south of the railroad, was divided into 2 to 5 acre lots on the original town plat. Space was intended here for gardens and small farms since town lots were small for those purposes. *Garden Place* was the identifier by convention and destined use.

Plot size in Garden Place was not changed when in 1894 the city administration downsized town lots on the new plat for future sales to accommodate many newcomers to the area. This resulted in a change from 350 to 300 square feet per lot.

Garden Place and other areas around the original town plat were early described as treeless open space with much prairie vegetation crossed by wagon and horse trails in the sandy soil. Some of these trails were the forerunners of numbered streets and tree-named avenues.

The countryside began to change with the development of Rocky Ford ditch, begun in 1877 and extended east of town by 1880. Three timber claims, firsts in the nation, soon were planted with trees watered by the ditch. Town plat of 1887 laid out lots for sale with ditch water running near each lot, to the delight of buyers.

Sometime after the first *unacceptable* July 4, 1876 plat of William Matthews, [*did not meet legal requirements for metes and bounds*] George Washington Swink conceived of and began construction of his second major water project. It became known as *Swink's Artificial Lake,* reported completed January 11, 1882 in the *Rocky Mountain News*.

Noticeably absent in public record are Mr. Swink's plan approval, support, location, or construction of his lake. Apart from naming *Lake Street* on the original plat of 1876 there are few recorded statements of earliest pioneers and citizens in local news.

Lake Street of the 1876 plat was renamed Eleventh Street on the 1887 re-plat and fifteen north-south streets were later numbered from west to east. Maple Avenue at its eastern end was joined at its crossing over Rocky Ford ditch with the north-south country road that became Nineteenth Street. This conjunction was near the site of the future Stauffer Packing Plant to open December 1933 and operate until 1972.

Unoccupied land was bordered on the north by the railroad and on the south by Rocky Ford ditch. The area, with levees at both east and west ends, offered the possibility within these man-made restrictive boundaries for construction of a lake. A source of supply from the Rocky Ford ditch was already present.

Satellite View. The facing page shows a lined enclosure, supported by this author as a plausible location of Swink's Artificial Lake. Area enclosed is 20 acres by computer design, size reported in the *RM News*. Depth also reported average of 10 feet. If accurate, one surface acre-foot times 20 calculates to 871,200 gallons. An average 10 foot depth multiplying this figure = 8,712,000 gallons in the lake.

Construction details of such a large impoundment completed by Mr. Swink aren't found in newsprint. However, his personal vision and will to get things done was well known.

Note: Calculating the area of a football field, including the end zones equals 57,600 sf (360 x 160). One acre equals 43,560 sf. A football field is (57,600/43,560) or about 1.32 acres. Swink lake of 20 acres (20 x 43,560) = 871,200 sf. Area of the lake, 871,200/57,600 = 15.1 football fields.

His first major effort in delivery and management of water for Rocky Ford and the Arkansas Valley, was already accomplished in the completion of the Rocky Ford ditch.

Design and construction of his lake would have made use of much the same earth-moving equipment as for the ditch. Identification of specific tools and machinery would be speculation but would include many hours of labor for man and animal.

Horses and mules would have provided power before advent of steam or traction engines although engines were later present in the area and used by American Beet Sugar Company late 1899 and early 1900. Mr. Swink also employed a traction engine in April 1900, 18 years after completion, to compact the lake bottom after significant water loss.

Excavation and removal of soil to the described 10 foot depth likely provided the bulk of levees required, especially at east and west ends.

Descriptive statements of the lake's size by pioneers and residents were of *a pond or a fenced pond,* and that it was *several hundred feet long.* The latter size description may be closer to the area suggested on the aerial view since the impound begins near the end of Maple Avenue and is defined by space between the railroad and the Rocky Ford ditch, an area much longer than wide.

Speculation about the location of Swink's Artificial Lake should also include what is known of the size of Rocky Ford in 1882 when the lake was completed. The census of 1880 counted 47 individuals two years before the article in the Rocky Mountain News and the number of homes and buildings described by the first residents was fewer than a dozen. A 20 acre body of water impounded five years before the town lot sale in 1887 must have appeared to the few who lived in the vicinity as a small inland ocean on the prairie.

Ice Production and Competition

Clean ice was possible after artesian wells supplied the town beginning 1895. Among the difficulties of maintaining an 'artificial lake' for ice was competition growing from commercial production. The Polar Ice & Storage Company began offering clean ice formed on site by machinery, ideal for human consumption. Production and sales began in 1905 at 100 South Tenth Street. A food storage business began with a subsequent owner who offered rental of lockers that were popular until home refrigeration and freezers were common.

Patrons subscribed by purchasing ice coupons redeemable for home needs.

Swink's Lake Ice blocks were carried by rail to Swink's icehouse near his store between Main and Tenth Streets. Some ice was also stored by an un-named 1897 group, forerunner of Rocky Ford Ice and Storage, 100 South Tenth Street where they had a storage structure. Ice demand decreased after Rocky Ford Ice and Mercantile Company began commercial production at that site in 1905.

Swink's Lake was extant from January 1882 coexistent with the 1893 Santa Fe cattle pens near the extension of Fifteenth Street. Although lake ice harvest declined with commercial production, demise of the lake apparently was not immediate. Just as the beginning of the lake, its history, longevity and other uses are not fully known. Mr. Swink died in 1910 and so far known, details of his lake and of his several other water-related projects in the Arkansas Valley passed with him.

Rocky Ford ditch was the source of water for Swink's Lake. Beginning May, 1874 to conjunction with Timpas Creek c. 1880, need for water was increasing for all growers, farmers, orchardists, poultry raisers, cattlemen, American Beet Sugar Company and town of Rocky Ford.

Demands for water were influenced by watershed in the mountains and rights of users downstream as the river flowed eastward to the Mississippi. Plentiful water in the good years fulfilled most needs; scarcity of water in low precipitation years caused users to do with less.

When ice was no longer a needed product of the winter, Swink's Lake would have become an idle resource on the edge of town. A town with a lake certainly has benefits such as natural attractiveness with trees growing around and water sports, as participated in then.

Demands for water from the Rocky Ford ditch and scarcity during lean years likely were the pressures on the existence of the lake. Users east of town, downstream must have been affected in some manner. Water was supplied to the ditch during growing seasons, spring, summer, and fall. In winter, water would have been scarce. Keeping water in the lake then must have made ice production a challenge some years. These considerations probably contributed to the end of the lake's usefulness with the ultimate end, abandonment to other development.

Others in the community were interested in lakes around Rocky Ford for sports of hunting and fishing, apparently not a desire of Mr. Swink whose other lakes were associated so only by lease to others. Neither were his lakes considered by him for the business of fish propagation.

Ice block harvesting operation, showing the storage house, boiler house and three elevators, as well as various operations on the ice. Ice was first cleared of snow before marking and cutting by hand saw. Blocks were elevated and stacked at several levels of storage leaving no air space, protecting against thawing, and covered with straw or sawdust for insulation. Boilers generated the power to operate lifts and conveyors for moving blocks.

Appletons' *Cyclopaedia of Applied Mechanics,* published in 1885.

Swink's 1876 Store

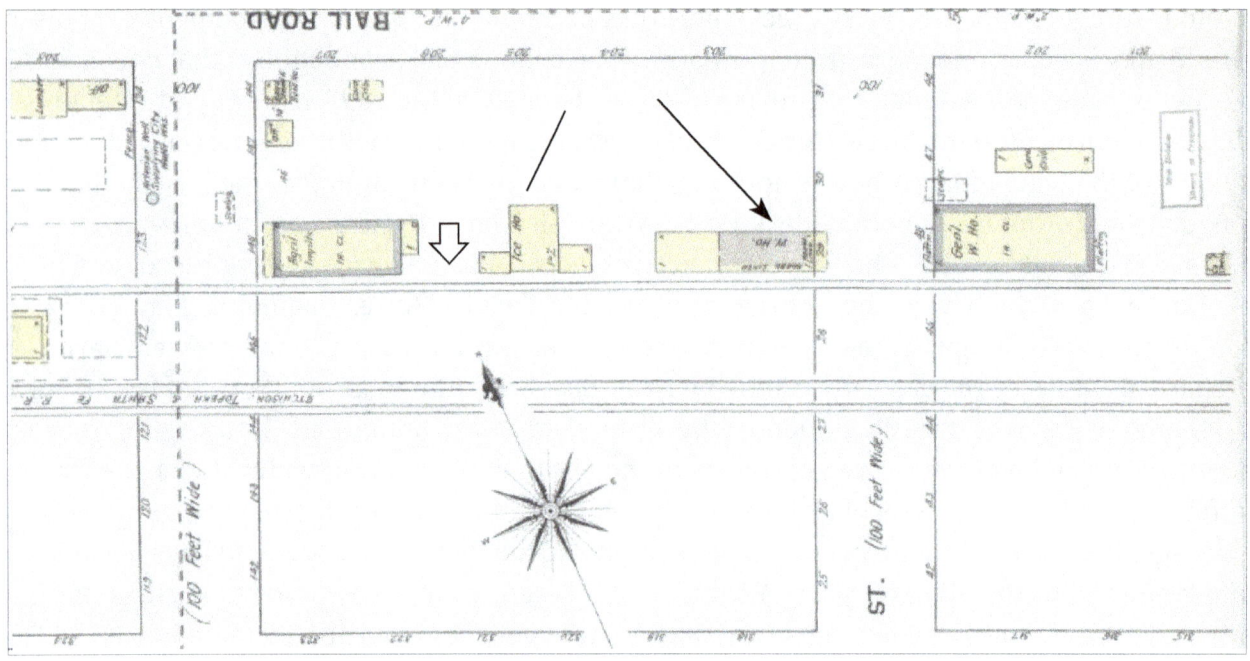

Main Street crossing at left, Tenth Street is right, Railroad Avenue, top, and Front Street is bottom in this 1901 Sanborn map segment.

G.W. Swink moved from *Old Rocky Ford* in 1875 after buying the inventory of their store from partner Asa Russell. Their former store of adobe -*page x*-was the successor to the first, a crude stockade of poles and logs with dirt roof placed near the river crossing.

The 1876 store-*arrow*- in *new* Rocky Ford was 18 x 40 ft. with frame addition-*yellow*-on the west end. Swink's ice house -*line marker*- was flanked by small frame additions for coal storage on the Sanford map of 1901. Site of the original small, sand-colored Santa Fe station was near the main tracks -*open arrow*- or possibly in the position of the later 1888 agricultural implement business, Rocky Ford Mercantile Co. of B.U. Dye. He built on railroad property west of the ice house after the 1887 wooden depot was in use. His business faced Gibson Lumber, later Newton Lumber, across Main Street where the current parking and open space is near the 1907 depot.

Inventory of Swink's store was developed to include the needs of travelers going west and for the needs of the pioneers building the town of *new* Rocky Ford.

Much is known of Swink's inventory gleaned from invoices, receipts, newspaper articles, and letters. The great number of goods, a sample of which appears on the following page, required the frame addition to the west end of his store. While these goods and more were on the shelves, Mr. Swink met personally with arriving immigrants where they camped when traveling west. He had only to walk or ride east from his Tenth Street location onto Railroad Avenue to the Fourteenth Street campgrounds. Wagons there were partly-shaded by cottonwoods planted by the Santa Fe.

Note: See *Rocky Ford, Colorado-A Walk Past Local Doors* p. 92 for photos of Swink's 1876 store.

Swink Store Partial Inventory:
Many items were included: baled hay-barbed wire-beef-beer-bullet lead-butter-candy-cement-clothing-coffee-crackers-cured meats-dishes-dried fish and dried fruit-farm implements-feed and grain-fenceposts-fencing-firewood-flour and fresh fruit, gunpowder-hardware-hides-lemons-medicine-melons and potatoes-seed-spirits, drugs-sugar and syrup-tobacco-vinegar-vegetables-and much free advice and direction.

Aside from the essentials sold from Swink's Store to citizenry and passing immigrants there might have been a scene such as described here during hunting season. The narrative was given by a local observer and critical commentator one winter:

> *"There are more ducks killed around the stoves at Swink and Swink's and on the dry goods boxes of G.W.'s store and such like places in town by the local Nimrods every mornin' between nine o'clock and noon than are killed in twenty-four hours along the Arkansas River, from here to the Mississippi. If the state lawmakers don't put some anchor on their wholesale carnage, the time will soon be here when the ducks won't be there, and nothin' to tell about that anybody will put any confidence in, 'cause there won't be any ducks."* Anon.

Proprietor of a circa 1880s general store would display every item of inventory to view for his customers.. Each bit of space would be used, even ceiling or rafters.

G.W, Swink added space to each end of his ice house out back for coal storage.

Conversation, as above around the stove at Swink's in winter, might have been in a cozy space as in this rough simile. His store was 20 x 40 ft. with space used to display his goods, away from stove heat if possible, so that storytellers could accommodate.

bing.com/images

Note: Swink and Swink Recreation Parlor, Mike Miller, proprietor, location probably 300 block South Main Street.
Nimrod, fiercely aggressive individual was believed to be the world's first great hunter/conqueror (Genesis 10:9).

Swink Timber Culture Claim No.1 Remnants

A description of the area under the claim was written by school children in their 1925 history *Rocky Ford As the School Children See It*:

"In 1882 it was seen that the crowd was outgrowing the store, so in 1883 Watermelon Day, as it had already begun to be called, was held in the outskirts of Mr. Swink's timber claim, in 'the grove just north of town'–that is on the land now occupied by the Amos Apartment Houses,[SW corner Chestnut and Main] *and the adjoining territory–north of Chestnut Avenue and west of Tenth Street".*

Soil Conservation photo AG-282-96, Oct. 4, 1936. Scale=1:20,000

Aerial view of trees in rank and file of Mr. Swink's Timber Culture Claim planted after November 3, 1887 when his application was approved. Many trees were removed over the years for development of the fairgrounds. Trees planted soon after the claim approval would be approaching fifty years in this 1936 photo. Main Street fairgrounds gate is at circle. Fair ground was eventually expanded eastward-*above right*-by addition of 53 acres more of Swink property.

Rocky Ford Cigars

Cigar making and use in Colorado became popular during the late 1800s, especially during the 1858-59 gold rush. *Segar* smoking among mining immigrants was viewed as far more sophisticated than smoking cigarettes or chewing tobacco. Because of this growing popularity making cigars became one of Colorado Territory's early industries.

Fifty-niners from the East and Midwest, arriving during the Colorado Gold Rush, brought a fascination for the popular *segar*. In the 1860s, European and English spelling, *segar,* was used but the higher quality *cigar* made in Cuba replaced the European and Engllish spelling.

US Census revealed that no cigar manufacturing business operated in Colorado in 1860 or 1870. The first business directories of Colorado Territory, published in 1866, advertised retail sale of cigars but they did not mention cigar manufacturers until 1873. On June 28, 1873, *Rocky Mountain News* printed an advertisement for John Winker, a cigar maker at 398 Larimer Street. Denver's business directory had listed him as seller of cigars two years prior. He may well have been rolling his own for sale by 1872. That year, $18,000 worth of cigars—about 250,000 of them—were made.

Cigar making employed thousands of Coloradans across the state during the late 1800s and early 1900s, before mechanization overtook the industry. Slowly, cigar shop owners changed the process. Instead of each cigar maker performing every step of the rolling process, owners divided the steps so that cheaper labor using machinery could do most of the work.

Manufacturing owners also tried to break unions by hiring women, particularly immigrants willing to work for lower wages.

Pocket Five Pack, illustration from a P. Lorillard Co. *Cigar Making in Colorado.* coloradoencyclopedia.org/artcle/cigar-making-colorado.

Nearly all Colorado cigar makers were men but some experienced women did come to the state to roll cigars and some had their own shops. The Solis Cigar Factory in 1914 Denver employed 32 women among 145 workers.

Women owned shops in Boulder, Denver, Florence, La Junta, Pueblo, Monte Vista, and Rocky Ford. Though none are known to have been recorded in Rocky Ford directories, women owned cigar manufacturing shops might also indicate the industry was a home-run business providing products to stores.

Rocky Ford Cigars

Cigars were two for five cents in some places in town, five cents in some stores. Entrepreneurs early saw a need and developed a container, the cigar box holding several with box size and shape determined by size of cigar. *Rocky Ford* brand, among their many labels, was one of the P. Lorillard Tobacco Company products.

Origin of the name isn't known but could have been influenced by any of similarly named locations; Rocky Ford, Georgia, Rocky Ford, Kansas, Rocky Ford, Oklahoma, Rocky Ford Township, South Dakota and Rocky Ford, Indiana.

Forty-two thousand factories were making cigars in 1895, and at least 50 today. Palma Cigar Company in Denver is the only company currently rolling hand-made cigars in Colorado.

Token dated 1909

Note: One of the earliest tokens struck may have been in 1863 by the Milwaukee firm Mossin & Marr who designed and engraved tokens for the 1859 Edward Aschermann Cigar & Tobacco Company, Milwaukee, Wisconsin.

The token illustrated was stuck by one of several companies dealing in merchandise tokens of different values used in sales incentives. Five cents was a common value in copper or aluminum but some were as high as one dollar and as low as one cent.

Labels were of paper printed for advertising and made into a 'ring' placed on each cigar. Highly prized and collectible as tokens they were also a toy for children growing up with a cigar-smoking father or other family member. Many rings were made of precious metals, some designed like fine jewelry but with a cigar manufacturer's motif.

Have a cigar! One way to celebrate an addition to the family, whether made of candy, bubble gum or rolled fine leaf tobacco.

F.Y. Hauck Hose Cart Company of 1894 preceded horse-drawn wagons with citizens Frank Y. Hauck as Assistant Chief and Leon R. Fenlason, Chief. Team members are not named but several men were enlisted, or volunteered.

There was a camaraderie among the athletic young men physically able for the strenuous work of a hose cart company. Both speed and coordination were essential to make a run and match the hose to hydrant.

Horses or mules were not considered for hose cart duty because the immediacy required during a conflagration proscribed time for harnessing and hitching to wagons or fire engines. Team members, often down town businessmen, were closer to the action. They pulled a two-wheeled cart bearing a hose reel near to a fire hydrant, connect and continue toward the fire.

City administration had provided six hydrants by 1891 in the business district and a fire hose pumping station by 1907. Location of this pumping station was directly behind the building at 110 North Main Street.

Hose cart team proficiency was a matter of home-town pride, not unlike the pride of horse owners in racing their best animal on the main streets of many western towns.. Proficiency was primary among hose cart companies and their speed demonstrated the result of their training. Periodic competition demonstrated their fine-tuned coordination and agility. State-wide competitions illustrated in photo and article their dedication. Description in photo of what a hose cart company is and does is demonstrated by a Fort Collins team.

Hose Cart Company Action

Courtesy, Fort Collins History connection, image H02346

Fort Collins, Colorado Hose Cart Team posing in racing demonstration c. 1897. Team was state champion that year among all the competing hose cart teams. Team positions were known as *pipe man*, *spike*, 2 man *first swing*, 2 man *second swing*, 2 man *tillers*, and *breaker*. Competition segments were *Hub to Hub Race* at a pistol start for 200 yards with 750 pounds and 200 feet of hose. Time, 21 4/5 sec. *Relay Team Race* for 1000 yards, 10 men each 100 yards [relaying] carrying [?] pounds. Time 109 ½ seconds.

Rocky Ford Fire Wagon

Discussion of Rocky Ford's first horse-drawn fire wagon on page 326 of *Rocky Ford, Colorado-A Walk Past Local Doors* might have caused discomfort, as it did for the author, and for those who appreciate horses and how they labor for us. No one could have predicted what would happen to the team, Prince and Alex, when they were urged to respond to what would be their *final bell*, and their sacrifice, necessary to prevent great suffering near the fire.

The team, pulling a four-wheeled cart with 500 feet of hose, 12 and 16 foot ladders, and other smaller equipment was called to a fire at a carpentry shop on North Eleventh Street. What happened next could have been prevented had some resident of the area not previously placed barbed wire across the alley near the shop. Both horses became entangled and because of their fright and capture by wire and harness, could not escape the flames. Delavan V. Burrell, who lived nearby at 404 North Tenth Street, brought his rifle to dispatch the horses.

Prior this fire on North Eleventh Street much discussion had taken place about new horse-drawn equipment to replace hose carts and buckets to bring to a fire. A topic current since a fire in 1898 destroyed the east side 200 block of North Main Street with its five businesses.

Mayor, Dr. R.M. Pollock and city council approved the purchase in 1901 of the horse-drawn wagon that was destroyed in the carpentry shop fire eight years later in 1909. The dollar cost was $735 for the four-wheeled cart and its equipment. Horses, well-trained for their duty, matched for light weight and speed, and their harness were other significant costs at $575.

Fire chief Fred A. Carpe and drivers Jack Tinsley and George Frantz, who were on duty for this fire must have felt this loss personally since they had all no doubt shared many hours of training and working together.

Pressure Pumping Station for fire hoses was successfully tested February 21, 1907. Location was in a two-story frame building, east across Main Street from the 1895 artesian well. A dedicated hydrant was located near the corner of Main and Railroad, front of 200 North Main. The hose frame structure was a dual-purpose one at 110 North Main on the 1901 Sanborn map. The flat roof was used as base for a bandstand as well.

First Fire Department, 1895 consisted of one hose reel company of 18 men, all volunteers, organized in 1894. They relied on artesian water stored in two open concrete reservoirs on Reservoir Hill-previously known until 1902 as Culling's Hill. One reservoir measured 175 ft. x 50 ft. x 6 ft., the other, 175 ft. x 30 ft. x 6 ft..

The reservoir hilltop was a maximum 100 ft. elevation above the fair grounds on North Main Street and an average 55 ft. above Main Street businesses. Significant pressure was available to firefighters who could deliver water via one first class hose reel of 500 ft. length by attachment to any of eight fire hydrants at that time in the business district.

Elaterite, possible Fire Hazard A new product among building materials was introduced in Rocky Ford September, 1900 by English Lumber Company. It was an elastic bituminous mineral resin, also known as caoutchouc-gum elastic or India rubber-promoted extensively by the company. It was naturally found as a dark brown-black mineral hydrocarbon, soft, elastic until it hardened in air. It appeared as soft flexible masses like crude natural latex in making rubber.

Elaterite was commercially produced and used in interior decoration, flooring, and building facing stone. It was used by the R.W. English Lumber Company to cover many of its buildings since it was found to be a good insulator against heat. Previous corrugated metal building cover was said by local carpenters to 'kill the life in lumber' by its ability to absorb intensive heat from the sun.

Sanborn map of 1919 identified the material on 100-104 South Main Street, extending to Tenth Street along the railroad. Few houses or out buildings were on the map using the material, one of which was on Maple Avenue between Main and Ninth Streets in 1901.

Other advantages of this material were not given. Because it was used only by English Lumber Company it appears that they were the sole outlet. Elaterite accepted paint so that its natural color could be covered but because of its composition was thought to have potential for fire, therefore did not appear on later Sanborn maps.

Rocky Ford Siege Gun

Photo courtesy of *Rocky Ford Public Museum*

These men sportively gathered together during Pueblo's *Pageant of States and Nations* for the Fourth of July celebration in 1898. Photo is in *Rocky Ford, Colorado–A Walk Past Local Doors,* page 299 to present an example of an exaggerated subject postal card, popular during the era.

Men in the photo were responsible for the construction, transportation and display of their 'gun' in the Pueblo parade of 55 minutes duration. One purpose was to join in the celebration just for the fun of participation. More than that, their float was a great advertisement for Rocky Ford, its melons, and the Arkansas Valley Fair to be held September 1, 1898.

Another Watermelon Day, celebrated in Omaha, Nebraska's on September 15, was also on the agenda for the float and its constructors. Details of transportation were not given.

Exaggerated subject post cards were produced by photographers to promote the town, the Arkansas Valley, its crops, and the Fair. Rocky Ford's own, J.E. Orr very likely produced some of them. Preparation of the *'Gun'* is not described in news articles but it was:

"*... an immense melon, 23 feet long and in correct proportions for the genuine Rocky Ford or Swink* [strain] *Melon.*" *Enterprise* July 7, 1898.

A banner was at each corner of the float, two inscribed *"Captured Great Britain, Canada and New England in 1897. We now besiege Pueblo."* The other banners read *"Watermelon Day at Omaha September 15. Come and see us* [at Rocky Ford] *Sept. 1."*

World's Fair in Chicago during 1897 had a delegation from Rocky Ford, relating to the references above. Produce from Rocky Ford and the Arkansas Valley experienced growing popularity with great reception in Chicago and other large eastern cities. Shipments of melons to countries in Europe were also written in contemporary news.

Platform for the bunting-covered float was *"... drawn by A.M. Jackson's six fine gray horses, proudly tossing handsome plumes."*

The foregoing photo may have been taken during construction of the float since neither banners nor signs are attached. Newspaper articles of the finished float in both Pueblo and Rocky Ford reported reception by parade viewers enthusiastic and accompanied by cheers.

Close inspection of the photo reveals some of the melon-men using spoons. There is reference in the *Enterprise* to spoons carried in jacket lapel button holes during Fair time for just the purpose of melon feasting. Men, women, and children joined in this custom using spoons rather than eating hand-held melon awkwardly while in some of their finer attire.

Watermelon Day, 1898

During this celebration, and up to a month and a half later, the townspeople complained of the careless disregard for disposal of melon rinds that occurred afterward. They were already dealing with English sparrows, tumbleweed, cottonwood seed, blow dirt, and now, flies and bees hovering over spoiling melon remains. City Council addressed the complaint by providing an ordinance dealing with the latter problem which was recurrent each year and getting more attention. Soon, the *Enterprise* editor was able to inform the public of council's specific action.

Enterprise August 18, 1898

—The town authorities are doing a good job in cleaning up the streets and alleys. They have adopted a most commendable prohibition ordinance —forbidding throwing the remains of second-hand watermelons into the streets and alleys. A penalty of $5 will be assessed for violation of this rule.

Watermelon Day popularity was increasing yearly with the crowds coming for the event. Education of those from out-of-town apparently was not enthusiastically or even willingly addressed, as witness the photos of discarded melon remains among the trees of the Fairgrounds. Photos by local photographers depicted Watermelon Day melon remnants well into the 1900s. The discard of remains, to be fair, was not entirely the action of visitors, but also included residents.

Hospitality was foremost among Fair committee members and City Council, who encouraged businessmen and citizens to the same. Hospitality helped business grow, in town and in the Arkansas Valley and there was an understandable reluctance among some to inhibit enthusiasm for the celebration by announcing rules.

The solution eventually and necessarily came to be a two-fold one. Each guest at the melon pile was to receive one of his or her choice, melon or cantaloupe. The person's choice was not to be eaten on the grounds without proper disposal of remains but preferably taken home.

Some who came to town on one of the special trains preferred keeping their memento of Watermelon Day for their train's departure. Forethought among visiting groups had designated some who would harbor their melons aboard until then. Local carriers, previously taking guests to the fairgrounds, now would lend their services returning them to their train for a fee.

West Hotel 1888=Swink Hotel=St. James Hotel 1892   IOOF Hall 1892

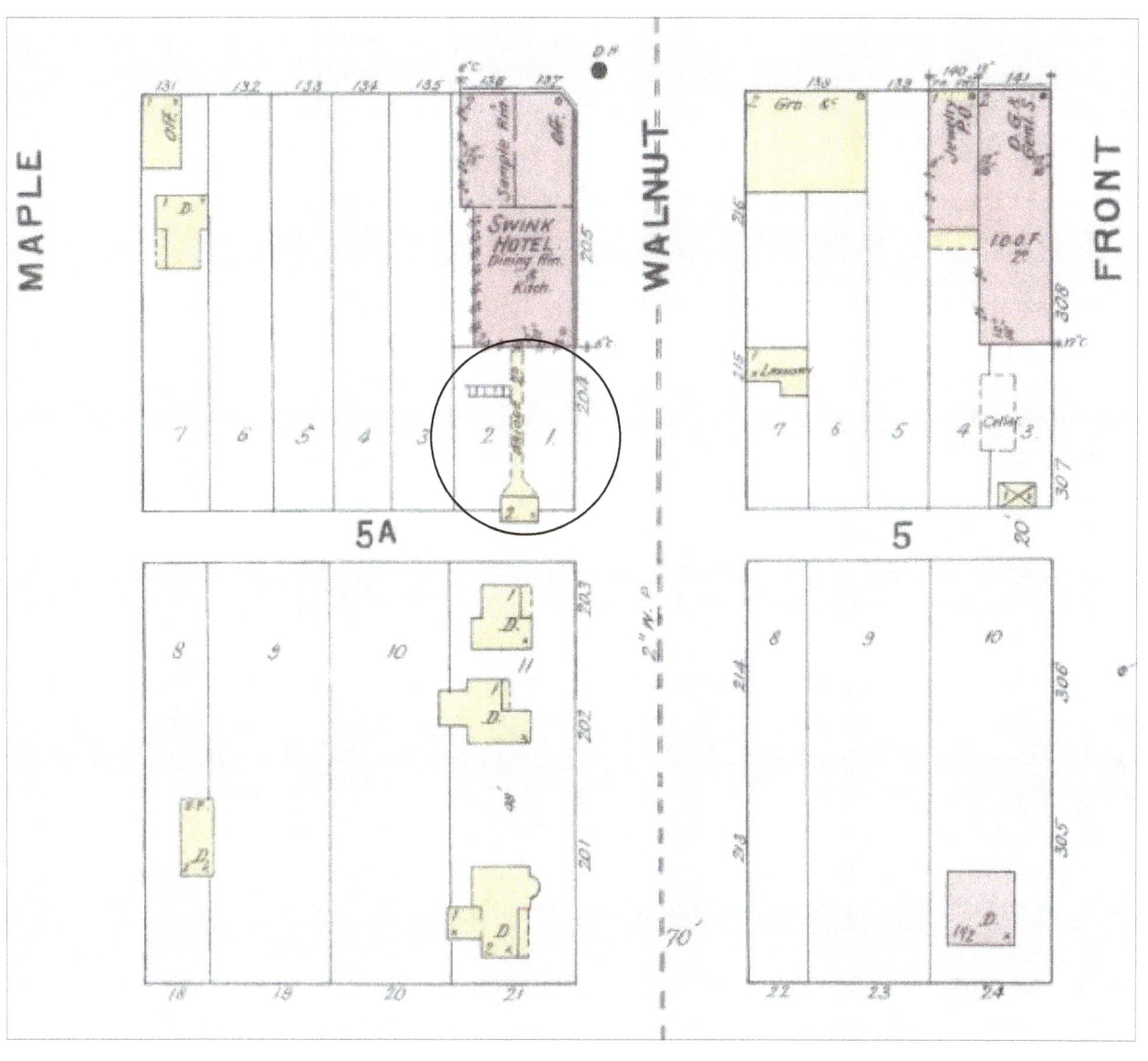

◯ = Bridge   Main Street at top and Tenth Street at bottom of illustration on this Sanborn map.

Sanborn Map of 1895, the 200 and 300 Blocks South Main Street

Map scale indicates a 40 ft. second-story walkway from a doorway on the wall of the Swink Hotel, 300 S Main Street to its novel outhouse at the rear. Walkway indicated as *'Bridge'* also had ground access via ladder or stairs. No reason for such an elevated, long 'bridge' type walkway is given in the hotel's history. Speculation might suggest it was more sanitary to better separate the privy from kitchen and dining areas at rear of the hotel. A later 1901 map shows an additional structure on the ground at the end of the walkway approximately 25' on a side-*page 23.* Atop the structure is a second-story 10' square framed cubicle housing a water closet, maybe the first in Rocky Ford.

Construction of the bridge might also have been to avoid a seepage area behind the hotel such as described for factory ground chosen for worker housing. Construction of the housing could not begin before site drainage and aeration. Existence of a cess pool is unlikely at the rear of the hotel such as the one behind the Longworth Hotel, 410-412 S Main in the block south of the Swink Hotel.

City Council referred to the Health Committee the fact that a cesspool was spilling from its confinement behind the Longworth Hotel, April 30, 1907.

The cellar or basement under the Elk Hotel at 311½ S main "... *contained a large quantity of unwholesome, filthy and stagnant water giving off strong offensive odor to the passers by....*" [witness testimony], June 3, !915.

Mr. Swink and his investors in the success of the hotel could not have been other than serious and deliberate regarding such a bridge-like structure behind their hotel. It must have been necessary and practical for hotel function rather than a whimsical addition to invite notoriety, as in some other towns. However, the structure was removed from service c. 1896 after eight years dating from 1888.

J.P. Salls and Charles Chandler from Colorado Springs [leased ?], then bought the building, made other modifications and renamed the hotel St. James September 27, 1894. Two store fronts, an office on the north, a sample room on the south were in the hotel front. Art goods and '*Notions*' were sold there by later occupants.

IOOF Building, upper right at 200 S Main Street of the previous illustration housed a dry goods and general store in 1895. Smirl's Shoe and Garment and Bonta Mercantile occupied later. A jewelry store next door and eventually the post office occupied store space until the postmaster moved it in 1898.

Frame buildings, *yellow*, are marked '*D*' for Dwelling, '*Off*' for Office, and one is marked '*Laundry*'. '*Gro*' for Grocery may indicate the site of the Big Four Cash Grocery operated by J.W. Leesing and J.W. Rex. This site later housed a barber shop.

Chinese Laundry was facing Walnut Avenue east of the grocery-later barbershop at Main and Walnut Streets. Gee Ging, active c. 1891 to 1901, operated his hand laundry on Walnut Avenue in a small frame building east of those businesses. He retired about 1901 and *John, The Chinaman*, possibly a partner or employee, assumed the business.

J. W. Wolf opened a steam laundry on Tenth Street and Walnut Avenue in 1901, east across the alley of John the Chinaman's business, formerly Gee Ging's. The steam laundry, new process for the time, also eventually influenced John to move on. A notice was posted to customers to come for their clothes and pay up because he was returning to China. The *Enterprise* wrote: *"John, the Chinaman who has served his customers the past ten years or so, could not compete with Mr. Wolf's Modern Steam Laundry, so is going home to China."*

Note: Sample rooms were provided for use by itinerant sales people who displayed wares and entertained prospective customers during their travels.

A Walk in the City

Calaboose was built October 1, 1887, east of Green and Babcock, a solid structure of 2 x 4s at 203 South Eleventh, south of Front Street near the railroad. The South Eleventh area had been ceded by Rocky Ford Town and Investment Company for administration and other buildings. The Investment Company dissolved March 28, 1902.

City marshal said the calaboose needed two locks, also a cleaning as he reported to the council meeting September 3, 1894. There is no known photo of the place and as related in city record, J.R. DeWeese was first marshal, paid $50.00 monthly in 1902. Police administration or law enforcement activity between 1887 and 1894 was not always known to be continuously staffed.

Sanborn Maps of Rocky Ford were not in existence until 1895. One small section of the two-page map of town is shown here. Buildings were sparse in number but for the enterprises located on the 200-300 blocks of N Main, *only east side shown* upper left in the map section.

Calaboose was relocated to 956 Elm Avenue in 1895 on the alley on the northwest corner of the lot at Elm Avenue where later would be part of June Chevrolet. The jail was eventually moved into the new 1919 City Hall at 203 North Ninth Street and enlarged in 1954. The former calaboose was later a tamale factory on the 1901 Sanborn map and vacant in 1906.

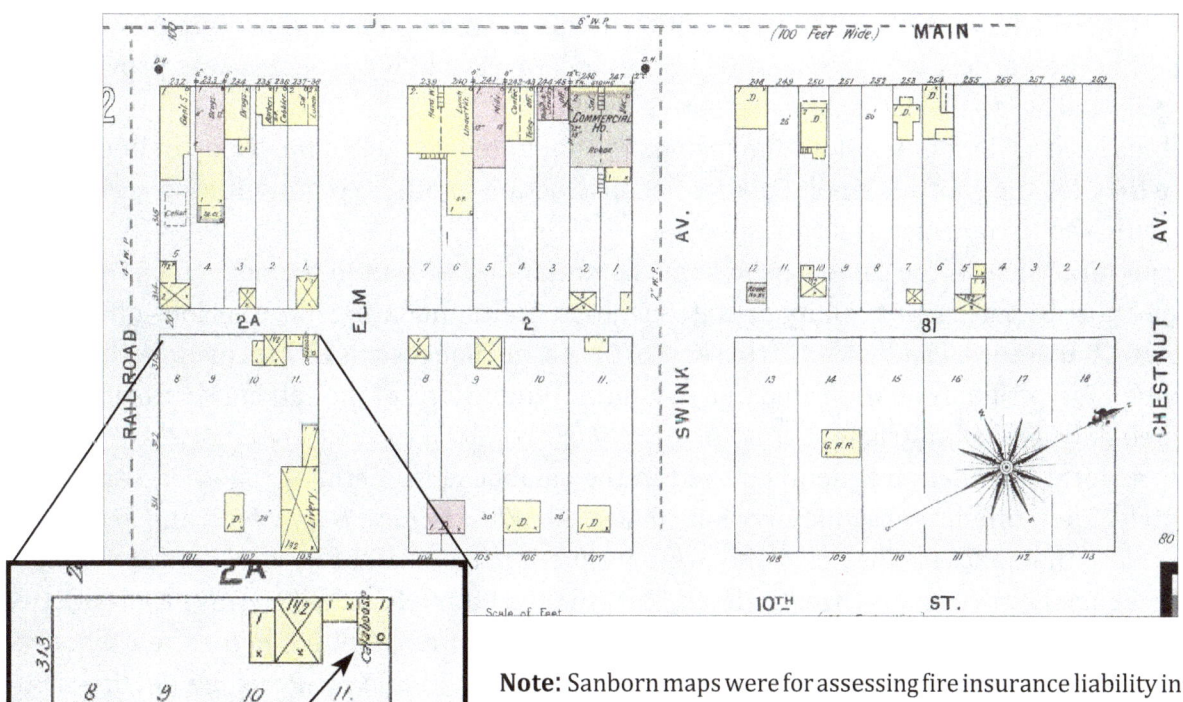

Note: Sanborn maps were for assessing fire insurance liability in urban areas across the US. Scale obscured on this map.

Section at left is part of block occupied once by June Chevrolet. It shows *calaboose* on the alley corner with Elm Avenue. Small building adjacent is likely an outhouse. Adjacent is a 1-1/2 story structure with attached building or shed. All are wooden framed. Structure marked 'D' is a one-story dwelling.

The livery is not named, one of several in town. Liveries were always identified, as well as buildings and businesses with furnaces, stoves and heaters, forges, electric motors, gasoline engines, and flammables.

cudl/.colorado.edu/luna/...and links

Calaboose Amenities

Historically the calaboose, hoosegow or jail in cities and towns in the west and mid-west was built and furnished for the towns' particular requirements with few extras for inmates. Most were small and plain thereby presenting to all as well as to potential miscreants the prospect of an undesirable and uncomfortable stay if warranted.

Stone or concrete formed some walls and roofs. Some were built of logs, the result resembling a small cabin in the mountains. Most had one small barred window with or without glass; many without. Some walls were built window-less in favor of a small barred one in a reinforced door.

Rocky Ford calaboose was built with 2 x 4 lumber, abutted flat side, which greatly increased strength of walls and door. Broad surfaces of the lumber were interfaced and the narrow edges formed the inner and outer walls. This arrangement resulted in a 'stacked' appearance of 2 x 4s.

Square foot dimensions were small, reducing cost and creating a close confining space. The consequence of such meager square footage must have had a stifling effect on the psyche of some. For the inebriate this did not matter possibly until his senses returned in a few hours or maybe by the next morning.

Some jails that were similarly sized and constructed were furnished with a rude bunk or stacked bunk beds for multiple inmates. Other items such as plumbing or lighting were not provided in the earliest jails nor was heating. A box or very likely a bucket was provided for seating as well as for the necessary alternative to plumbing.

Details such as door or window dimensions are not noted on the Sanborn map of Rocky Ford nor are they for the roof and floor. Calaboose construction in other communities describes dirt floors with a solid roof, materials not specified.

A temporary use of the calaboose in some communities was often the goal when offenders were en-route to permanent county or state facilities, accommodating more serious offenders.

Town Characters. The 2 x 4 construct east of Green and Babcock in 1895 provided a hot place in summer and probably an unheated one in winter. Dimensions of the calaboose are unknown, described only as a solid structure.

Three local offenders frequently stayed in the calaboose, sometimes together, sometimes separately. Their offenses are unknown but suspected. *Whiskey Jack, Happy Jack*, and *Peg-Leg* or *Ole Peg* were their aliases. They probably were frequent patrons of the several bars and saloons in town which they over-patronized at times. Early in the 1900s when Ole Peg was in jail with two others, probably the two already mentioned, he unwillingly or not abetted their escape when his jail mates took his leg off to knock a hole in the roof. They did leave Peg's leg outside as he declined escape for he felt the security of a sturdy bed.

Note: Calaboose had been part of the English language for almost a century when John S. Farmer included the term in his 1889 book *Americanisms - Old & New*, defining it as the common *gaol* or *prison*. Farmer also mentioned a verb calaboose, meaning *to imprison*, but that term was apparently lost in the years between then and now. *Calaboose* is Spanish in origin, from the Spanish word *calabozo*, meaning *dungeon*. **Synonyms**: bastille, big house [slang], bridewell, brig, can, clink [slang], cooler, coop, guardroom, hock, hold, hoosegow, jail, jailhouse, joint [slang], jug, lockup, pen, penitentiary, pokey [slang], prison, slam, slammer, stir [slang], stockade.

merriam-webster.com/dictionary/calaboose

A Walk in the City

Hospitals of Rocky Ford

Pollock's Hospital was opened in 1907 at 915 Chestnut Avenue, the current annex to El Capitan Hotel. Pollock's Hospital was built with leadership of Dr. R.M. Pollock who also organized the Rocky Ford Hospital Association. Though extant, the building remained as a hospital only from 1907 to 1915. Dr. Moody was on the staff with Dr. Pollock.

Physicians Hospital at 803-805 Maple was built by brothers Drs. B.F. and B.B. Blotz in 1915, succeeding Pollock's Hospital. Hospital care was offered there until c. 1954. Though extant, the building was later to become Bauer Home, a nursing care facility.

Pioneer Memorial Hospital was dedicated August, 1954 after deconstruction of Washington School at 900 S Twelfth Street. Hospital administration eventually ceased, with hospital care being obtained in La Junta.

Pioneer Health Care Center was the original 1954 hospital building, now home of nursing, rehabilitation, and respite care services for patients in the city.

TB Sanitarium on the grounds at Twelfth Street south of the railroad tracks in 1896 once served victims of tuberculosis and other upper respiratory ailments. Many came from the east for the sunshine supported by friends and relatives who gathered funds for them to come to Rocky Ford. Tents were set up for them among a grove of trees.

Van Antwerp Sanitarium at 401 S Main was so named for treatment of specific types of ailments. It opened early in Rocky Ford history offering services supportive of quiet and restful rehabilitation and convalescence for the invalid such as TB patients need.

Garden Place Hospital-Sanitarium, built by C.H. (Marshal) Baldwin was advertised January 16, 1903 in the *Enterprise* as opening of a new, well-lighted building having all the

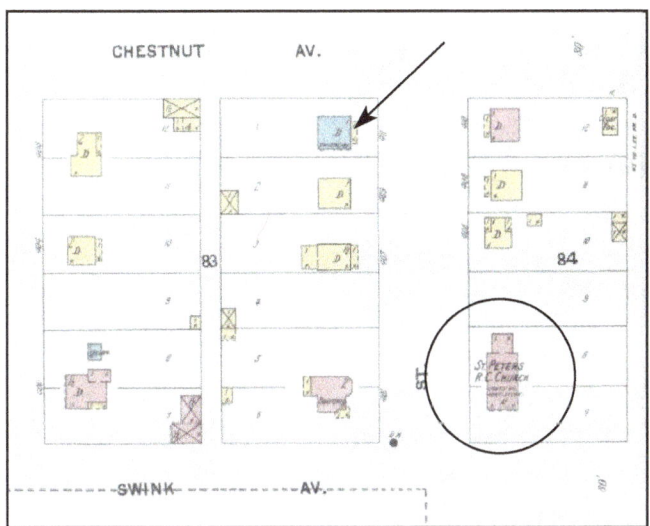

Sanford map portion, 1901

modern conveniences for care of "*... transient sufferers of accidents, the sick from TB who need the restorative climate of the Arkansas Valley.*" A street address, which included a number of "*Sanitary Tents*" for TB patients, was not printed.

Fisher Smith Hospital, operated by Dr. Smith, opened August 1, 1904 as a ten-bed hospital in the large concrete residence of W.P. Clark on the Southwest corner of Twelfth Street and Chestnut Avenue. Mrs. Smith, the doctor's wife, was a trained nurse and hospital administrator. Although this concrete home-hospital was extant on Sanborn maps of 1901 through 1919 it apparently did not survive as a hospital many years after Physicians Hospital open in 1915. A house, extant on location-*arrow*, is site of and possibly the original with siding.

In 1901, the original Catholic Church, Twelfth Street and Swink Avenue, *circle*, preceded construction of the rectory and is included for reference.

A search for hospitals among newspaper ads and articles yielded conjoined ads of two hospitals and their proprietors. Dr. Smith's, City Hospital, also called Fisher Smith Hospital described previously, and which was apparently simultaneously a residence at 411 North Twelfth Street. Another, the Red Cross Hospital of Dr. S.J. Greear indicates only South Main Street. It may have been part of the Van Antwerp Sanitarium at 401 although there is no confirmation. No other hospital was known on South Main Street.

Dr. Smith's hospital opened August 1, 1904 just a month prior the advertisement. Both doctors apparently cooperated in placement of their ad; perhaps they also cooperated in the medical profession. Longevity of either hospital isn't known but perhaps they were in operation until the Pollock hospital in 1907 or Physicians Hospital in 1915.

Physicians Hospital continued serving the community until August 1954 and the dedication of Pioneer Memorial Hospital.

Enterprise
September 2, 1904

Note: Dr. Paul P. Keck arrived September 1907, apparently the first veterinarian in town, to open a veterinary hospital at Ninth and Walnut, in the former Grand Valley Livery-page 7.

Santa Fe Stock Yard, 1902

South Fourth Street ends at the tracks-*line*-where a small corral-*circle*-held cattle for shipment. It was built in 1902 and used through the 1950s when field loading became common with advent of trailers and trucks. Decreasing use of this and the 1893 corral brought their removal in the 1960s.

Scale=1:20,000
Soil Conservation Service photo AG-282-96, Oct. 4, 1936

Supplemental feeding of cattle with beet pulp during beet sugar campaign was done here as well as in the yard east of Fifteenth Street. Rail sidings were near both for ease of loading. Users of the pens were farmers, ranchers and feeders associated with the American Beet Sugar Company and who also raised beets.

Upper left of photo shows west curve of two-lane US 50 traversing town. Three years prior the photo on November 7, 1933, city council arranged for paving US 50 in concrete.

Santa Fe Stock Yard, 1893

On the eastern edge of town just east of Fifteenth Street, the Santa Fe maintained its first cattle pens In Rocky Ford-*arrow*. The Soil Conservation Service (SCS) photo below shows them a few days after the 1902 corral at left.

Two-lane US 50 entering Rocky Ford from the east passes the gateway obelisks leading to Railroad Avenue and continues on Elm Avenue curving upper left traveling through town to the west curve of US 50.

The gateway obelisks-*circle*-are casting a shadow in late morning or early afternoon sun.

SCS photo AG-371-57, Nov. 20, 1936. Scale=1:20,000

Stauffer Packing and holding pens, opened December 15, 1914, are lower right View the 1893 pens in a 1931 photo following.

Santa Fe Stockyard, 1893

East of Fifteenth Street adjacent the tracks Santa Fe officials established holding pens for convenience of cattle shipment. This photo looking west April 16, 1931 is from top of a cattle car. Santa Fe Agent, D.K. Spencer in Rocky Ford, described this rail-side accommodation to shippers in the cattle raising industry:

kansasmemory.org/item/215841

"We ... had two stock yards, one on each end of town, and shipped a few cars of cattle after my arrival [transfer from Lamar]. *Several stock feeding operations had been formed after 1900 using the ample amount of sugar beet pulp that had been generated by the sugar factory as feed. This business* [shipping by rail] *died during the 1950's with the advent of "in the field" handling by motor carriers."*   D.K. Spencer, Station Agent, 1956-1979.

The area of these stock pens was at the western edge of the Artificial Lake site of G.W. Swink constructed to completion in January, 1882. The pens were co-existent with the lake, according to statements in the *Enterprise* by residents, and were in use approximately 50 years from c. 1900 before truck transport from the field reduced their need. These pens and those at the Fifth Street location were removed in the 1960s.

Note: Some townspeople, early in the sugar factory annual campaigns, complained to city council and through them to the factory officials about the odors coming from beet pulp. The two holding corals within the city were especially noted due to proximity to close neighborhoods. Fresh-from-the-factory pulp was not so noxious but as some uneaten by cattle stayed in feed bunkers it began to ferment and draw flies and other insects. Feeding times and amounts were modified to appease citizenry, but with time, as with 'the grandfather clock in the hall', the odor was all but ignored.

Ball Games

The editor of the *Bent County Register*, describing a local game, broadened his journalistic style to include poetic ability for the entertainment of his readers, and with a bit of humor. He never mentions the score. His description of the game, probably played in Lamar, ended by leaving the reader to determine whether or not the players were able to leave the field on their own.

Bent County Register, July 9, 1887

> Once upon a time, No matter when, A game of ball was played by men, This has oft been done before, But scarcely with such mirth and roar, For on each base, We believe t'was three, Stood the couse of all this glee, To mark each base and know each peg, There stood a familar looking keg, And before the batter dared to pass, He had to stop and take a glass, This rule is not laid down by Hoyle, But one adapted the score to spoil, So if a batter a base ran bye, The crowd set up a hue and cry, And amid the din and cheer, He was ordered back to take his beer, To play this game t'would take a year, If the kegs had not run out of beer, As it was the boys had fun, The only reason the game begun.

Many towns had baseball or softball teams, some made up of local businessmen, as in Rocky Ford, some by player-fans of all ages. Early 1900s teams included one representing Rocky Ford but with team members from other locations. The Rocky Ford Ball Club of 1907 played under that name but was based in Denver listed as a pro or semi-pro team. Perhaps the reason for location being business support in financing the team with pay, uniforms, equipment, and travel expenses. Advertising the town on uniforms was likely with the support of local businesses.

Rocky Ford High School fielded a team soon after their new 1908 building was completed on Sycamore Avenue between Eighth and Ninth Streets. They were known as the *Rocky Ford Melon Boys, Rocky Ford Nine* or *Rocky Ford Team*, well before the *Meloneer* name was adopted. The nine players and manager were photographed in 1912 after winning the Colorado-Northern New Mexico championship (see *Rocky Ford, Colorado-A Walk Past Local Doors* p. 31; p. 182).

A Game of *Base Ball*

A brief article in the Rocky Ford *Enterprise* informed readers in one sentence that the *Leans* beat the *Fats* in a game of *'base ball'*. Noted they; The *defeated* weren't even capitalized!

> —In the game of base ball between the Leans and the Fats of Rocky Ford, the fats were defeated.

Enterprise July 14, 1898

The statement apparently came under criticism immediately the day after the game but not until the following week could the Fats publish their condemnation of this false information. The news- *Fats actually beat the Leans*, could not be publicized sooner since the paper was a weekly on Thursday. For a whole week the Fats must have been laying for the editor, waiting for him to be out on the street, possibly to extract a public reversal.

In his effort to move past the subject the editor was animated in explaining that basically the information came to the *Enterprise* through a 'schoolboy's essay' written about a 'country editor'. The whole lengthy contrivance was placed before the public in the following week's edition.

The public, reading between the lines, appreciated the humor of the editor describing himself as the country editor who wrote the essay as would a 'schoolboy'. He did not, however, openly own up to the error regarding the winner but only a very few would not know who the *Philistine* was. (low-brow, uneducated, anti intellectual)

The editor did "Take it Back" however in his flamboyant and hidden self-chastising way in a journalistic style designed to generate interest among his readers.

> —Only our great personal courage prompted us to be on the streets of Rocky Ford on Friday last. Several of the weightiest men in town—regular athletes—were "laying for us," and our readers may be thankful that the Enterprise did not cease with our last issue. The schoolboy in his essay on the country editor said that he never knew of but one editor to get licked and the way that happened was that his paper stopped and he couldn't take it back. Fortunately the Enterprise has not stopped and we can "Take it back." The item which made all the trouble was that saying that the game between the Leans and the Fats, the latter were defeated. This statement the Fats emphatically declare to be a double-breasted falsification. And when nine robust, able-bodied men, whose average weight is 175 pounds, all sit down on us in that vigorous manner we feel like inquiring if we have not made a mistake. We were grossly in error in this matter. The facts are that the Fats beat the Leans two to one. It is a matter of deep regret that we can not recall the name of the Philistine who gave us the false information. It would be a genuine pleasure to turn upon him a portion of the wrath which has been generated by our getting the Fats roasted instead of the Leans.

bing.com/images

Enterprise July 21, 1898

Hay Palace, 1893

Before 1900, hay was cut by hand and stored in sheaves until placed later in stacks. Forks were used to rake and gather it into convenient sized stacks.

In the 1860s, mechanical cutters had developed from which came horse-drawn mechanized mowers and balers. In 1872, a reaper that used a knotting device to bundle and bind hay was invented. This was commercialized in 1874 by Cyrus McCormick. In 1936 the automatic baler was invented that tied bales with twine using knotters from a John Deere grain binder, improved in 1938.

The first *round* baler was probably invented in the late 1800s. An early one was shown in Paris demonstrating steam power in agriculture. This was a portable machine designed for baling straw near the threshing site.

Enterprise, August 31, 1893

Emphasis was placed on hay during agricultural displays at the Fair from 1893 to 1898, partially because of its abundance, but also because it could provide a suitable temporary display area for many agricultural products.

> **THE ALFALFA PALACE.**
>
> This unique structure is the first of this kind in the history of agricultural fairs. It will be in circular form and built wholly of baled alfalfa. A portion of the roof will be thatched with fresh, bright green alfalfa, giving it a very attractive appearance and most appropriately harmonizing with the fine display of farm products with wich it will be crowded. A table composed of baled hay will extend around the entire circumference of the palace, which, with the facilities for display upon the high alfalfa walls, will make the building difficult to excell for the purposes for which it is constructed. The alfalfa palace will be one of the great attractions of the fair and will be worthy of seeing both for itself and for the magnificent display of cereals, melons, fruits, etc., which it will contain.

Note: 'Hay' and 'alfalfa' are often used to identify the same thing. They both provide a fodder for farm animals and many herbivores in nature. *Hay* is basically a generic term identifying a grass, legume, or other herbaceous plant that is cut and dried for storage to be used for animal fodder. *Alfalfa* is a perennial flowering plant in the legume family and is one kind of hay. It is cultivated as an important forage crop in many countries around the world and is particularly attractive to honey bees when it flowers.

Hay Palace, 1898

The Arkansas Valley Fair in 1893 thru September 1, 1898 erected this agricultural products display area. A site on the fairgrounds was selected and this feature was re-built every year of hay bales covered partially by a canvas roof and thatched alfalfa.

While this seems novel to the Fair and the town of Rocky Ford there were in other communities such like structures, erected at regional fair times for display and judging of agricultural products. There were Hay Palaces so named in Sugar City and Greeley, Colorado. Likely in other areas of agricultural prominence as well.

These 'palaces' varied in size but were large enough to cover a significant display area. The one depicted in the photo was an overflow space adjunct to and near a permanent structure displaying other like products. It also provided a measure of relief from the summer sun for many fair-goers around harvest time.

The last Hay Palace (below) during the Arkansas Valley Fair of 1898 was dismantled and soon after replaced by a frame structure among the former Swink grove that remained from the Timber Culture Claim of November 3, 1887. Already 11 years old, trees planted then were large enough to supply abundant shade to modify the heat of the day.

Construction of a hay palace today likely would be discouraged because of fire danger. Smokers of the early day fairs might have felt at home in such an outdoor environment then but a careless person's actions could have ruined the day.

ARKANSAS VALLEY EXPERIMENT STATION Fair Display 1898

This heading was signed using sections of small tree branches fastened to a rigid background for this Hay Palace. Open sacks of seed types were displayed below grain shocks. Large squash are to the right above corn ears lying on a shelf. Jars of honey appear to be on the cabinet shelf. Bales of hay are visible below the sign and behind the display and the child. Courtesy Herman Boraker in *Rocky Ford, Colorado 100th Anniversary 1887-1987 Calendar*.

Sheets of canvas covered part of the roof. The Experiment Station, established 1888, and its staff have posted some photos and data on the bales left and center background.

Agricultural Building, 1898

> Carpenters are now at work on the new Agricultural building which takes the place of the temporary alfalfa palace of former years. This building will be 30 by 100 feet and will be situated in the fine grove recently purchased of Senator Swink. Just west of the Agricultural building will be erected a poultry house of much greater size than heretofore used. These two buildings will add much to the Fair's facilities for caring for exhibits and conduce much to the comfort and enjoyment of visitors.

Enterprise July 14, 1898

> To the left of the main entrance to the fair grounds stands the building erected to take the place of the Alfalfa palace. This building contains a dazzling array of the finest fruits and grains grown, and an entire day could be spent therein to great advantage, says the Pueblo Chieftain

Enterprise September 14, 1900

Enterprise, August 9, 1901

Rocky Ford's Tenth Fair

New Buildings and Other Extensive Improvements in Progress.

The officers of the Arkansas Valley Fair appreciate the importance it has attained and the growing interest of the people over a wide scope of country. This is demonstrated by the interest which the officers and directors take in all matters pertaining to the Fair and by the liberal appropriations for new buildings.

A large crowd of workmen are employed in various parts of the grounds. The judges' stand has been rebuilt and made much more sightly. The new and handsome ticket office has been erected just outside the grounds. The hall for the display of fruits and agricultural products, poultry, etc., has been doubled in size and built in a most substantial manner. At the western end of this long building ample provisions has been made for a very extensive poultry and Belgian hare display. Heretofore the accommodations for these departments have been so inadequate as to cause some of the leading exhibitors to remain away. They will have no cause to do so this year as most liberal space has been provided in a building of the best character, protected from drafts and well ventilated. A knowledge of the extensive arrangements made for their benefit should attract many new exhibitors of poultry and Belgian hares.

Last and best of all the improvements is the Art hall in the fine grove just south of the grand stand. This building is octagonal, about 300 feet in circumference. It is a frame structure, both substantial and ornamental. All around the outer circumference will be tables, and another circle of tables will be provided around the pillars supporting the center. The building will be lighted by windows on four sides, giving ample light. In this commodious structure the ladies will have facilities for the display of their handiwork far superior to the past. The various elegant articles which should be on exhibition will now have a degree of care and protection never before possible. The ladies of Otero county should take a renewed interest in this department and fill the Art building to its full capacity.

In the stables are an unusual number of fine and fast horses. The speed ring part of the Fair program promises to be more attractive than ever before.

From all reports the attendance from outside the county is going to be in excess of former years. The outlook is that the coming exhibition will be the best and most largely attended in the history of the association.

Arkansas Valley Fair Board, in 1897-1898, having completed much discussion and planning for improvements to a variety of projects, set contractors and their men to work. Many changes to the whole of the Fairgrounds were completed before the 1901 Fair opening. Several new additions were in place to receive displays of an agricultural nature, handiwork of those from different age brackets, and several forms of art to be displayed in a new setting, the Arts Building or Hall. Grooming of the 'speed ring' [race track] was done as well as maintenance and cleaning of the horse barns. Judges for the various events to take place in front of the Grandstand would view from a roofed high-rise structure on the infield. To take advantage of it all fair-goers would enter through a 'new and handsome ticket office' at the gate.

Note: highlights remain from a word search.

Arts Building, 1901

Built directly behind (south) of the grandstand in 1901, this building is now a registered national historical site.

Note: Spot blemishes damaged the photo in several places.

Interior furnishings are described in an August news article in the *Enterprise* just before the Fair of 1901 (following page). A small tree is planted inside a concrete ring at left front (spots are film damage).

Appearance then

Sanborn map section of 1901 Fairgrounds shows the hexagonal Arts building in relationship to other buildings. Far right narrow structure shows position of horse stalls along east boundary of the fairgrounds.

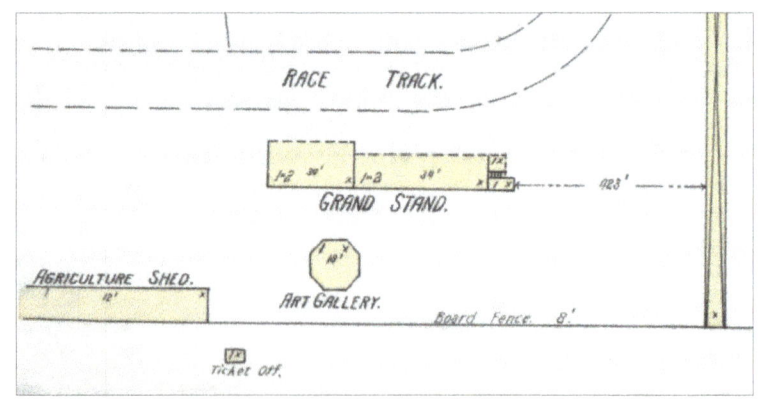

Appearance now

Present Site is near the exposition building. Exterior preserves original architecture, studiously maintained with a new roof. Original stepped concrete entryway was not preserved.

https://en.wikipedia.org/wiki/Art_Building_(Rocky Ford,_Colorado)

Fairground Construction and Additions

Many improvements were made to the fairgrounds before the Fair of 1901. Perhaps the most significant was the new Arts building.

Enterprise, August 9, 1901

> Last and best of all the improvements is the Art hall in the fine grove just south of the grand stand. This building is octagonal, about 300 feet in circumference. It is a frame structure, both substantial and ornamental. All around the outer circumference will be tables, and another circle of tables will be provided around the pillars supporting the center. The building will be lighted by windows on four sides, giving ample light. In this commodious structure the ladies will have facilities for the display of their handiwork far superior to the past. The various elegant articles which should be on exhibition will now have a degree of care and protection never before possible. The ladies of Otero county should take a renewed interest in this department and fill the Art building to its full capacity.

More improvements were planned, according to the 1908 article. Nature of the delay is not known but some of the Fair Association plans came later.

> Whereas, the necessity has become apparent for additional ground for the proper accommodation of the exhibitors and patrons of our Fair, and
>
> Whereas, a proposition has been secured from Geo. W. Swink, owner of ground adjoining our present Fair ground, for selling to the association the balance of the grove south and west of the ground (approximately 2 acres) for the sum of $2300, and for the 20 acres north of the present grounds (less 3 acres off the north side for railroad right of way) for the sum of $4,250; also for forty acres northeast of the Fair Ground (less 3 acres for railroad right of way) known as the old lake, for the sum of $3,700, with one-half share of Rocky Ford Ditch stock for the twenty acre tract and 46-100 of a share of the Rocky Ford Ditch stock for the forty acre tract.

Enterprise, September 23, 1910

> **Rocky Ford Fair Grounds Enlarged.**
>
> Following recent improvements at the Arkansas Valley Fair Association grounds at Rocky Ford, to the extent of nearly $6,000, comes the announcement of the purchase by the association of an additional tract of fifty-three acres adjoining the present grounds, which will be parked and fitted for conveniences for the fair visitors. The site, which was purchased from G. W. Swink for $10,000, includes a lake, which will be further improved and form an attractive feature of the big valley fair.

Enterprise, October 10, 1908

Arkansas Valley Fair Board moved significantly in 1910 by enlarging the fairgrounds with several purchases from G.W. Swink (see page 30).

Depot vs Station

The Atcheson, Topeka & Santa Fe Railroad in November, 1944 listed 2431 stations in settlements on their lines, not all of which had passenger depot facilities. There were stations, in the early development of its rail lines, that were on sidings with rudimentary or no facilities, and with business being taken care of by an Agent under a tent, in a shed or nearby established business.

In Rocky Ford, with no separate facilities initially, the Agent was G.W. Swink in his store. Many small stations were known as a *one person agency*, with Agent also performing every other duty.

A small, red, sand-painted frame depot was constructed just west of the Nichols Avenue or Kit Carson Road, later Tenth Street, crossing the main road from Kit Carson, Colorado to Mexico. George W. Swink moved his store from Old Rocky Ford river crossing to just east of the depot described above and became the first Agent for the Santa Fe in 1876.

Paraphrased from D. K. Spencer, 1987, *The History of the Rocky Ford, Colorado Depot.*

The small station described as preceding the Swink store in 1876 when it was built track-side is the one of author speculation as to size and tenure. Size has not been determined but longevity was about 11 years, 1876 to 1887.

Depots, Depots Everywhere, but not one to Spare! From Historical Material Provided by D.K. Spencer.

Note: *Sand-painted* was the descriptive term used by Agent D.K. Spencer, August 19, 1987. *Sand-painted* referred to *color* of sand in the Santa Fe color scheme for buildings and rolling stock rather than sand applied to paint or adhesive as in art of sand-painting by native tribes. Overall result was an attractive display of the tones and colors of the southwestern landscape.

Use of *depot* or *station* by railroaders was interchangeable and amounted nearly to personal preference. The former described a terminal, terminus (destination), or entrepot (transshipment center); the latter a base, place, or post.

Spoons were one of many types of souvenir presented each year at the Fair. Many souvenirs were offered free to the public by merchants in town and other Valley towns for the business of advertising. The spoon was a popular Fair memento presented as a practical aid in the couth consumption of melons on the celebration day. Rocky Ford, Colo. was engraved on the bowl, purchaser's name etched on the handle. Those who attended Watermelon Day and participated in the melon give-away quickly learned the use of spare button holes on collars, lapels, and other convenient locations of one's dress to carry the item.

Souvenir coins, belt buckles, wooden nickels, pinwheels, banners and pins were among many other mementos, the kinds of which changed in successive Fair years.

AT & SF RR Depot

Soon after G.W. Swink built his adobe store near the track in 1876 he was named Station Agent for the railroad. He also was US Postmaster in the same location. Mr. Swink continued his store business while the Santa Fe later installed Mr. Amos as Station Agent in the small building near Main Street and west of the store. This was the first building Telegrapher Horace Amos operated from, likely a small frame structure as depicted previously.

The 1880 census, first one available for town, counted 47 individuals living in the vicinity of the new Rocky Ford. Pioneer Mattie Swink, a daughter of the store owner, wrote 12 years later in the December, 1892 *Enterprise*:

> *"The only house at that time [1876] at the town site was a small adobe residence which had been erected a little while before by George W. Nichols."*

Other buildings were the Swink store, wood-frame hotel and a blacksmith shop. Some individuals were living in tents or rudimentary lean-to, actively filing or proving up on land claims. A *'station'* was spoken of at this time in pioneer LeRoy Elser's letter, rather than a depot along the tracks:

> *"The railroad station was a small, red, sandpainted (sic) building north of the tracks some distance east of Main Street."*   Rocky Ford Daily Gazette, August 26, 1955.

North of the tracks c. 1876 indicated one line through the small settlement with a siding for servicing the Swink store. There is a period of 11 years from the time of the small station to one identified as the board-battened depot built by the Santa Fe. The former is the building that was moved to Hoehne, Colorado c. 1887 when the latter depot was built at 105 South Main Street.

Existence of an emerging settlement, like the new Rocky Ford along the Santa Fe tracks, must have delayed investment in a new, larger depot until the town and its business had increased. Apparently, filing town incorporation papers was a signal the time was appropriate because this was accomplished August 19, 1887 in Denver.

D.K. Spencer, in his August 19, 1987 chronicle, *The History of the Rocky Ford, Colorado Depot*, had described the arrival in town of the railroad in 1876:

> *"A small, red, sand-painted frame depot was constructed just west of the Nichols Avenue (10th Street) crossing, which was the main road from Kit Carson, Colorado to Mexico. The state of Colorado was ratified in 1876, and New Mexico was not to be a state until 1912; therefore, the road was known as the Mexico Road. George W. Swink moved his store from the river crossing to just east of the depot and became the first agent for the Santa Fe in 1876. His store and post office became the hub of the area with all kinds of merchandise being brought in by railroad for the big task of building a new city."*

The move of store business from Old Rocky Ford to *'just east of the depot'* confirms the pre-existence of the depot and building of the adobe store soon after the Santa Fe track arrival.

Secret Societies

Organizations in the 1915 city directory are not all now currently represented but all were listed by the editor, F. A. McKinney, as *secret* in his publication.

Secret Society for the time simply was an organization, fraternal, sororal or communal whose members took secret [confidential] initiation oaths, shared secret passwords and rites, and were pledged to mutual support. They participated in social or service activities in their communities. Today, they may present different views of themselves to the public considering *secret* now has many shades of meaning, most benign and beneficial, but at least one, sinister.

Notably absent from the directory is the Ku Klux Klan (KKK) of the latter shade of meaning. Though not listed, the Klan was in Colorado. The first KKK. originated in 1866 Tennessee. A *Realm* was established in Colorado in 1915 and by the mid 1920s had significant influence, gaining control of the state legislature, governor's office, Denver mayor's office, Denver police department, and many among the Protestant community. The KKK. operated by exploiting local cultural and ethnic differences and prejudices with its message of "100 percent Americanism." Their slogan meant accord in thinking, cultural and ethnic appearance, and communal activity.

The Klan was active in Rocky Ford, but not discussed in the *Enterprise*. KKK activity in the Arkansas Valley is related on page 57.

Source: *City Directory of* **1915**
Benevolent and Protective Order of Elks (BPOE). Rocky Ford Lodge No. 1147
Brotherhood of American Yeomen. Rocky Ford Homestead No. 714
Court of Honor. Rocky Ford Lodge No 1053
Grand Army of the Republic (GAR). Wadsworth Post No 9
Women's Relief Corps. No. 16
Ladies of the GAR. Rocky Ford Circle No. 17
Independent Order of Odd Fellows (IOOF). Rocky Ford Lodge No 87
Daughters of Rebekah. Violet Rebekah Lodge No 3
Knights of Pythias (K of P). Valley Lodge No 98
Loyal Order of Moose. Rocky Ford Lodge No 306
Masonic. St John's Lodge No 75, AF and AM (Ancient Free and Accepted Masons)
Royal Arch Masons. Rocky Ford Chapter No 36
Order of Eastern Star (OES). Acacia Chapter No 38
Modern Woodmen of America (MWA). Rocky Ford Camp No 7473
Royal Neighbors of America. Woodbine Camp No 4221
PEO. Chapter R. Philanthropic Educational Organization. Original society letters had a different meaning that continues to be "reserved for members only" today.
United Spanish War Veterans. Fidus Camp No 10
Woodmen of the World. Rocky Ford Camp No 195
Women of Woodcraft. Gem Circle No 196

Membership in an organization did not always preclude simultaneous membership in another. The Business Men's Party, though political, had members in fraternal service organizations, also.

In May, 1914 a new 'secret society' was formed among the young ladies of town, mostly for fun.

Tuck-a-Batchee Club was named for *Tukabatchee* or Tuckabatchee, one of the four original towns of the Muscogee Creek Indian Confederacy. The tribal town was located on the Tallapoosa River in the present-day state of Alabama (statehood 1819).

Tukabatchee was the home of *Big Warrior*, one of the two principal Cree chiefs until his death in 1826. Chief Opothleyahola, born there in 1780, preceded him. *Enterprise* May 29, 1914

> "Tuck-a-Batchee" is the name of the new club organized by the younger set in Rocky Ford. The girls have not let us into the secret of the extraordinary name but we know it is all right anyway. Miss Leo Shelton was the hostess on Tuesday evening of this week and a most enjoyable time is reported.

In 1811, leaders Tecumseh and Tenskwatawa spoke to Creek leaders in the Tukabatchee town square to express their disappointment in American expansion into their confederacy. Tecumseh said Chalagawtha- their Prophet- would "...stamp his foot and all of Tukabatchee's cabins would fall." The town was leveled by an earthquake a month later. wikipedia.org/wiki/Tukabatchee

Note: In 1811–1812 New Madrid, Missouri, on the Mississippi River, experienced earthquakes beginning with one of magnitude 7.2–8.2 December 16, 1811, followed by a magnitude 7.4 aftershock the same day. Two additional earthquakes of similar magnitude followed in January and February 1812. The reputation of 'Prophet' Chalagawtha was thereby significantly enhanced.

The Tuck-a-Batchee girls were possibly inventing a fad among the town's *"younger set"* as the editor called them. Their club, with its ... *"extraordinary name"*... , might have been chosen simply because it was extraordinary. Some young people experiment with clothing arrangements, hair, or makeup and may have been setting such goals for their club.

A chewing gum *fad* a few years previous was the object of the *Enterprise* editor's counsel:

"Girls, if you must chew gum, don't do so at Sunday school and church. As you approach the church carefully, place the gum under the edge of the sidewalk [boardwalk, at this time] *where you can get it as you come out. Then as going home it would be well to forget the gum for three or four years."* *Enterprise* October 28, 1897

'*Tuck*' in Tuck-a-Batchee may be a clue to the club motive. Summer, warm in the Arkansas Valley, meant lighter clothes for girls, both in weight and color and looser belts. Blouses were partially tucked loosely at the waist or sleeve displaying a relaxed appearance.

Note: Post WW I cloth was scarce and expensive. Women wore shorter skirts with fewer undergarments. They cut their hair shorter. More clothing was store-bought, off-the-rack garments, changing the body silhouette. In 1915, girls wore dresses or skirts at the knee, with knee or ankle socks. Dress yokes dropped to the thigh. School girls wore skirts and middy blouses-shirts with sailor-style collar and loose waists. Fragile easily-soiled muslins of the previous decade were replaced with prints and bright-colored gingham. oureverydaylife.com/childrens-clothes-in-1915

Ersatz KKK in Rocky Ford

Only one article mentions the KKK in Rocky Ford news but not of the organization with many Klaverns; a benign one with an entirely different purpose from the sinister organization.

The choice of name for the 'Klub' must have been born of whimsey. Tenor of the faith community and its leaders concerning religious matters and functions in the community indicate they would support and counsel absolute distancing from the perverse national organization. Citizens in general likely were of similar mind, *so it seems*. However, the *sinister* Ku Klux Klan was once active in Rocky Ford, see pp. 57-58.

Organizers of sports activities in town were anticipating the start of summer team activities among the boys. Time of co-ed activities had not yet arrived. Not stated, but implied, some of the boys likely were involved at some level of school and probably on school sports teams. School administration, however, was not involved, noted by lack of reference.

Consideration for all ages isn't noted and likely involved Junior High and Senior levels rather than the elementary schools.

Reference to "new Gym" leads to speculation of meaning, group of people or virtual location. The high school might be considered. Although built in 1907-1908 with a large assembly hall on its third floor, the space was not originally considered for a gymnasium.

This former 1908 RFHS. building was incorporated into new construction completed February 1918. That building included a large library-study hall on the second floor, but not known or considered for a 'Gym.'

> **K. K. K.**
> **Not Meant for Ku-Klux Klan but is Initials of New Gym Club.**
>
> The K. K. Klub—which is the name of the new Gym—is growing and the boys are getting things fixed up in good shape. Ten new members have been voted in in the last two weeks.
>
> Track and baseball teams are being organized and outdoor work will be carried on in connection with the Gymnasium.
>
> All the members are taking an interest in this organization and are going through the different exercises daily, thus putting their spare time to a good advantage, and it looks like a long felt want has been filled in the starting of this "Klub."

Enterprise March 19, 1909

A commercial gym is not indicated but is another possibility since other spacious buildings were available in the community for theater gatherings, dance studios, or lectures and lyceums. School children, in their 1925 book, possibly gave a clue: "*The [Fair] Association has for its permanent grounds one of the largest amphitheaters of the State, located on the site of the old Swink timber claim, just at the head of Main Street.*" North Ninth Street at 705 is that "*amphitheater*" and possibly the 'Gym' of the new KK Klub. Showers and toilets were included with hardwood flooring in the large open area lined with bench seating, c. 1894.

Arkansas Valley Fair Exposition Building, though property of the Fair Association named for the commercial enterprise, has long been a shared-use building by agreement of the Fair Board and the School District. Was this the *'new Gym'*, now 15 years old?

Note: Klavern = blend of klan and cavern, first used in 1928; merriam-webster.com/dictionary/klavern.
Quote: *Rocky Ford As the School Children See It*, 1925, Blanche B. McFarland, editor.

KKK In the Arkansas Valley

Klan activity became evident early in the 1900s as Kleagles spread across the West. Peak of their activity surfaced in the 1924 Denver elections that soon spread across the state.

> *"For the Klan to exist its members had to have a group to fear and hate. In Colorado there were not enough Black Americans or Jews to make them the chosen ones, or perhaps the Realm in Denver fell into the pattern already chosen by the eastern Klan groups and that was fear and hatred of Catholics. In these two counties* [Crowley and Otero] *the largest minority was Hispanics (sic) and they were mostly Catholic, but the Klan was not apt to choose them because of the great need for their labor. What they did choose were the Anglo Catholics."*
>
> *The man in charge of all Colorado Realms was called the Imperial Wizard, and the head of each Realm was the King Kleagle. Every effort was made to keep the membership secret. In Ordway a secret did get out, and everyone knew the King Kleagle of the Ordway Realm was a prominent lawyer in that town.*
>
> *By 1926 Realms were organized in Otero and Crowley Counties. . . . In Ordway, Rocky Ford and Swink the organization staged parades, held at night with hundreds of spectators from miles around. The members marched or rode horseback three or four abreast or rode in horse-drawn vehicles The men were completely covered by long, white robes and peaked white hoods, which concealed their faces except for the holes cut out for their eyes. The parade was meant to impress and frighten the spectators with the power of these unknown men. Some were frightened but to most it was like a Halloween show to children, scary but exciting."* (Bollacker quote, see *Sources* page 184)

Attempts were made to intimidate voters to vote for Klansmen running for office or for particular ballot issues. Threats were made to those who were Catholic or to their relatives who might lose their jobs if voting was not favorable to the Klan. They would receive a burning cross in front of their home as a reminder.

> *"In Ordway, a small group of Klan members, dressed in their white robes, went into every Protestant church on a Sunday morning during services and asked the church members to join their cause and one Protestant church did become the church of the Klan. Its congregation grew and a new church was constructed for that denomination"* (ibid.).

In summary, African Americans as well as Jews, immigrants, leftists, homosexuals, Catholics, Muslims, and atheists were targeted by the Klan in many communities. Essentially, anyone who was not what the Klan thought reflected "100 percent Americanism" was vulnerable to their hate.

Note: Ku Klux Klan, the name was probably formed by combining Greek kyklos (κύκλος, which means circle) with clan. "C" in clan was replaced by "K" to favor alliteration. The word had previously been used for other fraternal organizations in the South such as Kuklos Adelphon, a fraternity founded at the University of North Carolina in 1812. It was also known as *old* Kappa Alpha, K. A., Kappa Alpha, Circle of Brothers and the Alpha Society.

Kleagle is an officer of the Ku Klux Klan whose role was to recruit new members while maintaining three guiding principles: recruit, maintain control, and safeguard [new members]. Kl-ansman + eagle, a true predatory bird with attributes applied to a man who was predacious regarding gathering new members.

Realm: Local areas of responsibility and Klan activity and members there, as in the Ordway Realm.

KKK - A Personal Anecdote

> Along in the middle 20's the Klu Klux Klan became very active. Charley Wanger, a little Jew, sold members bed sheets, and they would cover up with the sheets and a hood that looked like a dunce cap that a kid might have to wear in school. Many of our neighbors were klansmen and covered up to keep from being recognized, but you could tell some of them by the way than they walked. They were anti catholic, anti negro, anti Mexican or any the other race. They had a parade along about 1925. Vic and I were watching when a klansman came up and said he would give us a dollar to put out their handbills. We put out a few and shoved the rest under the gate at the R.W. Lumber Co. Then we went down to old lady Horton's and had a banana split with the doe. I have since learned that most of the old bastards that were in it weren't much in the way of men. They would burn crosses in front of your home or business if they din't like you. Sam Kitch was mayor of Rocky Ford then and he wouldn't join them so they started to burn a cross in his front yard and got kicked out in the street for their trouble.

Privately published memoir draft: *Papers of Frank Milenski, Water Resources Archive*, Colorado State University.

Francis (Frank) Raymond Milenski, Rocky Ford farmer for many years, was noted for his knowledge and work in the business of water use and administration in Colorado and the West. He began to write his memoirs (year of script uncertain) with suggestions from an unidentified mentor to place his knowledge in publication of a book. Apparently, this task was not completed before his death.

Among his many anecdotes was the paragraph above about the Klan in Rocky Ford when he was 12 years old. Frank and his brother Vic (Victor Edward) 13, were called upon to help with local advertisement while watching a KKK parade one day circa 1925, apparently on Main Street (reference to R.W. English Lumber Company 104 South Main Street).

Lulu G. and Arlyn Samuel Kitch at 301 North Twelfth Street; Horton's Market, 1309 Elm Avenue were within two blocks of each other. These two locations indicate that the Klan marchers possibly turned east onto Elm Avenue-US 50 during part of their parade route.

Since Mr. Kitch was Mayor of Rocky Ford then he would have been a target as he was anti-Klan. Mr. Milenski's anecdotal information is that when the Klan tried to burn a cross on the Kitch property Sam Kitch kicked it out into the street, possibly along with the perpetrators..

Note: Frank Milenski was born 8 Nov 1913; married 10 June 1935 to Eleanor Zumbrunnen; died 16 Nov. 1998. Typewritten text on *Mead Erasable Onion Skin* provides weak contrast and reproduction. Text was at the most a first draft with many notes and corrections.

Arkansas Valley Bed and Breakfest (website spelling), is currently at former Kitch home, 301 North 12th Street.

THE Clubs of Rocky Ford

THE is understood before each name which reflects use by Editors of Rocky Ford *Enterprise* in nearly all their publications in setting the adjective before article, in this case, club name. Foregoing use of *THE* here removes display of repetition.

This list of clubs is not all-inclusive because clubs formed for many social reasons and to follow many different interests. This happened frequently and almost as often a club seemed to disband or disappear from public view, probably after having accomplished a stated goal or sometimes having lost member interest or support.

National fraternal and sororal organizations are not included here although there were several involving many members (Eagles, VFW, GAR, Moose, Elks, Masons, IOOF, etc.). Associated with them were adjunct men's, women's and youth organizations, also not included here.

A club name was sometimes shortened to save page space, such as Every Tuesday Club to Tuesday Club, or Newdale Community Club to Newdale Club. Many articles used only the club acronym, easily recognized by subscribers.

Identification here of acronyms, though attempted, was not often assisted by text. Use of them was so frequent that original printing of meaning was lost in time. Yet, some are self-explanatory.

- AKA Club (1913 women graduates)
- Arkansas Valley Gun Club
- Alta Piensa Club (High Thoughts)
- Auction Bridge Club
- Banner Club
- Bide-a-Wee Club
- Businessman's Club
- Capitol Hill Club (Newdale)
- CFWO Club
    (City Federation of Women's Org.)
- Commercial Club
- Country Rook (cards) Club
- Country Club
- Coterie Club (Close Associates)
- CWBM Club
- Dramatic Club (High School)
- Embroidery Club
- Entre Nous Club (Between Us)
- Eureka Mother's Club (Ordway)
- Evening Whist Club, Whist Club (cards)
- Every Tuesday Reading Club, Tuesday Club
- FBG Club
- Farmers' Club
- Fathers Club (Eureka-Ordway)
- Five Hundred Club (bid Euchre)
- Fortnightly Club
- Forty Club (Home Protective Association)
- Home Missions Study Club
- JSIT Club
- La Fayette Club
- LCC Club
- LJ.-RF (dual city Auction Club)
- Melon Motorcycle Club
- MGR Club
- Monday Evening (Literary) Club
- Mothers Club (Weitzer-Vroman)
- Newdale Community Club
- Mu Ta Delta Club
- Neighbors Club (LaFayette)
- NB Club (Nota Bene-*note well*)
- Noekwil Club
- ODT Club (Our Day Together)
- Otero Agricultural Club
- Out-of-Club Guests Club
- Pinochle Club (cards)
- Rocky Ford Automobile (Motor) Club
- Rocky Ford Chess Club
- Rocky Ford Duck Shooting Club
- Rocky Ford Gun Club
- Rocky Ford Music Club
- Rocky Ford Outing Club (excursions)
- Safe-a-Pin Club (independent fraternity)
- Sans Souci Club (without care)
- Secret X-Nine Club (neighborhood boys)
- Senior Girl's Club

Standard Rod and Gun Club
TBG Club
Thirteen Club
TT Club
Tuck-a-Batchee Club*
Tuesday Reading Club (Circle)
Twentieth Century Club (Star Valley)
Tuxedo Club
West Swink Avenue Ladies Club
WFA Club (previously Neighbors Club)
WRC (Woman's Relief Club)
Woman's Club
WSA Club
WW Club
XI. Club
XTE Club
Young Mens (Progressive} Club
Young Women's Missionary Society (M. E. Church)

*Name change later to Tuck-a-Batche Club

Note: Card games, numerous throughout history, were part of club activities but seldom part of a club acronym.

Clubs of Rocky Ford were numerous over years yet among those listed not all were functioning at the same time. Many were of short duration serving a purpose until no longer maintained by membership. Examples of those were several clubs instituted by high school students of Junior or Senior classes wishing to maintain contact and fellowship with class friends after graduation.

Some clubs drew charters formally naming themselves and outlining goals. A few clubs were sophisticated to the extent of naming a manager or leader and other officers they viewed necessary to accomplish those goals. Some designed banners, chose colors and flowers or other symbols to represent or identify themselves among other clubs in town. Most were together in their chosen groups to socialize and have fun while working diligently toward goals.

One fraternal club was *Single Seven* or *The Seven*, Young bachelors who banded together only to socialize, not necessarily to proclaim their unmarried status. Related but not their only impetus, was that two of them co-owned and operated the bar and billiard parlor where they held meetings.

An association of native Americans in Las Animas formed in April 27, 1898. They were known as *IORM., Independent* [or Improved, in one article] *Order of Red Men* with a lodge to be formed in Rocky Ford. The Ordway Lodge reelected officers June 19, 1906 and from an article in the *Ordway New Era* we learn the officer designations: Sachem (chief, head, or principal), Chief of Records, Prophet, Senior Sagamore, and Junior Sagamore, both subordinate chiefs. Goals of the order were not given but assumed to be important and relevant to members of a distinctive minority, possibly only *because they were* a minority..

Out-of-Club Guests Club, previously mentioned, was a fictitious name stemming from the repetition of those *Enterprise* words noting meetings of numerous clubs and their guests. No meetings or associations were known among people who were *guests* of clubs.

Safe-a-Pin Club was an independent college fraternity of modest membership in answer to all Greek-lettered fraternities on campus. Club espoused alternative behavior to rife snobbery.

Secret X-9 Club was a neighborhood boys club known to have met only one time for naming, establishing rules and selection of aliases, then, disbanding at adjournment.

Blaze-A-Way Gun Club members hunted and entertained public with shooting demonstrations.

Red Men's Lodge

What is known of *Red Men* appears in few articles. Membership may have been modest or at least short-lived. Membership possibly was open to non-Natives.

> Pat Bradish, of La Junta, was in Las Animas this week with the purpose of organizing a Red Men's Lodge. —Las Animas Democrat.

La Junta *Tribune*, April 27, 1898

> The Red Men of Rocky Ford, to the considerable number of sixteen, went down to La Junta Wednesday night where the lodge was holding a special pow-wow. They took part in the street parade and drill, and the other exercises and festivities of the occasion, and gave special attention to the fine supper spread by La Junta braves and their squaws.

La Junta *Tribune,* August 10, 1898

> Several local Redmen went to Rocky Ford on the noon train yesterday to assist in organizing a lodge at that point last night.

La Junta *Tribune*, February 27, 1901

> G. M. Dameron is attending the annual grand powwow of the Independent Order of Red Men at Cripple Creek this week.

Enterprise, February 28, 1902

> The Improved Order of Red Men at their meeting last week, re-elected their old officers, as follows:
> Harry Feiser, Sachem.
> Wm. Edgar, Chief of Records.
> Dan Pettit, Prophet.
> Geo. Gallavan, Senior Sagamore.
> A. J. Evans, Junior Sagamore.

Ordway *New Era*, January 19, 1906

Re-election of previous office-holders at this publication may be due to limited membership.

Normalites

This word, *Normal-ites*, might suggest a kind of unique society, nationality or cryptic culture. Normalites would be first to agree the former description properly and accurately defines who they are, possibly with some professional pride.

This adjective is only one of many words fashioned for particular purpose and meaning. Some US schools beginning in the 1800s were established to train high school graduates for teaching elementary school classes. Origin in 1685 was by St. Jean-Baptiste de La Salle, founder of the *Institute of the Brothers of the Christian Schools*. He established the first school, the *École Normale*, in Reims, Champagne, France from which the 'Normal' school derives its name.

Normal schools were founded in the U. S. among New England states, the first in Lexington, Massachusetts in 1839. *Normal* refers to the goal of these institutions to foster particular life standards or models within students. Norms were acceptable individual behavior for the times, especially those that strengthened social values of society, political leaning and important narratives (subjects) taught in curriculum.

Normalites in Colorado

In 1890, the Colorado legislature established its first Normal school. The legislature passed Senate Bill 104 to establish *State Normal School of Colorado* in Greeley, which Governor Alva Adams (1889-1891) signed into law April 1, 1889. The school opened on October 6, 1890 to train qualified teachers for state public schools, with a staff of four instructors and 96 students, offering certification after completing a two-year course. Adams State University, Alamosa, was another 'Normal'.

Function Of The Normal School

"The function of the Normal School is to make teachers. To do this it must keep abreast of the times. It must lead in public education. It must project the future. The modern conception of education embraces all of human life. This wide and deep and rich notion enlarges the function of an institution that aims to prepare teachers. This function embraces in its relations: The faculty, the child, those preparing to teach, the home, the state, society, and the course of study."

From the Normal School 1901-02 Catalog, Greeley, Colorado.

Normalites Now

In 1911, the school's name was changed to Colorado State Teachers College and offered bachelor's degrees after completion of a four-year course. In 1935, the name changed again to Colorado State College of Education, recognizing the graduate program started in 1913. In 1957, the name was shortened to Colorado State College to recognize the further growth of programs. Finally, in 1970, the name was changed to the current University of Northern Colorado, with satellites in Loveland, Colorado Springs and Lowry neighborhood of Denver.

For this narrative *Normalites*, as found among archived *Enterprise* articles, refers to those who support, have attended, are attending, or who have graduated from a Normal school.

New Normal: A state to which an economy or society settles following a crisis differing from the situation that prevailed prior to the start of the crisis. The term was employed in relation to World War I, financial crisis of 2007-2008, September 11, 2001 attacks, aftermath of the 2008–2012 global recession, the COVID-19 pandemic and other events. *Wikipedia*

Scorching Automobiles

Automobiles appeared in town early 1900s. People, accustomed to avoiding slower moving horse and buggy or farmer's wagon took notice of their speed and noise. On their way about business, they were wary. Many dogs would challenge and bite the wheels that would often run over them.

Well before 1920 most in town were aware because the number of machines was growing in relation to horses and mules. City council had to deal with ordinances for automobile movement, identification (licensing), taxing and general rules of the road, where to drive and where to park. Some communities required a driver to be accompanied by at least one other to get out to help control frightened mules or horses. Auto breakdowns were frequent and liveries weren't immediately prepared for anything that wasn't four-legged.

Consideration was given of the noise and smells of automobiles. The noise was novel, unlike neighing and braying of animals. The smell of exhaust was not like the exhaust of animal digestion. That took getting used to and just had to be tolerated. Sanitary service by city street workers changed. Watermelon Day celebration clean-ups became prime as the animal population diminished along with their *road apples*. Fortunately, an ordnance was already in place.

> —The town authorities are doing a good job in cleaning up the streets and alleys. They have adopted a most commendable prohibition ordinance — forbidding throwing the remains of second-hand watermelons into the streets and alleys. A penalty of $5 will be assessed for violation of this rule.

Enterprise, August 18, 1898

Pedestrian safety became a consideration since many drivers were unschooled in road etiquette. Some 'mahouts' eagerly drove their new transportation, often with show-off cavalier mentality.

A new term was born describing an encounter with an automobile- *'Scorching.'* Boys on bicycles raced to stay with the new machine trying to keep up with their speed. 'Wheelers' were not always safe maneuvering near the vehicle when the driver decided to turn.

Near misses were common. A driver, going to a meeting at Liberty School, drove around a corner of the building, before streets, curbs, sidewalks, and surprised a circle of boys concentrating on their marble game. Participants were quick to avoid collision but now were aware of this new menace to their game.

Enterprise, February 9, 1906

> Mark Twain thinks that chauffeurs should be called "mahouts." Pedestrians who are run down by scorching automobiles can think of much harder names than that to call them.

Mark Twain's appraisal of early drivers showed his disdain. A *mahout* is an elephant rider, trainer, or keeper. The occupation starts in boyhood when a boy begins following a hereditary family profession. While young, he receives an elephant early in its life and cares for and keeps it near his family. They remain bonded to each other for life like some bond today to their autos.

Note: To be *scorched* was to experience a close call. Today's version might include *smoking, rolling coal*, or *wasting*, all unlawful, and subject the driver to arrest and fine. Perpetrators temporarily, but purposely, stress their diesel cars or truck engines to produce dense black smoke to envelop individuals or other vehicles along the street.

Repair was subject of a 1913 song, "*He'd Have to Get Under – Get Out and Get Under (to Fix Up His Automobile)*." Song was popular in the 1920 comedy "Get Out and Get Under," a movie about a new car owner's adventures with his Model T Ford.

Automobile Activity

Rocky Ford entered the automobile era in 1903 when D.W. Barkley, Jr., and D.V. Burrell drove their Cadillac one-cylinder horseless carriages into town. Not far into the future other drivers of "devil wagons" were on the streets. Drivers began to feel the need to organize and demonstrate their community responsibilities, toward farmers in particular. They had three goals; accommodating citizen concerns, planning for better roads, and developing accord with horse and mule owners.

Mayor's Proclamation

> **Rocky Ford Auto Owners and Drivers Organize.**
>
> A well attended meeting of automobile owners and drivers was held in this city on Tuesday evening when the organization of the Rocky Ford Motor Club was perfected. The following officers were elected:
>
> President—George Daring.
> Vice President—Dr. B. E. Moody.
> Secretary—B. A. Snelton.
> Treasurer—Cary Pollock.
>
> The purpose of the Motor Club is to strive to create a better feeling between farmers and drivers of "devil wagons;" to work for better roads and to see that tourists receive courteous treatment and a square deal.
>
> The club has a good membership to start with, and the prospects are that it will before long be one of the strongest organizations in Rocky Ford.

> I want to call the attention of those who run automobiles and motor cycles. Beware of breaking speed limits, as the marshals have instructions to strictly enforce this ordinance. If they can't do it any other way they will have to carry a pocket full of tacks and throw them in front of machine. This ordinance must be enforced.

Enterprise, July 14, 1911

Two named citizens each purchased the new 1903 Cadillac-*illustrated below*-built late year 1902. They were reliably powered by 10 hp (7 kW) single-cylinder engines. Their general appearance was that of leather bench seats perched high and open on the vehicle carriage that yet resembled some horse-powered ones. One cental head lamp and two dash board lanterns provided some light at night.

Images courtesy *yahoo.com royalty free*

Note: First vehicle headlamps were officially introduced during the 1880s based on acetylene and oil, similar to gas lamps. These fueled the headlamps, but because of high costs of both, improving the system was nearly impossible. They had the advantages of resistance to air currents and bad weather, like snow and rain, but before long, they were replaced. Cadillac changed to electric lights in 1912.

Cadillacs in Town

Rocky Ford Magazine, Summer 1998 vol. 1 no. 1.

This 1905 photo shows one automobile on the 300 block of South Main Street. At left is a *1903 Model A Cadillac Rear-Entry Tonneau.*

Drivers are not identified here but two owners of the same type of automobile are on the facing page as owners of the same manufacture and year, according to the *Enterprise*. Many autos of the era were fueled with benzine, some by gasoline, and later, by diesel or liquid propane. Fuel odors were a complaint that led French chemists to experiment with perfume additives in fuels to try to ameliorate odors.

Automobiles in Town

Repeated and frequent chest expansion shows when talking up or writing about town attributes in news editorials. This is uniform in articles of the *Enterprise*. Subject matter varies but the sentiment is generally consistent whether about numbers of honey bees or tons of beets. *"We have the Better, if not the Best in the Region, State and the Arkansas Valley,"* to paraphrase.

Frequently, issues printed the Editor's slight digs at other news articles and papers in the Valley. Not the least, Editors of other newspapers were game. Although mostly friendly and benign the point was made clear. We are the better, and quite likely, best, as you should rightly acknowledge!

This article glows with pride about the growing number of autos in a town of this size - boldly declaring, a small town but *huge* in the West country.

Enterprise, December 15, 1905

> **Rocky Ford's Automobile Club.**
>
> No town of its size in the west has as many automobiles as Rocky Ford, and the list is steadily growing. At present we have eleven autos, as follows:
>
> A. H. Griswold, an Oldsmobile and a Rambler.
> Dr. H. Van Buskirk, a Knox.
> Will Lockhart, a Franklin.
> W. B. Gobin, an Oldsmobile.
> D. V. Burrell, a Cadillac.
> D. W. Barkley, Jr., a Cadillac.
> Chas. Hushaw, an Oldsmobile.
> Goodner Bros., a Toledo.
> W. D. Ebbert, a Winton.
> F. W. Smith, a rebuilt gasoline.

All the gentlemen mentioned were businessmen, likely prosperous and therefore able to afford this upgrade in personal transportation averaging several hundred dollars.

- F.W. Smith was a blacksmith and a franchiser for a company that built small gasoline engines.
- A.H. Griswold operated The Novelty Works, dealing in guns, bicycles, and lathe work. Eventually, he became an automobile dealer.
- Dr. H. Van Buskirk was president of the Farmers and Merchants Bank.
- Will Lockhart was proprietor of Alfalfa Land and Cattle Co.
- W.B. Gobin was an attorney..
- D.W. Barkley was one of several *Enterprise* Editors over the years.
- Charles Hushaw, and Charles Cartwright were automobile dealers.
- Goodner Brothers manufactured pumps in conjunction with their foundry business.
- W.D. Ebbert was proprietor of Arkansas Valley Seeds Company.

There were many among the horse and mule owners who wondered at the appearance of automobiles on their streets where one learned to step lively, whether horses, mules, pedestrians or bicycle riders. In just two years the automobile census grew from two to eleven with more to come. There was temporary consternation about use of streets and roads, most earnestly felt by farmers whose animals were spooked and sometimes caused to run away or be injured.

New businesses were started for essential auto service and repair forcing the livery to transition from hay, oats, veterinary service and shoeing to fuel, oil, tires, air and insurance.

Clothiers, and milliners began advertising new styles of wearing apparel specially designed to keep ones' hat on and dust off. *Dusters* were made to cover the ladies from neck to shoes, also doubling as warm protection against rain and snow.

A week preceding the December 15, 1905 article the Editor declared a new *Winton* had been purchased by a local seed man. Five more autos had been added by February, 1910.

The Editor was keeping score because other newspapers in the Valley were doing the same. The machines were the *new* thing and worthy of the time spent to publicize them because they were visible measures of local sophistication and progress. *'Benzine Buggies'* became *boffo*.

> The indications are that Rocky Ford is to continue to lead all towns of its size in the West in the number of automobiles owned by its citizens. The latest purchaser of an auto is W. D. Ebbert, of the Arkansas Valley Seed House, who will hereafter ride in a Winton.

Enterprise, December 8, 1905

> Building permits were granted A. H. Griswold for his automobile garage south of the McPherson Lumber Co. and to H. A. Dawley and Boone Bacon.

Enterprise, October 6, 1905

Enterprise, September 29, 1905

> **Boom in Autos**
>
> The automobile business has picked up considerable during the past week, five new machines having been added to the list of those owned by Rocky Ford parties. The new buzz wagon proprietors are George Lackey, S. A. Mathews, G. P. Randall and Walter Bishop, who have purchased Studebaker E. M. F. machines, while George Meador is engaged in breaking in an Oldsmobile for use in making his frequent trips to and from his ranch near the Meador reservoir.

Enterprise February 18, 1910

> As an indication of the enterprise of Rocky Ford we will mention that the number of automobiles owned here has made a demand for a garage, a want which will be supplied by A. H. Griswold. The building will be of brick and frost proof so that the water in the cooling tanks of the benzine buggies will not freeze. Such a place of storage will be a great convenience to our automobile owners.

Entrepreneurs were quick to see the need for a different kind of business, the kind that provided service for 'buzz wagons' rather than, or in addition to, horses and mules. Some were livery owners of which there were several in town.

Others, as in the October 6, 1905 article were starting up with all new buildings along Ninth Street south of Elm Avenue and the railroad. Another was on Main Street and Swink Avenue at 400 North Main. Description of the construction using brick and of being 'frost proof' suggests insulation as would be referred to now. A new location at the southwest corner of Swink and Tenth Street-now 305 North Tenth Street-was large enough to house 100 cars. This business site, indicated on Sanborn map of 1919, is now part of Loaf 'N Jug.

Rocky Ford Cafe
Advertising in the 1920s increasingly displayed the fact of motor traffic in town. Vintage menu art such as this humorous example, was seen in many places with script tailored to double as a menu.

Details and ads of this café are missing from among the pages of the *Enterprise* except for references to large groups being entertained there.

Wording of the included articles suggest that the café was near the Santa Fe Depot, possibly 914 Front Street across the tracks where Karl Weid operated a bakery and served lunches. The Pacific House Hotel was in the same building

Charles Recker, known for serving large numbers, owned a bakery and restaurant on Ninth Street between Front Street and Walnut Avenue. His business was just across Ninth from

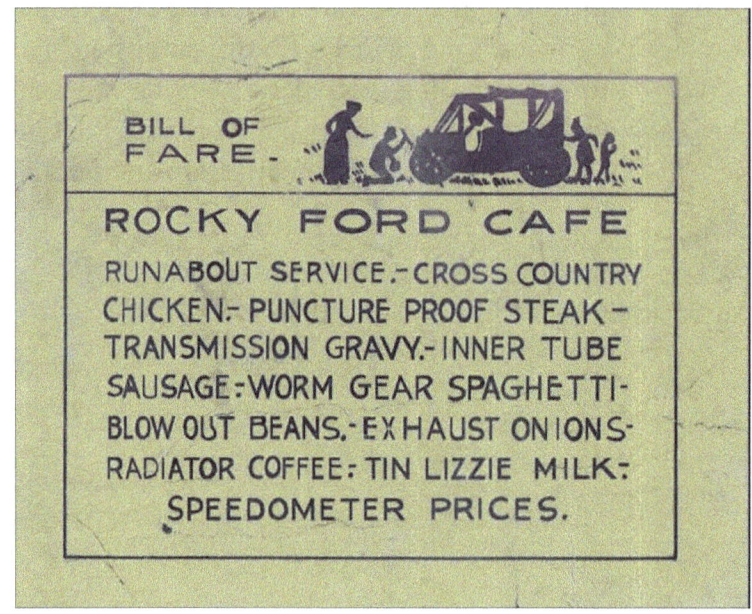

site of the 1909 First Church of Christ Scientist, later Otero County Health Department building.

> As it has now been arranged, the special agricultural demonstration train will be met by the mayor and his Rocky Ford guests at the Santa Fe depot at 6 p. m. this (Friday) evening and the representatives of the Colorado Agricultural College, U. S. Department of Agriculture and others accompanying the train will be escorted to the Rocky Ford cafe, for the banquet to which they had been invited by Mayor Coffman.

Enterprise, February 28, 1913

Enterprise, March 7, 1913

> Headed by Mayor Coffman, the visitors were met at the depot on Friday evening by a big delegation of city and club officials and were at once escorted to the Rocky Ford cafe, where one of the finest banquets ever served in this city awaited them.

Charles Recker also operated the Park Hotel at the same location, possibly accommodating several of the noted visitors.

Wherever the sign was displayed it was sure to amuse patrons while presenting some humor of the time by the establishment's owner.

Café sign: bing.com/images/search?q=rockyford

Floods in the Arkansas Valley

Arkansas River Basin drains 85,350 square miles monitored by gauging stations at Canon City to Holly near the state line. These stations, now many years post-publication of *Floods in Colorado* by the US Department of the Interior in 1948, will reflect many changes. Data included in that publication about frequent floods during history of the Arkansas still serves us today.

Estimates of floods before the time gauging stations were established relies upon memory of native Americans, early travelers, explorers and settlers, not always written as historical record but passed by memory. The government publication distills what is known of these through recollection and oral tradition, sometimes corroborated by multiple witnesses. Acknowledged history of flooding begins with the first settlers and keeping of written records.

1826: Earliest of known floods occurred well before permanent settlements along the river. A Mr. Traber, employee of Hudson's Bay Company worked in vicinity of the old site of Fort Lyon when in that year water was estimated at 15 feet at the future site of Las Animas.

1859: A flood circa 1859, occurred on the Arkansas River downstream of the tributary Purgatoire River, affecting the area near Lamar. Depth of water was also estimated by previous camping visitors to have been 15 feet. This flood originated on the plains rather than the mountains, observed by travelers on the Santa Fe Trail.

1864: First flood detailed by much information occurred June 11. A storm over much of eastern Colorado caused a similar amount of damage as the later 1921 flood, according to settlers in Pueblo. All streams were very high and overflowed for great distances.

1867: Flooding during May was extensive enough to cause the move of Fort Lyon 17 miles to a new site farther west. Fast-melting snow during May was estimated to be the chief cause by observers in Canon City where streams were overflowing. The Arkansas and Purgatoire were flooding at the same time causing the future site of Lamar to be a lake from sand hills on the south to the first hills north of the river.

1869: There was a flood this year, noted only by its occurrence, but not documented. According to the previously mentioned publication, *"It was an immense amount of water."*

1875: The flood of September 16 was the next of record, caused primarily by a swollen Purgatoire River after heavy rains on the prairie. Arkansas flooding, therefore, was below the mouth of the Purgatoire, affecting the area downstream. News reported of the event:

> *"At Fort Lyon* [4 miles below the mouth of the Purgatoire] *the water was 4 feet higher than ever known before. The bottom land between the bridge and the post trader's* [a distance of three-fourths of a mile] *was a swift, raging flood."*   Las Animas Leader, September 18, 1875.

The upper river was also in flood west to Pueblo but since newspapers in Pueblo gave no notice, it was apparently not serious.

1884: During June, accumulating runoff from melting snow flooded the Arkansas from above the 'Grand Canyon' west of the Royal Gorge and Pueblo. The *Canon City Record* reported the water two feet deep on the railroad tracks in the canyon.

Note: Grand Canyon used here denotes that of the Arkansas River upstream of Canon City.

1886: Downstream of the Purgatoire River the Arkansas flooded extensively July 20-25. Flooding was not occurring west of the Purgatoire. Rains were heaviest in the vicinity of La Junta and Las Animas:

"Wednesday morning the water in the Arkansas River was within 1 foot of the bottom of the sleepers of the wagon bridge. There were 5 wash-outs [on the railroad] *between La Junta and a point 6 miles east.*   La Junta Tribune, July 22, 1886.

The *Tribune* article continued with;

"In King Arroyo, east of town, the water came down in a wave 12 feet high. In Anderson Arroyo just west of town the water was at least 20 feet deep, running over the Santa Fe Co.'s bridge. . . . Johnson was sleeping in the [his] *house . . . 10 miles up Anderson Arroyo. About midnight he was awakened by the storm. He had been up but a few minutes when the house began to tremble, a wave about 8 feet high struck the south end, forcing in the window and almost in an instant the house went to pieces and was floating down this newly-formed river."*

Fate of Mr. Johnson was not revealed.

1889: Grape Creek, west of Pueblo, flooded, the result of a cloudburst. This and rains lasting two hours in the Pueblo area flooded the Arkansas August 9, 1889. Rain began about 5:30 p. m. and flooded both Pueblo and Florence, the latter particularly suffered great damage. Denver and Rio Grande lost the Hardscrabble bridge near Florence and several other untold damages.

1893: A very dry year, one of the driest on record at Pueblo, produced eight feet of rise in the Arkansas during a two-hour rainstorm July 26. After the storm estimates [no gauging station data of record] placed peak discharge at between 20,000 and 25,000 second-feet, a unit for gauging stream flow that is equal to one cubic foot per second past a stream mark.

1894: May 29-31 that year noted a storm lasting at least 36 hours at Salida. Estimates of 3 to 4 inches had fallen at Florence in the preceding 24 hours. Rain upriver of Canon City was considered of low influence but much damage occurred down river. Levees in Pueblo were breached in six areas flooding many of the businesses near the breaks.

The Denver and Rio Grande freight yard was flooded at least three feet. Water was seven feet at the highest stage of the flood and five lives were lost in Pueblo with an estimated $2,000,000 in damages. Water flowed in swift current adding to the destruction.

In Rocky Ford, significant precipitation May 24 was followed by much more May 30. Flow in the river from earlier storms around Salida and Florence was notably adding to the flood with crest estimated at twelve feet at West Ranch. The wagon road bridge was lost and the Rocky Ford bridge damaged.

Post-flood analysis by Pueblo's city engineer determined peak discharge to have been 39,100 second-feet, warranting a channel enlargement in the city to 40,000 second-feet.

Note: *Sleepers,* in the 1886 article, referred to additional ties supporting rails under the wagon bridge. Grape Creek, in the 1889 reference, flows through Custer and Fremont counties to the Arkansas. The creek drains much of Wet Mountain Valley, located between the Sangre de Cristo and Wet Mountains.

Floods in the Arkansas Valley

1904: A flood on the Purgatoire River, September 29-30, has to be estimated from data of peak discharge at Trinidad since no gauging station was operative at the river mouth entering the Arkansas. Purgatoire discharge at Trinidad was 44,300 second-feet and likely more at entry into the Arkansas near Las Animas.

The gauge near the Colorado-Kansas Diversion Dam, three miles west of Prowers, was indicating about 70,000 second-feet. Water rose so fast the gate tender at the dam had to swim his horses and himself out of danger.

News accounts told of the Arkansas River bottom flooded from the entry of the Purgatoire to the state line. Because the flood was in September and unexpected that late in the year, farmers and the railroad were unprepared. Damages were much greater as a result.

1908: Heavy rains the night of October 18 caused the flood of October 19-20 in the area close-in west of La Junta. Rain gauges recorded 6.25 inches 40 miles northwest of Holly, 6 inches near Prowers, and 6.34 inches just north of Lamar.

Heavy rain runoff north of the river was caused by extensive and close grazing, leaving almost no ground cover on a hard surface. Water entered the Arkansas mostly below Amity Dam at Prowers. Runoff reached Holly before midnight October 19 and registered 9.8 feet.

Water from Two-Butte Creek and smaller tributaries to the south added to that from the north which had only receded about six inches.

A second mass of water came down the Purgatoire River contributing to a peak volume at Holly of 11 feet. Essentially, the latter was considered a 'second flood' by record keepers. Water was still at three feet October 22. Peak discharge at Amity Dam was more than 100,000 second-feet. At Holly, the peak was estimated 136,000 second-feet.

Several lives were lost along with thousands of sheep, other animals, many homes, with extensive damage to railroad structures. Rail traffic was delayed six days and most highway bridges washed away from the Purgatoire to Kansas.

1921: Upstream of the Purgatoire damaging floods did not occur until 1921. Then, a general storm covered the state June 2-5, 1921 that was concentrated in cloudbursts between Canon City and Pueblo. The storm covered about 550 square miles in two large areas producing runoff converging at Pueblo, where the damage was greatest.

1929: August 7, the Purgatoire flooded with peak discharge 52,800 second-feet at its mouth and a peak discharge at Lamar of 45,300.

Twenty-one years from 1908 to 1929 were not identified as flood years in the 1948 publication *Floods in Colorado* by the US Department of the Interior. The history of floods on the river strongly suggest some did occur, but of non-noteworthy character or significance for substantial damage.

Note: Purgatoire River, in southeastern Colorado, is also known locally as the Purgatory River or the Picketwire River. Purgatoire (French for Puratory), named by French trappers to commemorate Spanish explorers killed in a Native American attack.

Amity Canal head gate is in Bent County on the north bank of the Arkansas, approximately 10 miles downstream from John Martin Reservoir and dam. Canal is approximately 80 miles long, from head gate to near the Colorado Kansas border.

Floods in the Arkansas Valley

1934: Purgatoire River flooded again September 15 as also the Apishapa and Timpas Creeks. Latter two flooded areas do not have surviving records but the cumulative effect was seen at Lamar. There, 2,800 second-feet were recorded on September 15, day of the flood, and 9,600 the day after the flood.

Apishapa and Timpas Creeks enter the Arkansas between Nepesta and La Junta, the Purgatoire between La Junta and Lamar. No damages were recorded in the Department of Interior publication, although there is little doubt that some did occur, possibly to canal and head gate structures and to farmers' fields bordering the river.

1944: Wilson Creek, a tributary to Oil Creek, flooded July 4 and caused a flood in the Arkansas downstream of the latter. At a diversion dam three miles west of Florence the crest, lasting a half hour, arrived July 5 with 19,000 second-feet recorded. By the time water reached Pueblo 33 miles later the flow was down to 5,980 second-feet.

Note: Oil Creek is located 6.4 miles from Cripple Creek in Teller County. Wilson Creek is a stream in Fremont County.

Floods near Rocky Ford

The authors of *Floods in Colorado* necessarily ended their publication to date 1944. Their research was summarized in following years and published by the Government Printing Office in 1948. Particular detail of local city and town flood damage was not the goal of the authors, only documentation of the Colorado floods as they affected the state and the valleys they coursed.

A search of the news, primarily Rocky ford *Enterprise,* La Junta *Tribune,* Ordway *New Era,* Las Animas *Leader,* and Lamar *Ledger* recovers news of several small floods of local interest to Rocky Ford and neighbors along the Arkansas. Many of those caused little concern although some channel shifts resulted in changes to some fields at riverside. Damage may also have occurred to canal head gates, diversion structures, levees, or conduits crossing the Arkansas. Significantly, there was little loss of livestock or farm structures, and few lives.

Floods of note to early Rocky Ford, by no means the only, were those in, 1894, 1921, 1935, 1955, and 1965. Others are briefly recounted on pages 69-71.

1921: Information of this flood has been described in the *Rocky Ford Daily Gazette* of June 3, 1970 and June 3, 1982 quoting the *Enterprise* edition of June 10, 1921.

The town was spared great loss but waters in 1921 actually reached lower streets of town on the north side, and covered the fairgrounds. Mayor Joel W. Todd, after the tragedy, issued a proclamation; *"Rocky Ford Escapes All Serious Flood Damage."* The damage was to the northwest, north and east in the fields among the homes, farms and livestock there.

Great loss occurred at West Ranch, the headquarters of the field operations of the American Beet Sugar Company. Witnesses described a wall of water twelve feet high as the crest reached the bridge nearby on State Highway 71. Many mules, horses and swine were carried away along with several buildings and corrals. *Old Rocky Ford* structures, particularly the Swink-Russell 1871 adobe store were carried away and the rocky river crossing completely obscured from that time by a change in the river channel and heavy sediment and silting.

Some time after 1921, while leveling a fence row built up with silt by the flood, a farmer uncovered skeletal remains of a woman who had been with child. That discovery was closure for relatives of the victims but much doubt remained for finding others among the missing since the devastation was so widespread.

Events of damage and loss were described in the *Enterprise* article, most importantly the loss of lives. Arthur Darr, his four children, and neighbor Mrs. Pratt and her granddaughter. They all lived on small ranches northwest of town.

Other fatalities include one man from Vroman and three men found in the river, two of them near Manzanola, and one man near Fowler. About two hundred refugees were housed in the American Beet Sugar Company laboratory building in Rocky Ford. Many were tenants and employees of West Ranch among other homeless from near the river.

Electric power was disrupted for cities from Pueblo to La Junta until power plants were made operable. In Rocky Ford all of June 4 and most of June 5, 1921 were without electricity but city generators were operating late on June 5 to supply power to pumps delivering water from city wells, safe from contamination.

Numerous ditch and canal structures were destroyed along with several bridges. The Santa Fe bridge at Nepesta was destroyed requiring rail traffic to travel through Trinidad for two weeks. Of all destruction, the city of Pueblo endured the most.

On June 4, 1921 one of the three spans of the Rocky Ford bridge on Hwy 266 toward Holbrook Valley was left in place. Both approaches and part of the roadway on the town-side were destroyed.

Photo courtesy Rock Ford *Daily Gazette* June 3, 1970.

Note: In 1921, county roads were not then designated as they are now with letters and numbers. However, well-defined roads along farm and ranch boundaries were in place. County Road 18.50 today is the first north-south road east of State Highway 71. Coincidence of the road in the story relative to CR 18.50 of today cannot be fixed with certainty but is within the area.

A comprehensive account of the 1921 flood, *Pueblo's Flood in Pictures*, was written by Willis H. Parker, illustrated with many high resolution monochrome photos among the text pages. It was printed by O'Brien Printing Company with plates by Schultz Engraving Company in Pueblo, c. 1921-1929.

In the Wake, June 4-5, 1921

Whatever solid evidence the flood of 1921 has left us to remember around Rocky Ford may be described as very little after 100 years but the house at 600 South Main Street is one such article, the only substantial article that is on hand today.

There were other structures and homes affected by the flood but with few remnants or points of reference given in the news. Some houses, sheds and fences were destroyed and floated away in the debris, mostly splintered wood and tangled wire. Some foundations and fences were silted heavily as they acted as levees, catching and retaining objects in the current.

Livestock losses were notable, nearly completely enumerated with many animals lost, especially at West Ranch. Bridges have been replaced, some at least twice since 1921. Ordinary things such as trees were stripped of bark and branches or completely uprooted and swept away.

People Affected

Rocky Ford citizens, Arthur Darr and four children along with neighbor, Mrs. Pratt and grand daughter were those to lose their lives northwest of town. A man from Vroman and three other unidentified men were taken from the river, one at Manzanola and two at Fowler.

Imagination will run its course as we try to comprehend the emotions of Lucas B. Gorsuch as he held to life while trapped in his house clutching sodden furniture. He endured for 18 hours floating next to the ceiling of one of his rooms, hoping to survive that long night. Very fortunately his wife Eula and daughter Della apparently were not home when the waters reached their house.

River Changes

In its violent weaving through the Valley during floods the Arkansas River changed course in several areas near Rocky Ford. These changes are easily seen in the aerial and satellite images included in this narrative.

Lower ends of some fields were shortened and carried away with their soils to be deposited on the inner meanders of new oxbows downstream. Older curves were cut off and bypassed by the strong current, some filled with heavier deposits from upstream as the velocity of the current slowed and sediments formed. It is likely much debris removed from upstream was deposited and buried in these areas.

Straight segments were widened some places and gouged deeper where confined by a narrower channel. Crossings such as at Point of Rocks, near North La Junta, and King's Crossing, east of La Junta lost their bridges, ferries and other structures nearby.

The *Old Rocky Ford* and its rocky crossing were destroyed, or totally silted over. All structures, along with the first store of G.W. Swink, were washed away.

It is likely that force of current scattered and pushed the stones of the crossing downstream. Observations of the river by residents of the countryside and of West Ranch were of a '... *wall of water 12 feet high* ... ' near the ranch site, easily supplying the power for this.

In hydrologist utterance, the river bottom was forcefully cleansed resulting in a renewed appearance. However the Flood of 1921 was analyzed, many Valley residents ultimately bore considerable losses. Though Rocky Ford was spared the greatest, terrible loss occurred in Pueblo where the Fountain River converged with the Arkansas.

Flood Restoration, 1921

Soon after the 1921 mud had dried, making it possible to move the house, it was taken to a new location, placed on a new foundation, refurbished, and with some additions was home to new owners at 600 South Main Street.

Mr. and Mrs. L.B. Gorsuch owned the house while in the country just east of State Highway 71 northwest of town. They owned and operated The Union Cleaners and Pressers, a dry cleaning shop at 420-422 North Main Street.

Neither stonework nor foundation were moved by the raging waters.

After the move, Mr. and Mrs. L.P. Clark made the house their home. Leo and Bill Clark owned and operated Clark's Food Market at 208 North Second Street, intersecting with US 50, where they also rented small cabins.

Enterprise monochrome 1921 photos were reprinted in the *Daily Gazette* June 3, 1970. Color photos by *Zillo.com*.

Weid Bakery, An example of family-owned building, built by them as a combined residence and place of business. Tragedy occurred Tuesday May 12, 1908 when the daughter of the Karl Weid family fell from an apartment window above the family bakery. The 1916 building has been occupied by several businesses since and is extant at 966 Front Street. Family name K WEID remains visible in the entablature above the central arch.

SHOCKING ACCIDENT
Little Daughter of Karl Weid Killed by Fall from Upstairs Window.

This community was greatly shocked on Tuesday afternoon by an unfortunate accident that befell little Lucile, the three-year-old daughter of Mr. and Mrs. Karl Weid. The little girl was playing in the apartments above her father's bakery on Front street and had apparently leaned over a window sill to call to her father below when she lost her balance and fell head foremost to the cement pavement, a distance of some 17 feet. A hurry call was sent for Dr. Pollock, who was in a few moments bending over the unconscious form of the little child, but a cursory examination showed that the skull had been badly fractured and there was no chance for recovery. The doctor had the little one removed to his hospital in the forlorn hope that an operation to relieve the pressure upon the brain might be of benefit, but it was found that the injury had been too severe and in a few hours the vital spark had left the little broken frame.

With all that was mortal of their child the stricken parents departed yesterday morning for Perry, Okla., where the remains will be interred.

The building has been occupied most recently by a tavern, after the David Stanbridge Post No. 8 American Legion. Upper windows were sealed with brick, lower windows reduced and along with the street entrance were modified with brick. The building was painted white.

Enterprise, May 15, 1908

Address is given as 966 for the bakery, 970 Front Street for the Weid residence; according to the 1914-1915 city directory. Walnut Avenue between Tenth and Main Street alley was closed to accommodate large markets on Main Street. Walnut is entered from Tenth Street or alleyways from Front Street or Maple Avenue.

Photo courtesy Rocky Ford Public Library

Part 2: A Walk in the Country

Significant Events

Boardwalk to the Country School

Three 1888-1889 school board members were charged with setting the location for a new school voted by the people June 7, 1888. Two sites were proposed, one at town center, another at center of School District No. 4. The latter was chosen for relationship to District boundaries and anticipated travel of prospective students.

Location was on land previously owned by G.W. Swink, sold to the Rocky Ford Town and Investment Company. This company was Santa Fe Railway effort to develop land on the right-of-way. Mr. W.C. Steele, local agent for the company and headquartered in Denver, offered any block in town for the school. Five acres were selected by the District and gratefully accepted free of cost.

A country lane, Washington Road, was on the southern boundary, the course to be Thirteenth Street on the east, and the road to Santa Fe, New Mexico, to be Twelfth Street, on the west.

Kit Carson Road-Tenth Street-would join Eleventh and Twelfth near the new school after crossing Pine Avenue. Tenth was once a main street past Swink's store and De Seeley Hotel that would eventually connect with the Santa Fe Trail several miles south of town.

The Country School, three rooms on upper and three at ground level, was finished spring of 1889 but not named until nine years later after more rooms were added. The *Enterprise* editor suggested several names then for both this school and another recently built. Final names were selected by the school children. *Washington,* often called Boardwalk School, was voted for the Country School and *Liberty* for the new one September 1898.

The center of town, supported by one board member, was the *irrigation ditch*-Rocky Ford Canal. The center of District 4, the other option, was south of town in the countryside, opposed by many. Two board members out-voted the third for the latter site which had several disadvantages the townspeople noted; travel to the new school for small children and few options for shelter.

Weather had to be considered for those who walked to school. Few dwellings or people along the way could harbor children or give aid if needed. More objections were likely expressed for edge of town at the time was near or contiguous with the Washington Road. Distance to the new school was considered too great from the irrigation ditch, then on the edge of town business development. [*Distance from the Rocky Ford Ditch south to Washington Road, is approximately one third mile-1396 ft.- in a straight line*].

Outhouses were provided on the school site at Washington Road, and today's Twelfth Street–SH 71. Nothing more is known of the buildings since description was not provided. Further and only concerning note is in city council minutes about the fire damage that occurred July 27, 1904. Other small fires before had drawn the attention of city council and although no more was said of them these episodes were generally assumed to be *'pranks of the younger generation.'*

Getting to Washington School was important to townspeople who volunteered their time, labor, and materials to build boardwalks-*plural indicated*-for their children to get to school. Time and labor to complete the walkways wasn't mentioned however both would have been substantial for the ones provided.

One boardwalk possibly was from the original Main Street near Swink Store and De Seeley Hotel, then thought of as the town center. That course would conveniently follow the Kit Carson Road south to the school. Another walkway possibly was built from the modern Main Street to

Washington Road and then east to the school.

The boardwalks were of lumber and used for many years until eventually gravel walks were put down followed by cement walks with street improvement. Apparently construction methods were not standard among the volunteer builders so that a variance in width and elevation occurred crossing the open ground to the school. One comment was that at least one of the walkways was very narrow in places.

Even so, these walks no doubt saved many small feet from encounters with dust, snow, and prairie mud ever present in the early history of town. Exceptions could be anticipated, those bolder ones who rather favored the cross-country route over a more direct line from their own starting points. A straight line between two points, so goes the axiom.

No one anticipated the wear of time and weather until boardwalks would be a topic of Council proceedings. Complaints were growing about loose nail heads surfacing as a menace to pedestrians. Removal of boardwalks was not noted in the news however they were, eventually, The first permanent walkways were gravel, then concrete with street and storm sewers.

Specimen Room

This name was applied by students and faculty to a space in the original upstairs portion of the Country School on Washington Road:

"This room was used for the storing of maps, chalk and any other school material, together with the modest library at that time owned by the school. Along with these was a miscellaneous collection of shells, minerals, horticultural freaks, and a few odds and ends–hence the name. All this sounds innocent enough, and to the unsophisticated high school student so it seemed. But justice was administered here and when a sobbing youngster crept with hanging head down the stairs, the whisper went around, 'He's been to the specimen room.' "

Many years later the *Teachers' Lounge* of the high school held a similar distinction on the third floor–actually a semifinished attic–where miscreants were isolated for a time to ruminate over infractions until a faculty member arrived for counseling or administrating corrective measures.

Note: Information, however brief, of other Rocky Ford Schools was included in *Rocky Ford, Colorado–A Walk Past local Doors*. Much of the information about Washington comes from personal experience of attendance there and living across the street from the grounds.

A detailed history of the *White School House* was prepared by Donna Abert in support of consideration of the school by the Otero County Register of Historic Places and Sites for inclusion as part of county schools history, circa January 2009.

Ruth (Muth) Grenard and Donna Abert collaborated in writing a summary of each known country school in Otero County through time. Publication date uncertain but their information may be viewed online at *washingtonprimary.cp.rfp.schoolinsites.com/?PageName='AboutTheSchool'* and links.. My printed copy is dated 2/27/2015.

Joyce (Bitter) Clute prepared: *Rocky Ford Schools Started in 1872 in One Room Cabin On Center Ranch*. Her article was published by *Rocky Ford Daily Gazette* in 1956 while a student in RFHS.

Author's License

Washington School ground was my front yard, just across Thirteenth from home. My closest friends lived over on Washington Avenue and two others on Fourteenth near Pine. We were all to be Juniors or Seniors in high school nearing graduation in the next few months.

School Board had moved classes from Washington School to the new combined elementary and Junior High over on Eleventh near Pine. Our *alma mater* was abandoned in 1954. After 65 years, Washington, the old Country School was condemned. A contractor was waiting to do his work but my friends and I were going to see the place once more before the bricks came down.

Summer was warm and moonlit that night. Entry double doors were not locked, unusual for a condemned building, We went in and stood in the Grand Entry directly front of the central stairway. This led to a landing and left and right stairs to the second floor. While we stood to calm our nerves, listening, every movement caused a squeak from wooden floors that years of oiling had not silenced. The noise was amplified in the half-light.

We moved to the room that was the First Grade. Each had a memory where we had begun to socialize as students for the first time. Second Grade across the Grand Entry was pleasant, mostly because of our teacher. She let everyone read, no matter how haltingly. Our First Grade teacher had been like the dark-clad individual in scenes of *The Wizard of Oz*, Miss Almira Gulch, Wicked Witch of the West, the one Aunt Em's house fell on. She was a near match to the character, I thought. Second Grade teacher was my crush. Her room opened to afternoon sun making the day bright and pleasant. But, it was really Miss Summers who did that.

While we stopped to remember the Christmas programs and other celebrations in the Grand Entry on the elevation between the stairs we thought to ring the bell one more time. The rope was there, so was the bell. That thought was abandoned in a hurry. The whole town would have known someone was in the old school.

We went to the stairs and the upper grade rooms. In the Sixth Grade room chalk and erasers were left behind. We chalked our messages on the blackboard, signing our farewells. It was there our final grade school days were spent before we met again in Jr. High School.

We wanted to see the principal's office where generations of students knew it to be the place where *the rubber hose* was kept. The item rumored to be administered for corrective behavior in miscreants over the years. Entering this creepy place we saw the door to the room where it all took place; the *rubber hose* treatment. The room was really a cloak closet with its door near the principal's desk. I remembered that no one could recall ever having seen the rubber hose, but we were about to!

'It' hung on a nail on the inside of the door facing the wall where the hook was; the hook that held the coat of the one receiving the hose. Just then I recalled we had never heard that girls were ever involved in hose treatment. Opening the door to the cloak room we all looked in. There was the clothes hook, but no nail behind the door! *And no rubber hose!*

What a relief, but at the same time a disappointment at believing something so long to have turned out to be only a well-polished and traded rumor! Then, memory of all the tales of the hose and its history changed. Only nostalgia and memory could make it real again.

The Country School on Washington Road

"One of the finest drives in the vicinity of Rocky Ford is the east and west street directly south of the Washington school and running through Garden Place [to the east]. It is now being put in splendid shape by Street Supervisor Dukes under the direction of the street and alley committee jointly with County Road Com. [Commissioner] Frank Green, and ought to have a name. Its relation to the Washington school has suggested the name of Washington avenue [sic], and the Enterprise hereby confirms that name. It will be known as Washington Avenue until some official authority shall rule otherwise." Enterprise July 15, 1904.

Photo courtesy, Rocky Ford Public Library

Country School of 1889 had a new front in 1902. It was first built with 6 rooms, now the rear section of this elevation. Six new rooms, along with other improvements, were added creating the 1902 front above. Classes had been held in the *Old School*, also called *Country School* nine years before students voted the name Washington.

Students also named Liberty School, completed in 1900, to note Cuban independence from Spain after the 1898 Spanish-American War. Washington remained red brick for years until the additional rooms and improvements in 1902. The exterior was eventually painted white.

Later photos show playground equipment, low wooden benches, a maypole, concrete walkways, trees, flower beds and grass close to the building. A flagpole was erected on the west lawn and a drinking fountain under a large tree to the left. A bicycle rack was provided near the tree for those who wheeled to school.

Washington School.
John Doll's history *The Story of Early Rocky Ford* cites the first use of the school in 1889. It was of brick *locally-fired* but not identified as to providing kiln. There were at least two.

The *Enterprise*, about the time of construction, briefly mentioned a brick yard existing on the western side of town, vintage not known, but without the mention of a kiln operating there. It is likely there was a kiln and the reader was left to assume the bricks were supplied from there for the 1888-1889 first part of Washington School construction.

Students, in their 1925 book *Rocky Ford as the School Children See It,* wrote:

"The bricks used in this building were obtained from the brick plant in Rocky Ford. The rocks [lintels, sills and keystones] *were gotten from Coolidge, Kansas. A great deal of the lumber was purchased in Chicago. Some of the material used in making the foundation* [limestone or shale block] *was obtained at Timpas Creek, south of Rocky Ford. The exterior of the building was very plain in appearance. There was a small projecting entrance on the north side. On the top of the building was a small tower. The original part of Washington building is the rear portion of the present* [1902] *building. ... There was no basement. The building was heated by means of stoves."*

The school, after the 1902 addition, in *Rocky Ford, Colorado–A Walk Past Local Doors*, (p. 164) shows the *"small tower,"* now supporting the bell, and at least two relic chimneys above stoves for heating the 1888-1889 part of the building. Chimneys were non-functional after 1902. A new, larger central chimney for the coal furnace of the 1902 addition then appeared near the bell tower.

The children wrote: *"There was no basement* [under the original 1888-1889 building]." The 1902 addition was designed with a basement, housing a furnace and coal storage area. From there, steam from the boiler circulated to radiators in each room. Adjacent the furnace room, separated by a wall, was a lunch room with tables and benches. There was no refrigeration.

Larmore Brick Kiln, possibly the *"brick plant"* written of by the children was a business referred to only vaguely in news articles. Fortunately, Rocky Ford school children placed the yard location in their book. The Larmore business was located at Sixth Street and Maple Avenue, on the western side of town..

This area became residential and new house-building and other changes contributed to the end of business and movement of this brick yard. Brothers L.W. and G.H. Larmore, owners, fired bricks there for early 1900s businesses and homes in their work as general contractors.

N.W. Terry Brick Kiln was the supplier of brick for the sugar factory, El Capitan Hotel, and many large business houses. The business began in 1894 at the end of Maple avenue on the eastern side of town. Operation was well after the first part of construction of Washington School but ahead of the addition completed in 1902. It is likely the Terry business supplied those brick. Sometime after completion of the ABSC factory order of one million bricks, the Terry business was sold to Fred Cheek and Sons, general contractors.

Cement Stone Company, 209 South Twelfth Street at Walnut Avenue began production of large plain blocks in 1904, and decorative ones in 1906 with new molds. These products greatly expanded choices for builders that were not available for Washington or Liberty schools.

Dye's Lake Improvements

September, 1901 *Enterprise* Editor Barkley reminded the public that duck hunting would start soon that year and was the best at Dye's Lake where the sporting club prepared barrels sunk in the ground for cover. Boats were provided and lunch was available. Members were wanted, twenty desired for a fee of only $10.00 each.

Hunting at Dye's was well-known along Colorado's eastern slope as well as its fishing. Ever promoting advantages of Colorado living, especially in the Arkansas Valley, Publisher D.W. Barkley wasn't instituting a new policy for his paper because all previous editors had done the same kind of drumming for town and its events ever since first editor Harry V. Alexander in 1887.

April 18, 1902 account of activity by the Dyes, who needed only slight urging, began several improvements to the resources at their lake. Something new was developing on the prairie:

"The growing population of Rocky Ford and vicinity makes it evident that we shall soon have a demand for some sort of a summer garden or grove resort, and with a view to supplying that need just as soon as it becomes . . . . [missing]. B. U. Dye and son Horace Dye have set about the adornment of Dye's lake (sic). They have a gang of fourteen men busy out there moving buildings, grading ground and putting in trees. They will plant over a thousand trees of different kinds. There will be a double line of trees extending entirely around the lake, shading a driveway, and then a grove of trees at one end of it. Later on the necessary buildings for such a resort will be constructed on the banks of this attractive little body of water, and boat houses and boats supplied. The fishing in the lake is already good."

Enterprise April 18, 1902

"Dye's lake just across the river, is a scene of active fishing operations just now, Mr. Dye has demands for fish to stock about twenty lakes in various parts of the state. The fish wanted are channel cat and small-mouthed bass, of all sizes and from one to fifteen pounds. A large seine is being used and great quantities of fish taken. . . . Dye's lake is proving quite a profitable piece of property just now. Mr. Ginger is getting from the lake a large amount of fine fish for the general market, including catfish weighing as high as eighteen pounds. Mr. Dye is also called on to supply other lakes with the large catfish for the purpose of stocking them. One shipment was made on Saturday to Charles W. Harris, Denver, state fish commissioner, consisting of Tennessee and channel cat. Ten other lakes in the state are waiting shipments of Mr. Dye's fish. By September 1st he will have such an arrangement of ponds at the lake as to be able to supply any kind of fish wanted at any time. A few days since, Mr. Dye placed in the lake 47,000 rainbow trout, a splendid fish for both sport and table." Enterprise July 18, 1902.

October, 1904 a clubhouse was in place for Rocky Ford gun club members who could entertain guests and visitors. Spartan club building facilities were known to have been dressing and sleeping areas, a meager kitchen and a large porch. Shelter was provided for both horse and carriage with other buildings planned. Works-in-progress were not described well in later news. Aerial photos in 1934 and 1936 of the area show no foundations or structure outlines, no remnants of buildings, trees, shrubs, sink boxes, driveways or roads as once planned.

Plants around Dye's Lake

April 5, 1894

—B. U. Dye yesterday planted two rows of wildgoose plums around the lake across the river. In September he will plant another double row of the Chickasaw plums, which will make a total of eight miles of plum trees on the margin of this beautiful lake.

August 9, 1894

—Dye's lake promises to be one of the most attractive spots in Otero county and also a source of great profit. B. U. Dye informs us that he contemplates setting out around the lake next spring 4,000 apple trees and 4,000 of other nursery stock.

A High-Toned Shooting Club.

Messrs. Aldrich and Reese, of Colorado Springs, have been corresponding with Stevenson & Dye, owners of the big lake across the river, with a view of leasing it for a term of years. A score of wealthy Colorado Springs parties—(everybody is rich there) propose to build a club house and erect shooting booths. Their plans also include the sowing of wild rice and celery to attract the ducks and geese. Grasses and willows will be planted for blinds and the lake in every way fixed up to be one of the most attractive spots for sportsmen in Colorado. The lake covers 120 acres and is only two miles from Rocky Ford. The negotiations have not been completed but the deal will probably be made.

February 21, 1895

Results of planting and improvement efforts around the lake are not reported in these *Enterprise* articles of the era. Finished as designed, or not, all improvements were ambitious, certainly expensive, but were ultimately unsuccessful.

Dye's Lake Improvements.

The growing population of Rocky Ford and vicinity makes it evident that we shall soon have a demand for some sort of a summer garden or grove resort, and with a view to supplying that need just as soon as it comes B. U. Dye and Horace Dye have set about the adornment of Dye's lake. They have a gang of fourteen men busy out there moving buildings, grading ground and putting in trees. They will plant over a thousand trees of different kinds. There will be a double line of trees extending entirely around the lake, shading a driveway, and then a grove of trees at one end of it. Later on the necessary buildings for such a resort will be constructed on the banks of this attractive little body of water, and boat houses and boats supplied. The fishing in the lake is already good.

April 18, 1902

Tuesday G. E. Preble, H. I. Maxwell and Game Warden Anderson planted a large lot of willows in Dye's Lake, which has been under the control of the Standard Rod and Gun Club for the past year or more. The willows were sent to the club by Dr. Carrier of Canon City who recently enjoyed the fine sporting facilities of the club. The willows were planted in 15 places, to provide a "blind" for each member of the club.

April 22, 1904

Note : Highlights remain from word search.

Descriptions of planting around Dye's Lake offer no mention of maintenance of that investment over the several years the lake was operated as a fishery or hunting area. Attempts likely were made early but apparently abandoned when plant failure-to-thrive became evident.

Dye's Lake Fishery

Origin of this water storage facility on the bluffs north of the river escapes discovery, partly for lack of record in available newspapers or public archives but likely existing somewhere in historical minutes of the agency or investor group at conception. We know the lake was an important early interest of B.U. Dye, and other investors.

One of the first notices of Dye's Lake was in the *Enterprise* January 10, 1895: Ice of "*... excellent quality...*" was filling G.W. Swink's ice house in January at his facility along the tracks between Main and Tenth Street. Ice was from "*... the Dye lake on the north side* [of the river].... ."

A view of the area when dry reveals a wide shallow dip in the prairie that grows wider and deepens as it slopes toward the Arkansas River. A narrow runnel on the bottom reaches a man-made embankment supporting a road on a concrete-covered dike. An outlet structure was placed at the dike in the deepest area with a gate that controls release of water to the Arkansas River under the Holbrook Canal and Rocky Ford Dyke Road.

Dye Reservoir has always been known as 'Dye's Lake', named so for the major investors from Rocky Ford, B.U. and son Horace Dye. Their intention was to develop a hunting and fishing leasing business but which resulted in a full-blown commercial enterprise.

It was apparent that water is also important for ventures other than agriculture. First indication of use beyond storage for irrigation came from the *Enterprise* November 15, 1894:

> "*... B U Dye received 100 black bass from the government fisheries, which were placed in his big lake across the river.*"

This 120 acre lake impounds 2400 acre feet of water which is in the reservoir only if there is need and other lakes are full. Holbrook Canal supplies water through a gate at the southwest shore.

In 1897 the *Enterprise* wrote of our "*... minor resources ...*" and "*... our numerous lakes*" which "*... attract thousands of ducks and geese.*" The editor proposed that since the area was widely known as a sporting location by many hunters and fishermen that we offer "*... unusual attractions to hunters ... by fitting it up* [the lake] *with a number of sink boxes ... .*" Providing good boats for hunting and fishing was proposed as an important adjunct.

Later in 1897 the *Enterprise* suggested that since Dye's Lake was already so well stocked that it would be possible to furnish fresh-caught fish to the public through local stores. Gerbing's Meat Market at 206 North Main was already supplying catfish to Pueblo restaurants, fish from Dye's Lake. The idea took some time to develop and eventually B.U. Dye and H.M. Ginger entered into a partnership to do just what the *Enterprise* suggested.

Mr. Ginger, experienced in wholesale fish trade in Indiana, was ready to search the possibilities of the business in Rocky Ford. He began trials in the lake to prove the efficacy of the idea, stated the *Enterprise* August 31, 1900.

Several food markets in Rocky Ford were advertising poultry, fish, beef, pork, and lamb at the time but source of the *fish* is not known. Some fish were imported because there had not been a commercial fishery in the Valley to that time. Local enterprising fishermen may also have been another source selling their catch to grocers. There seemed to B.U. Dye and H.M. Ginger an opportunity to grasp.

Fish Culture in Dye's Lake.
Having bodies of water close by Rocky Ford positively influenced the thinking of at least two early residents of town. H.M. Ginger and Bloomfield Usher Dye. Both became interested in raising fish, partly for sport but primarily for sale to residents of town and the Arkansas Valley. Entrepreneur G.W. Swink apparently was not interested in developing fisheries in his artificial lake near town for the business was not known to be linked to him.

A city council note of November 5, 1894 stated that B.U. Dye *received '100 black bass'* from a government fishery which he placed in his lake across the river. That brief mention in the *Enterprise* was eventually followed by this *Tribune* article of March 22, 1901:

"B.U. Dye, a few days since placed in his large lake 15,000 rainbow trout obtained from the state hatchery. The lake is already finely stocked with this fish, as well as black bass and suckers with a few German carp, which got in without Mr. Dye's knowledge. Fish weighing 20 pounds can now be found in the lake. H. M. Ginger will soon have his nets completed and be in shape to supply the market."

Methods used by Mr. Ginger for keeping species separate were not given in news accounts, other than that he had constructed *'several ponds'* within the lake. Possibly nets were anchored or weighted to the lake bottom and held upright by floats at the surface, allowing capture of fish by nets or seines. Floating boxes constructed with wire screening or netting might also have been the way species were kept separate. Neither method would eliminate unwanted species but accomplished separation of the desired fish well.

News over the next nine years was of continued interest in activities at the lake, both in fishing and hunting. However, not explicitly stated in the news during that time, was the gradual decline of business until a June 2, 1905 *Enterprise* article appeared to point that way: *"Rancher J.G. Hamilton of La Veta was unable to get catfish or bass to stock his own lakes."*

Bass and catfish are among the hardy of warm-water species, much more than trout, for example. They are also among the natives in warm waters, those east or west of the mountains in Colorado. Trout thrive in the cold of mountain lakes, streams and rivers, and will, also in warmer waters but cannot spawn naturally above 21 degrees C. The species can be maintained in warm waters only by introducing juveniles from hatcheries or collecting eggs from wild stock elsewhere.

There are many requirements for raising fish commercially in pond, lake, or river. Many would not be understood for several decades and it was credit to Mr. Ginger that he was able to do so well. Beside fulfilling requirements of species in isolated confinement, such as in his ponds within the lake, he had to deal with the carp and suckers entering the 2400 acre-foot lake. Its inlet and water from the Holbrook Canal originating upriver a few miles to the west were not protected against those species. Many would also enter as eggs on feet and feathers of waterfowl to mature and proliferate. This competition among species would alter the number and kind of survivors.

Placing fish in a lake with fluctuating storage will eventually result in fish loss. Lakes designed for agricultural use, as in the Arkansas Valley, might occasionally empty completely, as Dye Reservoir often has. Dye fishery ultimately failed, but after some years of profitable success.

The Big Fire

During fair week September, 1898, a fire involved the buildings on the entire east side of 200 North Main block which consumed several businesses, including Gerbing's Meat Market- *page 205.* Although all those buildings were replaced and holding businesses in a few months, Gerbing's stock of meats had been taken to La Junta for sale. After fire damage was repaired, the meat market returned.

Several food stores continued to advertise fresh fish until April, 1901 when Govreau's, at 204 South Main, entered an exclusive contract to sell fish from Dye's Lake. Mr. Ginger had perfected his fishery for several species and was ready to seine fish for sale locally and for a growing transplanting business in other lakes in the state. Supplying needs for lakes in the Arkansas Valley became especially good business. May, 1901 the *Enterprise* told of a variety of fish transported to Pueblo to stock the private pond of Irrigation Superintendent Chew. Numerous other lakes in the state received Dye Lake fish of different species for several years.

End of a Good Business

What happened to this fishery is not detailed in the *Enterprise* probably because it happened over time. As the need for irrigation increased in and around Rocky Ford owners of the water in Dye's Lake viewed it as more valuable for crops in the soil rather than fishing, hunting or water sports.

Fisheries require a dependable steady supply of good water. The use of the lake's water was more in demand as time passed and development of farms with irrigated fields and orchards increased. When growing seasons were not supplied with water from distant melting snows or frequent local rains the stored water in lakes had to be used.

Mr. Ginger's tremendous effort at fish culture was highly successful, according to the *Enterprise,* but his efforts were to gradually fail. Water levels were beginning to fluctuate with growing seasons. Maintenance of fish species was difficult because increasing stress affected productivity and numbers.

Frequent introduction of unwanted species, primarily carp and suckers, increased competition for space and food. Their spawn is abundant and hardy even in harsh environment and flourish in waters with meager food supply.

Lakes, rivers and streams are open to receive fish eggs flown in by waterfowl on feet and feathers. Where propagation is supported eggs hatch and the species develop where possibly they had not been before. Desirable fish are stressed competing for food and space.

Carp and suckers also entered Dye's Lake fishery through the inlet and water from the Holbrook Canal, originating from the Arkansas. These could be eliminated from Mr. Ginger's seines, easily at first, with difficulty later when the fish for market were outnumbered in his nets. Carp and suckers, taken by some for food, weren't considered desirable by others because of their feeding habit and boney constitution.

Note: Mr. Ginger offers no indication of feeding his various species with commercial or locally prepared feeds. Feeds and feeding for the larval fish are crucial to hatchery success. In freshwater, commercially manufactured feeds are the first-feeding after hatching for many species. These fish typically have large hatchlings with well-developed digestive tracts and include carp, salmonids and catfish. *sciencedirect.com*

Apparently, Mr. Ginger relied on the natural foods delivered in canal and river water.

Failure Too Soon came to B.U. and son Horace Dye and their partner H.M. Ginger. The lake gradually failed to produce the desired quantity of food fish for the market and for customers dependent on stock for their lakes.

Several ponds within the lake built for separation of species were removed along with all other equipment, boats, seines, transport containers and docks. Leasing of the lake to sportsmen's clubs began a new investment for the Dyes, bringing them back to their original ideas. Events would develop in the future that would limit these also, eventually ending their operations. Water was returning to the needs of agriculture as it had first helped develop it.

Note: In the 1950s the author witnessed emptying of Dye's Lake. Dyke Road and Holbrook Canal courses over the Dye outlet. Before effluent entered the Arkansas from a large culvert underneath there lay a large pool of viscous mud full of carp and suckers, many hundreds trapped. With dorsal fins exposed and mouths taking air from above the mud they were able to survive only a few hours before gills failed.

Description of carp as *German Carp* is inaccurate. *German Carp* does not describe a specie, rather a regional or locally popular name. Carp from the genus *Cyprinidae* were introduced by Eastern European immigrants early in US history as a prolific supply of a protein food source. They have proven to be hardy in poor environment, and just as the introduction of the English Sparrow, have become ubiquitous throughout the US.

During food rationed years of WW II, our family and neighbors living on East Ranch gathered carp, a bony fish, during spring spawning season at Holbrook Lake. When scaled, cleaned and pressure-cooked bone-in, were ground and easily shaped into cakes or loaves by adding dry cereals or oatmeal, eggs and spices. Baked or fried loaves or *pats* provided a nutritious protein source in times of meat rationing.

Success in Another Direction

Increasing concern of community and government, regarding out-of-town hunters, especially on the lakes, continued to grow.

> *"The Rocky Ford lakes are winning wide-spread popularity with sportsmen who enjoy successful hunting. A few days since J.E. Kane and H.S. Beatty of Pueblo came down for a day's hunt. They were accompanied by J.C. Gracey and S.W. Creasy, and in the evening they returned with 51 ducks. And there is plenty more left. George H. Thomas claims the honor of piloting them to the choice hunting ground."* Enterprise April 18, 1894.

> *"Colorado Springs parties have leased Harsin's lake thereby reserving to themselves the exclusive privilege of duck-shooting thereon."* Enterprise April 1, 1897.

The growing popularity of hunting Harsin's and Dye's Lake is described in other sections. Beside leasing water bodies for use of private hunting clubs and out of town individuals, merchants appreciated the hunter who also shopped in town and bought his room and board there for extended visits. Though many came by personal conveyance several were known to have come by train, a plus also for the railroad.

Dye's Lake Hunting

Much hunting activity was enjoyed at this lake because of its location on the migratory path of many species of waterfowl each year. Nearness to Rocky Ford was a great convenience to the hunter for one only had to ride his horse, drive a rig, or ride his bicycle two miles north of town. Roads were wagon paths but walking was within easy distance. Fishing or hunting gear and food for lunch was all that was necessary for the trip.

Bing.com/images

When hunting was the reason for being at the lake a *sink box* was helpful. No trees were available for cover with a prairie landscape all around, occupied only by a few grazing cattle and horses.

The type of sink box for the times may have been of canvas over a frame, metal-sided, or wooden. This particular one in the photo is described having attached extensions on each dimension that floated and were held steady by stones, leaded decoys or other heavy objects. Purpose was wave control. The whole device could be floated above lake bottom anchored to it by wire or cable or simply rested on the bottom.

It was necessary for the occupant to be clad in waders or hip boots unless wading was preferred.

A simple variation mentioned in the October 1898 *Enterprise* was to bury barrels near waterline or in the water so that the hunter could sit low against the horizon hoping to escape detection by his prey.

For any type of concealment a method of retrieval was necessary if birds were downed by shot over water. Rowboats were on hand or sometimes an eager retrieving canine.

> **Gun Club Organized.**
>
> The Rocky Ford gun club was organized last week with a membership of 15 and officered as follows:
> Bert Beymer, President.
> R. S. Beall, Secretary.
> Harry Morse, Treasurer.
> The large lake near the former site of Gerbing's slaughter house has been leased by the club and no other parties will be allowed to shoot ducks thereon.

October 13, 1898 the *Enterprise* printed an announcement of what was apparently organization of the first hunting club with charter membership of 15. Hunting was already popular with the public and a hunter was not restricted in his choice of hunting sites, except by posting of landowners. Sometimes they were taking more game than statutes allowed and several townspeople saw a need for controlled access that also provided disciplined hunting and observance of state law.

A grateful friend of the Standard Rod and Gun Club of Rocky Ford-apparently a name change- provided 15 large lots of willows in 1904 which were placed by members and Game Warden Anderson in various locations about the lake so that each member "... *may have a blind of their own.*" Few succeeding generations of those willows may exist on the west shore of the lake but nowhere else.

Types of concealment described above do not now exist at the lake. Cottonwoods along the south shore developed and matured many years since now are in decline or removed. The time of a once fine fishery and migratory waterfowl environment had passed. The hollow that once was prairie draining to the Arkansas is again prairie with intermittent annual bodies of water.

Water Sports and fishing through the ice were little mentioned in area newspapers. At least ice fishing may not have been practiced by many to make noteworthy news. Ice skating was an activity that drew interest of singles and groups written in news accounts, notably on Harsin Lake and Swink's Artificial lake east of town.

During the 1940s this author recalls being on Holbrook Lake when the ice was enough to support a car. Occupants of which parked out at a distance from the west shore to fish and had built a fire on the ice for warmth. The sensation of walking on ice even at my small weight caused some unease. Concern did not leave me while watching a skater across the lake near the eastern dike to see the ice depress as he skated. He appeared half-sunken while the surface seemed to roll as he moved. He appeared to be in the water, so flexible was the ice.

During another winter, Dye's Lake was visited by those with similar interests as at Holbrook. Fishing through the ice was popular, perhaps because the reservoir was much closer to town than other lakes. The deepest area near the outlet structure drew the fishermen. That day no one was on the ice although several areas bore signs of ice openings now frozen over.

Two vehicles were on the ice several yards out. One was a vintage truck with side racks on a flat bed sitting out from the concrete dike. Tracks showed that joy-riding was the reason for leaving a series of circles and skid marks. Something happened to cause the driver to leave the vehicle, maybe out of gas or because of some malfunction. No impulse could lead us to investigate since there were cracks in the ice near the truck.

Another vehicle, even less likely to be found out on a lake in winter, was a *Cletrac*, a small crawler tractor possibly to retrieve the truck. Not knowing the reason the tractor was stalled, we left the scene until the ice was gone in spring. We never knew the fate of the two vehicles, nor was there news in the *Enterprise* of consumption of vehicles by lake ice.

Note: *Cletrac*, Inc. was a manufacturer of tractors for military and civilian use, organized by Rollin H. White as the Cleveland Motor Plow Co. in 1916. White, a founder of the White Motor Company, had 10 years earlier formed this new firm to produce the crawler-type tractor he had developed for general farm use.

Dye's Lake Aerial View

Dye Reservoir has been a receiving impoundment for water coming from Holbrook Canal after Holbrook was filled. In times of less water the reservoir was by-passed for storage and therefore gradually lost its birds and fish and in recent years is often empty.

January 21, 2019 aerial photo shows a near empty reservoir. Google Maps.

Sports club members of the past could not anticipate the failure that was ahead. Survival of their plans to lease Dye's Lake and its amenities depended on availability of water, abundant then, less so with the years. Reservoir value today lies in additional storage in seasons of abundant water.

Dye's Lake Transition to Dye Reservoir

The immediate environs of Dye's Lake were and are not hospitable to introduction of trees and other plants. If any survived from the efforts of the owners to develop a grove-like park it was evident in a short while of failure to thrive. Livestock in the area would have eaten tender new plants. Deficient soil, wildlife, insects, broiling sun and lack of frequent watering and care by those with grounds responsibility finally saw extinction of all introduced plant life.

Dye's Lake Chronology

The *Enterprise* existed from 1887 to 1954. Editions before 1893 and after 1908 are not in the digitalized collection online and therefore some events, with exception, may not appear in the following list. Digitalized news begins with August 31, 1893 and ends with the May 29, 1908 weekly on Thursdays.

July 1, 1893: A drowning at the lake.
April 5, 1894: Wealthy hunters from Colorado Springs want to lease Dye's Lake, build a club house and 'shooting booths' and sow wild rice and celery to attract waterfowl.
April 18, 1894: Lake popularity grows among hunters.
May 3, 1894: New York party bags 60 ducks on area lakes.
November 15, 1894: B.U. Dye added 100 black bass.
January 10, 1895: G.W. Swink harvested ice.
February 21, 1895: B.U. Dye to plant 4000 apple and 4000 other trees around the lake in spring.
April 29, 1897: Sink boxes and boats proposed.
October 7, 1897: Gerbing's Meat Market shipping catfish and trout caught from the lake.
October 13, 1898: Rocky Ford Gun Club organized.
April 31, 1900: H.M. Ginger fisheries trial.
March 16, 1901: H.M. Ginger repairs running gear for fish net [seines] at Dawley's workshop.
April 2, 1901: Another drowning at the lake.
April 19, 1901: Govreau's Meat Market exclusive local agent for Dye's Lake fish.
May 17, 1901: Irrigation Superintendent Chew stocks private pond at Pueblo with Dye's Lake fish.
May 31, 1901: H.M. Ginger netted 1200 pounds of fish in two days, weighing from 2 to 20 pounds.
September 27, 1901: Hunting club wants 10 new members.
April 18, 1902: Proposal by B.U. and Horace Dye for *'summer garden'* or *'grove resort.'*
   H.M. Ginger, formerly of Dye's Lake Ranch visited from New Mexico for a stay of several months [apparently having moved to monitor his other business interests].
July 18, 1902: Demand grows for stocking other lakes and in general food marketing.
April 22, 1904: Standard Rod and Gun Club plant willows in 15 areas around the shore for individual member blinds.
May 20, 1904: Two went missing at the lake, were found after extended stay to cook their catch.
October 7, 1904: Standard Rod and Gun Club's 25 members completed their clubhouse for $750. Bedroom, dining room, kitchen were enhanced by a 15 x 40 foot porch. A large stable was provided for member's horses.
February 11, 1905: Articles of Incorporation of the Dye Canal and Reservoir Company of Manzanola by Horace B. Dye, James W. Beaty, and B.U. Dye. One purpose in forming this company and incorporation was *". . . to acquire, by purchase, gift or any other lawful means title to and ownership in irrigating canals and storage reservoirs in Otero County, taking their supply from the Arkansas River or its tributaries, but more especially to purchase a certain reservoir known as Dye's Lake, and to construct, own and operate parks and pleasure resorts."* The three Directors operated with capital stock $50,000 or 500 shares of $100. Future plans for Dye's Lake *'park'* were to change.
June 2, 1905: Rancher J.G. Hamilton of La Veta was unable to get catfish or bass to stock his own lake
September 2, 1909: *"The farmers living under the Holbrook Ditch near La Junta have organized the Holbrook irrigation district and have purchased the canal and all the water rights therein from the owners and are now surveying for an intake ditch from the river to Dye Lake. This ditch will be 20 miles long, 40 feet wide and seven feet deep. The Dye reservoir will probably hold 50,000 acre feet of water."*

Sale of the lake and water rights to Holbrook Irrigation District signaled the approaching end of approximately 12 years of a commercial fishery. Private use by hunting and fishing clubs and public excursions to the lake continued for a while but all appurtenances related to fisheries and hunting were eventually removed.

September 10, 1909
> Eight days after the September 2 announcement another *Enterprise* article appeared:

> **Dye Lake Sold**
> B. U. Dye on Tuesday disposed of what is known as the Dye Lake, north of the river, to the Holbrook Resevoir and Irrigation Co. The purchase price was $35,000 which encludes a large tract of land surrounding the reservoir.
> The lake has a capacity of 4,000 acre feet of water and it is the intention of the new company to greatly increase the capacity, so that when completed the Holbrook Irrigation district will have one of the best systems of storage reservoirs in the state.

May 6, 1910
> The *Enterprise* printed these small articles of what was soon to happen regarding the improvements ordered and publicized September 2, 1909.

> Harry McDowell, the Lamar contractor who has the Holbrook ditching contract, is this week moving his outfit out to the Dye reservoir where he will on Monday begin work upon the extensive improvements ordered some time since.

July 15, 1910
> Increased capacity and ready for water.

> Contractor H. H. McDowell on Wednesday completed his job of excavating and enlarging Dye's lake, and with a few finishing touches in the way of connecting up the Holbrook Irrigation Co. will be able to place their new reservoir in commission.

Priorities

On the western prairie landscape once described as the *Great American Desert*, a lament sometimes is heard from among those who see lakes and reservoirs around them diminish in summer to the lowest surface of the impoundment. The cry is often from the late-comers to our environment where we all thrive on very little annual downfall moisture as in our Arkansas River Valley. Until they are aware of use of water in the West they do not understand that our disappearing water will soon reappear as food on our tables, if we are prudent. Water means survival here.

Note: Rocky Ford, Colorado gets 13 inches of rain, on average, per year. The US average is 38 inches. Rocky Ford averages 29 inches of snow while the US average is 28 inches. Yearly, there averages 255 sunny days locally.

Earl Zimmerman Airport 1936

Established May 1, 1927 as Earl Zimmerman *Airfield* by local flight enthusiasts near the southeast shore of Dye Reservoir and dedicated as *Earl Zimmerman Airport* by the American Legion September 8, 1929.

The honor was for Rocky Ford pilot, Earl Henry Zimmerman who served in WW I. He died at Colorado Springs during flight of a test plane in 1928.

Several local area pilots learned basic flying skills here before entering military service in WW II. The field was used at least into 1929, according to records of Colorado Flight Fields.

Field location was recorded on this Soil Conservation Service aerial photo in 1936. Airfield buildings or other structures appear only as traces in the soil. The runways were not paved as were later WW II auxiliary fields.

Three small circles locate the vertices of the triangular runway system and the reach of each leg of the field.

cudl.colorado.edu/luna/servlet/detail/links

The three-span steel bridge over the Arkansas River, now replaced-*arrow at bottom*. Holbrook Canal and Rocky Ford Dyke Road angle center left to lower right. Upper arrow indicates CR 22.00. City dump–*enclosure*–appears sectioned showing some separation of materials. Fence lines and tree-lined roads are darker, some filled in by soil and vegetation. Airfield is no longer completely visible on USDA Farm Service Agency map of 2018–*following page*.

Note: Reservoir is near capacity. Compare to small volume pool in lake basin 82 years later, following page.

Earl Zimmerman Airport 2018

Land features were significantly changed over the years by weather, farming, and grazing activity. Dye Reservoir is seasonally dry because of irrigation demands. Ninety-one years after the airport dedication nearly all traces of runway legs are overgrown and filled by sand and vegetation.

This field was not built with passengers in mind. It was basically an unpaved facility for pilot training developed by and for flying enthusiasts.

A trace of one leg of the triad is near CR 22.00 indicated by the circle and white line. Other circles mark the vertices of the landing field's other sides. Farming activity is visible south of this country airfield near SH 266.

City refuse was dumped, since 1927-in the enclosure at *lower left*. See also page 82 in the book *Rocky Ford, Colorado–A Walk Past Local Doors*.

24timezones.com/mapa/usa/co_otero/rocky_ford.php

Dump activity over 41 years added layers of articles, glass, metal, and every other kind of discard, all left open to weather. Site has since been transformed for use as a tree dump. In 1968 a sanitary landfill was established south of SH 10 on CR 21.00 where all is now soil-covered.

Note: A portion of the runnel in lake bottom at upper left margin is visible extending into the only remaining water.

Rocky Ford Air Circus of 1930 showed interest in flying and flying machines increased all over the United States before and after the Lindbergh Atlantic flight to Paris in 1927.

Rocky Ford was not without some early aviation notoriety. Several local individuals learned to fly from rudimentary fields before WW II. Art Goebel won the Honolulu Airplane Race August 18, 1927. Just prior. Zimmerman Field, near Dye Reservoir was established May 1, likely a place known to Goebel.

September 8, 1929 the American Legion dedicated and officially named the field Earl Zimmerman Airport honoring the Rocky Ford man who was a WW I pilot. The air circus during the field dedication was probably the first organized event for presentation as a local show.

The field was to have a short life as an organized civilian airfield, until late 1929. Information after then is not known.

The Air Commerce Act of May 20, 1926 began the federal government's formal regulation of civil aviation. This dulled interest in flying for a while. Aviation up to then was a free-spirited activity engaged in by those who were willing and able to fly sometimes flimsy airframes.

Legislation urged by aviation industry leaders was designed to help develop full commercial potential while improving and maintaining safety. The Act made the Secretary of Commerce responsible for promoting air commerce, issuing and enforcing air traffic rules, licensing pilots, certifying aircraft, establishing airways, and operating and maintaining air navigation aids.

Cottonwood Field, another airstrip, has a turf surface near CR 23.00 and CR FF.00. The road north of US 50 and the river, strip is of private ownership, frequency of use is not known. There are no buildings or structures there.

The newly created Aeronautics Branch, under the Department of Commerce was responsible for oversight of this new industry. Those who were active locally in civil aviation were caught up in the cost and increasing regulation and Zimmerman Airport, a new enterprise, did not survive. A faint triangular runway pattern is visible in satellite view (see *Earl Zimmerman Airport 1936*).

Air Navigation Ground Markings
Pilots were beginning to fly the countryside without maps or printed visual aids, relying on things on the ground. Roads, highways, and known geologic landmarks such as lakes and rivers, were principal guides before development of radio. When airmail service was developing in the 1920s the US Postoffice installed a system of marks on the ground from New York to San Francisco that were identified easily by even inexperienced pilots. On August 20, 1920, the United States opened its first coast-to-coast airmail delivery route, just 60 years after trains ended the Pony Express.

In 1924 the Postal Service, knowing that pilots needed more help finding their way, began placing a series of large concrete arrows lighted by beacons along its designed airmail routes.

Large concrete arrows pointed the way across the US. This location is in Sweetwater County, Wyoming.
Courtesy, Tom Johnson, Bryan #14 Wyoming.

Approximately every ten miles mail pilots could see a 50-70 foot yellow-painted arrow supporting a 50-foot tower with a rotating million-candlepower light. These course lights flashed a code to identify each beacon's number. When visibility wasn't impaired by weather, the light of the next beacon could be seen from the one currently being flown over. Each arrow pointed to the next, a feature that kept pilots on course. A generator shed at the tail of each arrow powered the beacon.

Frequent maintenance of beacons and generators for day and night operation was essential. This necessary task was accomplished at remote sites by ground-based maintenance personnel. Markers near airfields were maintained by facility staff.

Federal markers facilitated US mail service from Atlantic to Pacific in about 30 hours. By 1924, a year after Congress provided funds the line of concrete markers stretched from Rock Springs, Wyoming to Cleveland, Ohio. The next summer, it reached all the way to New York, and by 1929 it spanned the continent uninterrupted.   Paraphrased from *Snopes* Staff, published August 30, 2013.

In 1926, the Post Office Department turned management of the markers and beacons over to the Department of Commerce. The project was finished in 1929, after completing a route from New York to San Francisco. But, the arrow-and-beacon system did not last long because by early 1930s, technological advances-radio and radar-began to supply much more reliable navigation.

Today, few towers remain but many once yellow-painted concrete arrows may be found out on the prairies between airfields. Towers were long ago salvaged and recycled for WW II. New advances in communication and navigation technology made the big arrows obsolete, and the Commerce Department decommissioned the beacons in the 1940s.

Published 30 August 2013 by *Snopes Staff,* filed under *Air Apparent* u.s. postal service sources.

Preserved beacon tower on its navigation arrow with generator shed.

apex.aero/2016/02/18/concrete-arrows-civilian-navigation-systems.

Beacon, tower and generator shed on arrow marker, c. 1920-1930s. Numbers and letters both sides of roof identify station number and location.

faa.gov/about/history/photo_album/foundation/?cid=building

Note: Concrete arrow markers were not installed in Colorado but there were 12 beacon towers placed across the state with large rotating lights, each providing one million candlepower.

Swink Lake east of the fairgrounds was a small natural lake on property owned or controlled by E.E. Swink and Mr. and Mrs. William Matthews. Notice was given to the public as duck hunting season approached that the area was posted against camping, fishing, hunting, shooting, and trespassing in general. Rocky Ford Duck Shooting Club, lessee, advertised that *"Violators will be dealt with as the law provides."* The notice applied to *". . . ranches owned or controlled by . . . the Swink and Matthews families."* Enterprise, September 28, 1900.

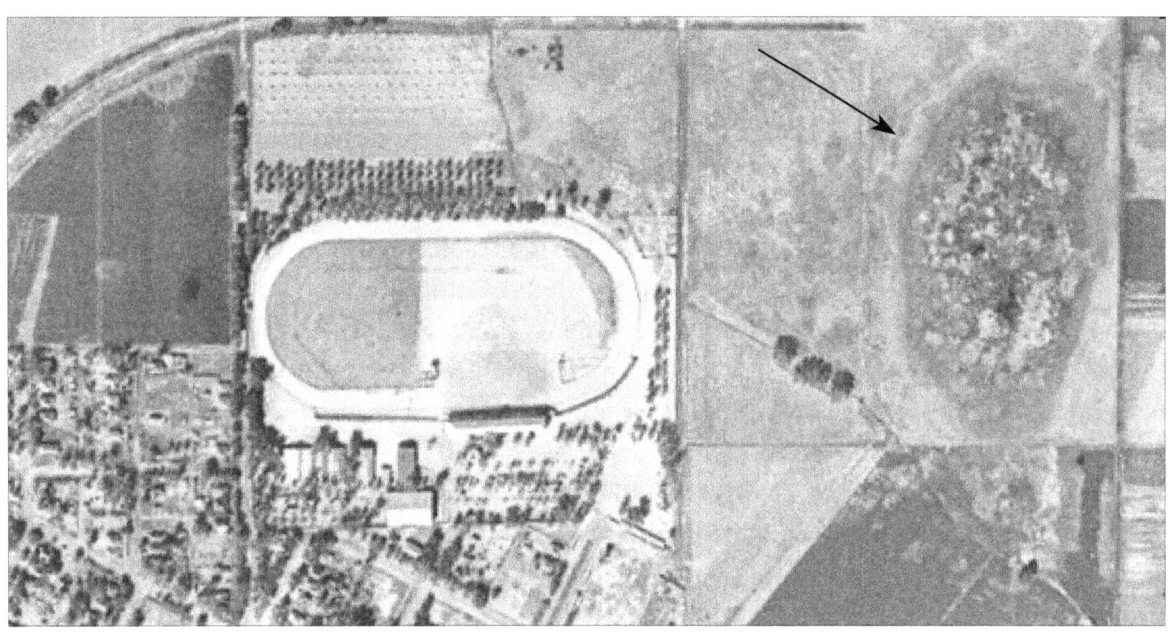

Photo AG 82-296 Soil Conservation Service October 4, 1936, scale 1:20,000

A 1936 aerial photo shows the lake now grown over with trees-*arrow*-and other vegetation. The lake size approximates that of the fairgrounds racetrack. Loss of water may be explained by a lower water table or active draining and filling as later photos show a partially tilled field. North of the fairgrounds, for example, G.W. Swink installed a network of tiles to remove surface water on his farm there. Perhaps a similar method was applied to this lake.

Hunting on Swink Lake

Mr. L.R. Fenlason, president, Arkansas Valley Gun Club, posted notice three years later in the *Enterprise* October, 1903 reserving hunting and shooting privileges for his club. Not only were local hunters informed of the restrictions placed on leased lakes around Rocky Ford they were reminded by the *Enterprise* editor in the issue of December 9, 1897 that hunters have limits:

". . . our sportsmen should remember that the law proscribes that one person in one day shall till (sic) no more than twenty ducks." Enterprise, .December 9, 1897.

Although sportsmen's clubs opted for leasing several ponds, lakes and the river bottom remained open to the public. Waterways developed as leach channels also provided miles of hunting space as did the river. All one needed was permission of land owners, reminded the *Enterprise* editor.

Swink Lake Sold

G.W. Swink died September 24, 1910. His land east of the fairgrounds, including the lake bed on the previous page and in this article, was sold thereby dispersing more of his real estate holdings.

G.W. Swink moved his stock of goods to Rocky Ford in 1876, partnering with Isaiah Denness, and to eventually procure a thousand acres of land, which he obtained by homestead, pre-emption and purchase. Preemption Act, also known as the Distributive Preemption Act, was a federal law of September 4, 1841 designed to:

"... appropriate the proceeds of the sales of public lands... and to grant 'pre-emption rights' (sic) *to individuals who were living on federal lands."*

Those individuals were commonly referred to as squatters, who were originally viewed by many to be less than legitimate but related to the original idea of land colonization. They were those who settled on property without right or title or payment of rent. The term remained in common use when applied to those now legally improving their claims, those who settled on public land under government regulation with the purpose of obtaining legal possession under a title.

President Abraham Lincoln signed the Homestead Act on May 20, 1862. On January 1, 1863, the first claim was made under the Act, which gave citizens or future citizens up to 160 acres of public land provided they live on it in a homestead of required minimum size, improve it, and pay a small registration fee. More than 160 million acres (650 thousand km2; 250 thousand sq. mi.) of public land, or nearly 10 percent of the total area of the United States, was given away free to 1.6 million homesteaders, most of whom had settled land west of the Mississippi River.

G.W. Swink's thousand acres included the town site of Rocky Ford and many acres surrounding. Because of his generosity many acres were either sold at reasonable terms or granted outright over his lifetime. Purchase by Arkansas Valley Fair Association of the 53 acres in the article was apparently not followed by the developments listed in the article. Improvements were set aside for reasons not explained.

Rocky Ford Fair Grounds Enlarged.

Following recent improvements at the Arkansas Valley Fair Association grounds at Rocky Ford, to the extent of nearly $6,000, comes the announcement of the purchase by the association of an additional tract of fifty-three acres adjoining the present grounds, which will be parked and fitted for conveniences for the fair visitors. The site, which was purchased from G. W. Swink for $10,000, includes a lake, which will be further improved and form an attractive feature of the big valley fair.

Enterprise October 1, 1910

Aerial view of the property on the previous page taken 26 years after purchase shows no parked improvements nor lake developments to enhance attractiveness. Instead, it seems maintenance of a lake without visible water supply stalled Fair Association plans. A lower water table and loss of above ground water developed into the wooded marsh or swamp it became.

Many years later a local sportsmen's club would use the space outside the existing boundary of horse stalls for public exhibition and demonstration of shooting sports.

A notice referring to *all* the ranch properties of the Swinks' and Matthews' is excerpted here. In the future, notices were published in the *Enterprise* October 9 and 23, 1903 about the particular wet area in the previous photograph and below, referring to it as *Swink Lake*. Another more notable lake in Rocky Ford was *Swink's Artificial Lake* near the east end of Maple Avenue in 1882, not involved in hunting.

Club President, L.R. Fenlason, reminded hunters of the sections of the law with its warnings in a news article. Postings in the *Enterprise* by The Arkansas Valley Gun Club referred to:

> "... the Swink lake near the fairgrounds, ... for ... shooting privileges .... Trespassers will be promptly prosecuted as the State Game Laws provide ... ."

The area was a naturally formed shallow lake, a wooded marsh or swamp on property of William Matthews north of the terminus of Tenth Street, east of the fairgrounds-*arrow*. Mr. and Mrs. Matthews owned the property which they leased to the Arkansas Valley Gun Club. Because of its location near town and ease of access it was necessary to post restrictions to maintain rights of the gun club until fulfilment or termination of lease. The area is now dry.

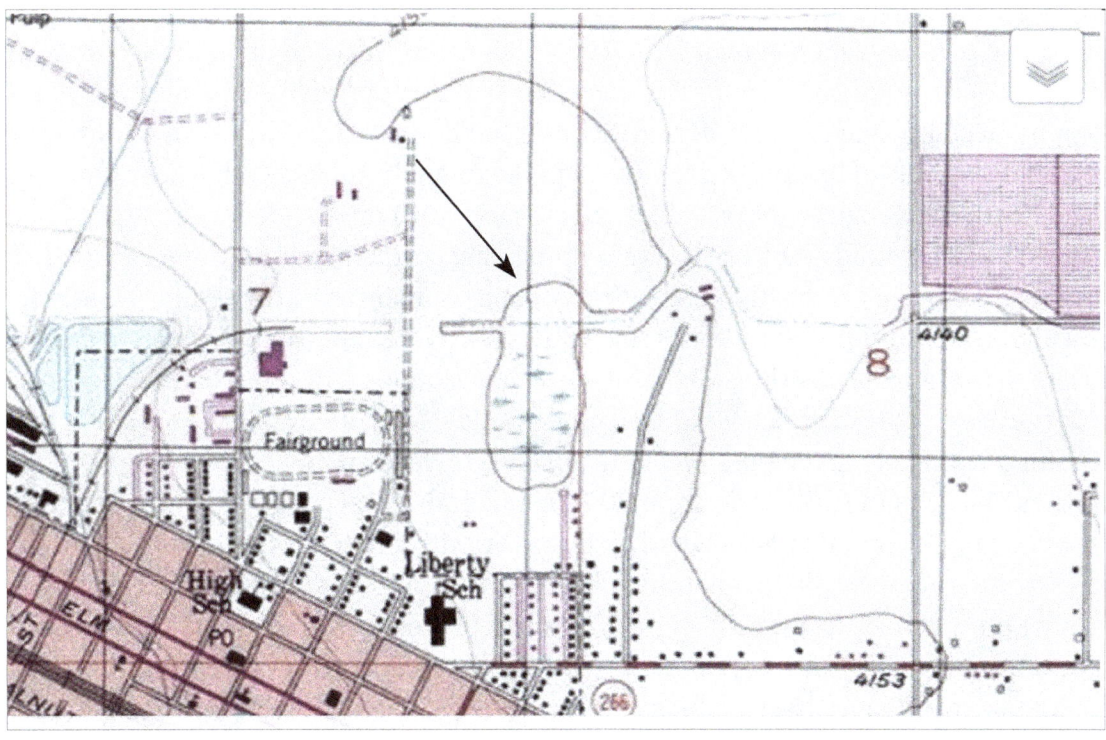

topozone.com/colorado/otero-co

Age of this map precedes closure of Liberty School. County roads are not yet identified.

Note: Topographic maps on TopoZone are created by the US Geological Survey (USGS) and have evolved for more than a century. Over time maps become more detailed as symbols are added or remove, terrain changes, natural features, land boundaries, and man-made structures are depicted by surveyors. The extensive legend-not shown-is now a complex document that explains the refinements within each category of features. [Evolutions of this map not dated]

Municipal Reservoir, 1936

North Rocky Ford is captured in this aerial photo with the *municipal reservoir* northeast of town between delimiters. A large area of arable land is to right center. The dark straight-line structure from center to left distance appears to be remnant pipe line to the factory from water well across the river. Arrow indicates North Main Street fairground entrance.

Time difference of fifty years between 1886 and 1936, *Frontispiece* photo and the *First Business Block* in *Rocky Ford, Colorado-A Walk Past Local Doors*, is impressive when considering all the development accomplished in that period. Several buildings in the full aerial photo are easily identified on the streets of Rocky Ford today. In this segment both Elks Lodge near the lower left corner and Rocky Ford High School at center left are circled. At upper left is a dense group of trees just north of the fairgrounds race track, a remaining part of G. W. Swink's timber culture claim.

Right of top center in this portion of the *Frontispiece*, is an intermittent body of water formed mostly by high water table. The author of this 1936 photo titled this body *Municipal Reservoir* in the desire for a caption. Its position northeast of the fairgrounds and south of the Arkansas River covers a large area, some of which would become arable land. How water was removed and the land reclaimed was likely made possible naturally by a lowered water table.

Other land, such as the 160 acres from G.W. Swink and 20 each from S.H. Young and Naomi Fielder, were soggy, unstable soils included in the factory site. Engineers employed steam engines, placed as stationary power plants on either side of a tract, and connected by cables alternately pulled a large plow across the area. An eight foot swath turned by the plow exposed the soil to air and sun, eventually drying it. In areas that were designated for farming this soil was further treated with lime to enhance its usefulness for crops. G.W. Swink successfully reclaimed some of his farmland north of the fairgrounds by laying underground a system of tiles to drain off excess water and allow cultivation.

Notes: Text below the photo refers to *the Frontispiece, Rocky Ford, Colorado, 1936* and *First Business Block in Rocky Ford circa 1886* of *Rocky Ford, Colorado--A Walk Past Local Doors*.

Municipal Reservoir, describing the marked area in the photo, was a name of expediency by the aerial photographer. Not a reservoir, it was a high water table marsh with waterfowl in abundance.

More on Swink's Artificial Lake

Photo is matted, identified as to location and date, April 1, 1910. Initials G.W.L. identify the sender as George W. Lenty who posted this card to his wife in Iowa. Nothing is known of Mr. Lenty's business in Rocky Ford. Lake is the *presumed artificial lake* of Mr. G.W. Swink.

Swink's Artificial Lake, *Perhaps*

Photo enlarged from postal card image page 103.

Artificial Lake classifies a body of water as man made. Creation of such a lake is assisted by natural depressions or elevations of surrounding terrain where excavation and filling can create an impoundment. This lake may have been so created. Photograph appears to have been taken from atop a levee. This photo from a photographer's collection was for advertising and sale in 1910, purchased in Rocky Ford as a postal card, prepared by a Chicago photography studio with its trademark on obverse.

Evidence for the Lake.

Type and abundance of trees in the previous photos reflect early resident desire and fondness for shade emphasized in this area designed by G.W. Swink, *if this is Swink's Lake*. Many young trees border the water and appear to be about the same age and development. Trees planted at or sometime after completion of the Lake in 1882 would have aged up to 28 years in 1910, the time of this photo.

An area beyond the trees in large photo page 104, right center, appears to be a field or possibly a road. Absence of visible current, bank erosion, driftwood and other flotsam indicate a stationary body of water, lake or pond such as described in news publications and interviews of Rocky Ford citizenry. Foreground-possibly a levee-appears higher than those visible right and at distance.

A fenced enclosure does not appear unless of wire or something poorly visible that blends with shore vegetation. A wire fence *is* mentioned in a 1905 *Enterprise* article–see *A Possible Suicide*.

Swink Lake in History. Swink's Lake was completed and publicized in the *Rocky Mountain News* in a two-sentence notice:

> "Mr. G. W. Swink of Rocky Ford, Las Animas County* has just completed one of the finest artificial lakes in the State. It covers an area of 20 acres, and has an average depth of ten feet."   R. M. *News*, Jan. 11, 1882 p. 6c. 2.

Passage of time may preclude surfacing of details of this venture of George W. Swink since it seems little was published when the lake was extant. Original 1876 town plat included a *Lake Street* at its eastern border. Senator Swink's daughter, Mattie (Swink) Lamon in a January 26, 1981 *Gazette* article, cited p. 298 of *Rocky Ford, Colorado, A Walk Past Local Doors* refers to the *pond* as source of ice blocks for storage in her father's ice house near his store. Then, *Enterprise* observed:

> "Senator Swink's lake near the stockyards is being treated for seepage. A traction engine is meandering over the bottom of the lake, hour after hour, in order to pack the earth more solidly."   *Enterprise*, April 6, 1900.

Another reference to the lake was by early Rocky Ford barber Fred Knaus, interviewed by the *Gazette* for the 75th anniversary of Rocky Ford. He described skating on a *fenced pond* near the Stauffer Packing Plant. His words indicate *possibly* the pond and packing plant were co-existent. He might have known Mr. Ray Keith, a delivery man for Fluke and Ritchie grocery at 303 South Main Sreet, who sprained an ankle skating on Swink Lake one evening.   *Enterprise* Dec. 20, 1907.

The lake then would have been east of Stauffer's extending some distance to accommodate the size stated in the *Rocky Mountain News*. However, the plant began operations in 1933, after supposed demise of the lake. Part, or all of the former lake site would have been covered by Stauffer's packing plant.

Another early resident interviewed by the *Gazette* for the anniversary issue of 1962 said that the lake was "*... several hundred feet long.*" This description implies the length exceeded width in its 20 acres as stated in the *Rocky Mountain News*.

Note: Otero County was formed from Las Animas and Bent Counties in 1889. In 1893 stock pens were built on the east edge of Fifteenth Street. Corral was contemporary with Swink's Lake; remained until the 1960s, then removal.

Author John Doll wrote of the storage building south of the railroad on Tenth Street built by the *Rocky Ford Ice and Storage Company* for ice from Swink's Lake. Article was written in the *Enterprise*, March 10, 1898 and indicates 100 South Tenth Street. The lake ice would have been transported by rail approximately 6 to 7 blocks from the lake to this storage place.

Some ice was taken from mountain lakes and locally, stated the *Enterprise* January 10, 1895.

"G. W. Swink commenced filling his large ice house near the Santa Fe tracks Monday morning. The ice is being taken from the Dye lake on the north side and is of excellent quality."

Ice from mountain lakes was harvested when temperatures were not low to freeze local sources.

A Possible Suicide

These words heading an *Enterprise* article must have been of concern to some:

"Yesterday a woman was seen running in a wild manner toward Swink's Lake. She was seen to crawl through the wire fence and disappear over the high bank. She was followed in a few minutes but no trace of her could be found. Foot prints were seen leading to the water but none showing that the woman had left the bank of the lake. If a suicide has been committed the victim is from a distance [out of town] *as no inquiry has been instituted as to any resident being missing. The fact will doubtless be shown in a day or two as the body will rise if a life has been taken by a demented mind."* May 25, 1900

Later issues of the weekly *Enterprise* reveal no more of this episode. Perhaps *corpus delicti*-no body of concern, was operative and the episode, though witnessed, was simply misinterpreted.

Stauffer Packing Plant opened in 1933, closed in 1972 after 39 plus years of business. *Valley Concrete* and others would occupy the area later. East of the Stauffer plant, the northern part of Garden Place was the probable location of Swink's Artificial Lake. Homes on small farms and many trees stood between Rocky Ford Ditch and Santa Fe railroad years after the lake.

Santa Fe cattle pens were built in 1893 just east of Fifteenth Street where the street met the railroad. The lake was then in existence, written of in the *Enterprise*. Forty years later the Stauffer plant was opened in 1933. Swink's Lake by then likely had been abandoned c. 1905. After 1905 sanitary ice was being produced commercially with machinery designed for that purpose at *Rocky Ford Ice and Mercantile Company*. Lake ice would no longer have been used for human consumption, though probably for other uses and cold storage of perishables.

News articles and residents' observations tend to describe non-use or abandonment well before the construction of the Stauffer plant. Nothing physical remains of Mr. Swink's Lake nor of more maintenance or of abandonment. Neither is it known whether Mr. Swink had provided for the future of his lake before his death in 1910.

Possibly the lake was losing so much of its storage capacity through seepage life of the lake was becoming unsustainable. This was indicated at least one time by the use of a traction engine to increase compaction of the lake bottom. Repeated effort to stop water loss would have been too costly but Mr. Swink's strong desire to improve Valley agriculture through irrigation was well known and would not be ended here. Ice production began c. 1882 and lasted at least 23 years through 1905 when commercial ice became available.

Baptism at Swink Lake

Numerous articles about the Peoples Mission were in the *Enterprise* during years the Mission was active in town. The leadership, as well as meeting location, changed often. Over time the Mission met above City Drug at 209 North Main Street, also at 712 South Main and other locations.

The Mission being affiliated with Christian teaching was likely inter-denominational or non-denominational in association. Information in the article of June 19, 1908 places the address at 406 South Main Street, once location in succession of at least two billiard halls.

Swink's Artificial Lake near the east end of Maple Avenue was the likely baptism site, rather than the Swink Lake just east of the fairgrounds, basically a marsh. The artificial lake was but a few blocks east on Maple Avenue from the Main Street location of the Mission.

Enterprise June 19, 1908

> **New Man in Charge.**
> Rev. and Mrs. C. C. Beatty, Evangelists of Indiana, have come here to take charge of the Peoples Mission. Mr. Beatty was for many years a railroad train dispatcher and Mrs. Beatty was at one time a city missionary in Chicago under Dwight L. Moody, the great evangelist.
> The Peoples Mission are changing their location to the store room on South Main street recently vacated by the millinery store. They expect to be moved in time for Saturday night meeting and will have a grand opening on Sunday. It is hoped that Rev. W. H. Lee, General Supt. of the church will be present for the occasion.

> The Peoples Mission had a baptismal service at Swink Lake last Sunday afternoon. Geo. Manney and wife and Joseph Salien were baptised.

Enterprise July 4, 1908

The baptism was a private event but performed in the open and available to public view at the lake. Not stated but family and friends along with the Mission congregation were very likely witnesses.

The west shore of the lake at this time likely was between modern era Fifteenth and Nineteenth Streets. This event is the final one which refers to 'Swink's Lake in the news, presumably Swink's Artificial Lake.

Harsin's Lake, by an 1893 map was a natural lake, apparently later enlarged as a source of gravel, indicated by the current shape of its shoreline, possibly the work of F.M. Harsin and successors.

I offer this *supposition*. There is frequent early reference to the lake in the *Enterprise* with *no physical evidence of its existence later in 1936 aerial photos.* Speculation leads to the lake being naturally reduced before 1936, succumbing to drought, return to farming and later gravel mining. Assumptions of water appearance, disappearance and reappearance are offered in a later section.

Note: Gravel mining was profitable business during building activity 1887 to 1920 when brick and mortar construction was increasingly used in town. The countryside of Otero County, prairie and river bottom, are dotted with active and abandoned gravel mines today.

County Site and Road identification

Following pages with aerial photos were of parts of county map sections 15, 16, 21, and 22, below. Dotted lines are irrigation or leach canals, all eventually emptying into the river, Rocky Ford Canal by joining Timpas Creek. The small body of water-*circle*-is the pond or lake Harsin, not known by name until F.M. Harsin operated a sheep ranch in the area.

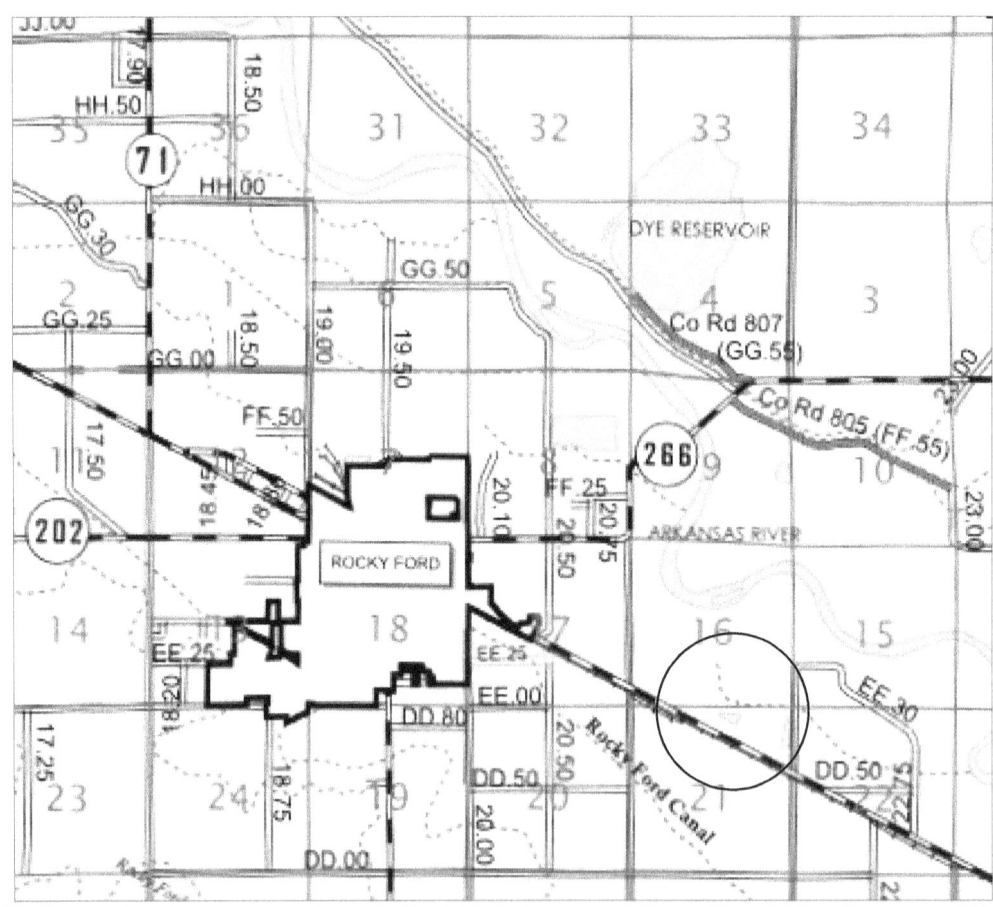

otero.gov/image/gis/oteromap.pdf October 2005.

Hospitality of the Harsins and proximity to town early made the lake a popular destination.

Harsin Lake

Often referred to in the *Enterprise* as a popular waterfowl hunter's destination, its attraction also included ice skating and fishing, sports as well among several other lakes and ponds on the countryside. Editor Barkley once offered this ode in the January 6, 1898 *Enterprise* about a young skater there:

> "He thought to glide 'cross Harsin's lake with wondrous ease and grace,
> But sad to say his thoughts went wrong. He glode upon his face."

The young man is not named, perhaps preserving some dignity when among his skating friends. Lakes of the countryside were very popular with hunters and fishermen, partly because they were easily reached. Several were listed in the *Enterprise;* Harsin and Dye's lakes, Swink's Lake northeast of the fairgrounds and Swink's Artificial Lake east of Rocky Ford. The river was also a popular destination during waterfowl hunting season.

Historical Mystery is presented by the lake's location. The recent county map section, page 108, does show a small body of water within two miles of Rocky Ford but it appears shaped as a gravel mine excavation in later photos. However, there are articles in the news of a natural lake in that area during late 1800s and early 1900s, not a gravel mine.

> "The lake on F.M. Harsin's farm two miles east of Rocky Ford has been a favorite skating place for our young people during the past fine skating season."   *Enterprise* December 20, 1907.

Another article identified the distance from town differently more than five years earlier.

> "On and after March 1st. All Hunting or Fishing on Harsin lake situated 5 miles east of Rocky Ford, is positively prohibited."   *Enterprise* April 11, 1902.

That notice was placed by Fred Chappell acting for a sportsman's club. The 5 mile distance would place the lake near city limits of Swink. No lake existed there according to available maps. The distance may have been in error by estimate. An early note of the lake in the news:

> "Colorado Springs parties have leased Harsin's lake (sic), thereby reserving to themselves the exclusive privilege of duck shooting thereon."   *Enterprise* April 1, 1897.

East and north of Rocky Ford from U. S. 50 have been sites of gravel mines. High water table was also evident several places north of Rocky Ford, east, southeast and southwest parts of town. G.W. Swink, and possibly others, were modifying their properties to remove water from their fields.

> "Senator Swink is putting in four cars of tiling on a farm [his] north of town which has been injured by seepage. The work is partially done yet the land has been greatly improved. The experiment promises to be highly successful."   *Enterprise* May 12, 1898.

Farms Where a Lake Was

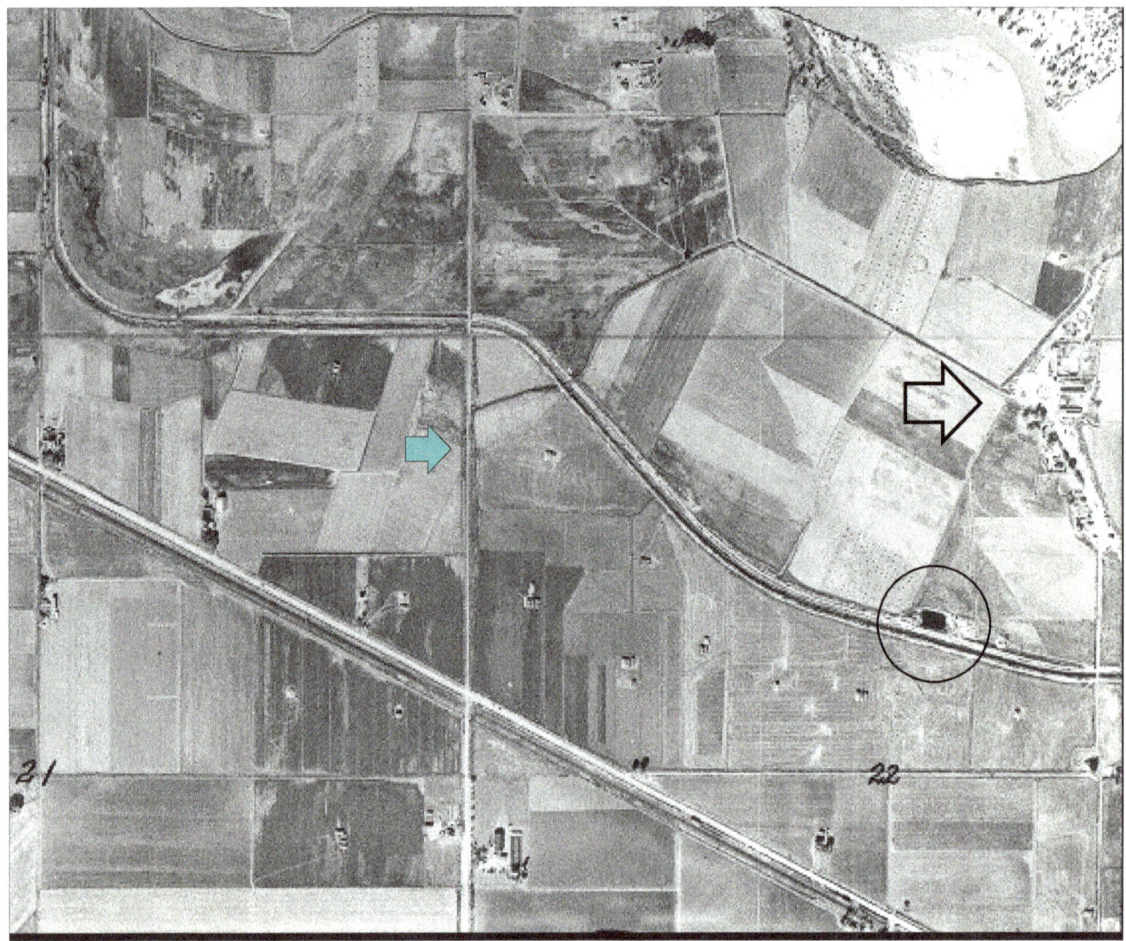

Soil Conservation Service, 309-29, October 28, 1936. Scale 1:20,000

Aerial view, 1936, showing CR 22.00-*green arrow*-and the same area as the photo on page 111. Photo reveals no lakes, gravel mines or open water except for a small pond along a leach canal below a bend of the Arkansas River at right-*circle*. Development of roads, appearance of farm buildings, haystacks, and extension of the leach canal from the upper left are the noticeable differences. The leach canal, partially removed or obscured in the following photo, is unnamed on maps.

East Ranch of the American Crystal Sugar Company (ACS)-*open arrow*-and tenant farmers were very active at this time raising beets, cattle feed, and feeding cattle supplemented with beet pulp. Wheat, onions, and alfalfa were other crops raised after beet acreage contracts were filled.

Newdale siding of the railroad, lower right out of photo near CR 22.75, was site of a beet dump for rail car loading.

Changes in the river channel-upper right in both photos-resulted in loss of some farmland, also evident in other photos of the river after flooding. US 50 is a narrow two-lane concrete highway.

A Walk in the Country

Satellite View

Imagery c 2021, Maxar Technologies, USDA Farm Service Agency, Map Data c 2021.

Area about 2 miles east of Rocky Ford along US 50 displays a difference in proportion to the aerial photo of this area previous page due to camera lenses and altitude. County Road (CR) 21.50-*small arrow*-and CR 22.00-*green arrow*-bracket the property with the body of water, *probably* the remnant Harsin Lake, now modified by gravel mining. Smaller ponds to the right also have the appearance of gravel mining and present a possibility of having been connected in the past. One small pond persists in both photos-*circle*.

Remnants of East Ranch of the American Crystal Sugar Company are visible at the north end of CR 22.75 off US 50-*large arrow*. A metal-enclosed maintenance shop housing a granary and a forge remain, *photo back cover*. Tenant housing and other structures for equipment and livestock were removed long ago with only footers, foundations, concrete cattle loading ramp and a concrete-lined pit for wagon and truck scales remaining.

Traces of former cattle corals around the maintenance shop indicate the extent of cattle feeding activity during history of the ABSC at the Ranch. Newdale siding, extreme lower right corner, was loading site for beets, and during WW II, horses and mules used in the war effort.

111

Walking Rocky Ford and the Arkansas Valley

A Natural Lake in 1893

Maps of the state before 1891 show no lake in the area just east of Rocky Ford but one appears on this 1893 map approximately two miles east of town, the future Harsin Lake. Other towns in the Arkansas Valley, Ordway, Swink, Fowler, and Cheraw do not appear. Rocky Ford, Olney [Olney Springs], Catlin [Manzanola] and Meredith [Sugar City] appear as the only towns or settlements located in the region by the cartographer.

An un-named lake-*arrow*- lies north of the river, later to be the improved Dye's Lake. Contour lines showing 25 feet elevation between them and with the river and railroad are prominent features of the map topography. Disproportionate size of features, when comparing lake to lake and town with river, seem only to show their placement and existence on the landscape.

Historical Enigma

Grove Karl Gilbert of the Department of the Interior-US Geological Survey in 1895-1896 published *The Underground Water of the Arkansas Valley in Eastern Colorado*. He found the flow of water below or at ground surface was related to restrictions of the width of gravel and sand beds under the ground. Flowing water *appears above* [up gradient] of the constriction and *disappears below* [down gradient] of the constriction, as is the case with the Arkansas River.

"The underflow of the Arkansas River is rarely demonstrated by the phenomena of disappearance and reappearance, but there can be no doubt that it is greater than that of any tributary." G.K.G.

Harsin Lake may be influenced by one or more of the under-surface phenomena Mr. Gilbert found, therefore explaining the appearance, disappearance, and re-appearance of the lake between 1893-1936, all well before gravel mining as in its current 2020 appearance.

Future lakes: Dye at arrow; Harsin's Lake in circle.

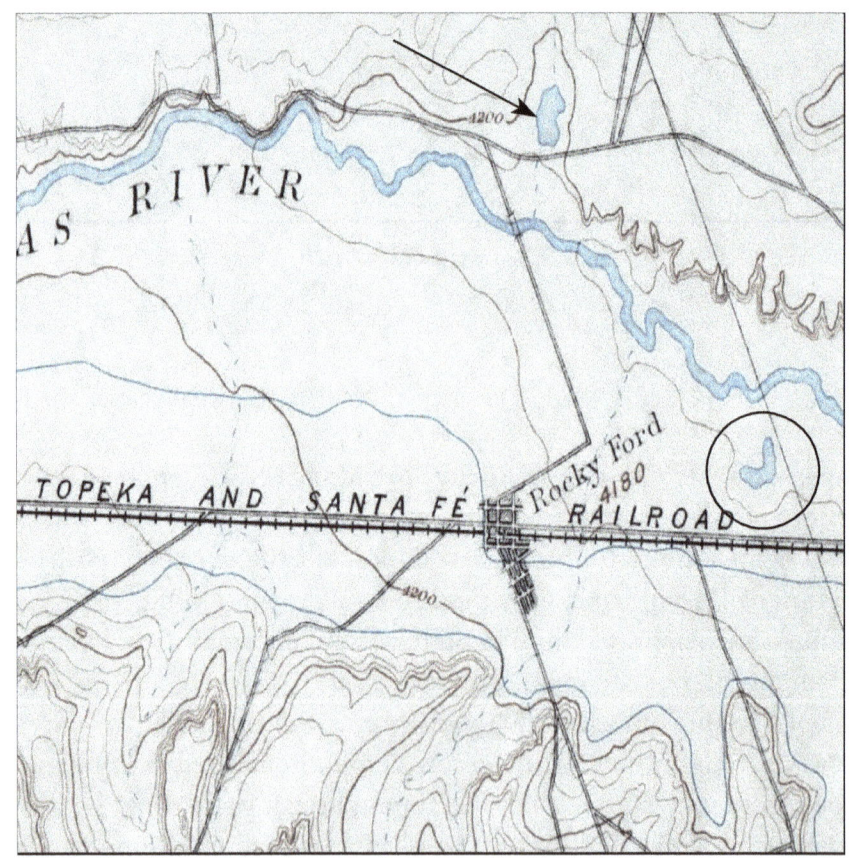

US Department of Agriculture Recon Map 1893.

Note: Rudimentary wagon trails connected valley towns along the railroad in 1893. The road that would become US Hwy 50 would be graded to La Junta beginning April, 1899. Commercial travel was on wagon roads between Valley towns. Wagon roads north of the river from Kit Carson generally followed the river to Pueblo.

Flood Interaction and Harsin Lake

Harsin Lake appearance or non-appearance, disappearance and re-appearance and eventual persistence as a water body is shown on previous pages. To this point little information of the possible influence of river flooding has been noted.

There have been many floods on the Arkansas River. Notable are those during times of human habitation, June 1864 and June 1894, 1921, 1955 and 1965 nearest the locality of the lake. Many other floods have rerouted the Arkansas, causing some property loss and lives, but they did not directly effect Harsin Lake because they were either well up or down river.

Before the 1880s and much settlement along the river there was an abundance of water to the Little Arkansas River near Wichita. Occasionally, however, the river was a bed of dry sand upstream of the Little Arkansas during July and August. During this prolonged dry spell, water in the channel was known to disappear suddenly, only to make its reappearance as unexpectedly within the next day or two.

This phenomenon was observed by G.K. Gilbert in his 1896 publication for the Department of the Interior-US Geological Survey. Although his observations had been farther away in Eastern Colorado this action apparently was not uncommon in other places along other rivers. Altered features of river flow manifested themselves also in underground streams confined by sand, gravel and bedrock strata. These apparently mimicked the visible river bed although in different scale.

Curious Water Flow

Medano Creek of the Great Sand Dunes National Park, Colorado fluctuates in size and depth during its visible flow May and June when snow melt from the Sangre de Cristo mountains swell the *June Rise*. A phenomenon then occurs when the flow exhibits a series of surges, two or three per minute in shallow wave-like movement. During other times of the year the flow may be beneath the sandy bottom, reduced, continuous, sometimes resurfacing, as in the Little Arkansas.

The responsible feature for the surge develops in the creek which borders the east, west and northern edges of the dunes. Sand continually slides into the creek never forming a permanent or stable streambed. Small underwater dunes (moving ripple marks) form to act like dams continually forming and breaking down, releasing water to surge where a stable bed would allow a smooth, laminar flow.

The creek flows seasonally around the dune field of about 30 square miles and carries sand from the eastern, western, and northern edges to redeposit it to the south where winds recycle it back into the dune field.

The normal flow of the Arkansas and other rivers usually does not exhibit surge action except dramatically in flood but have undersurface flow, even in arid conditions. Those who have ventured near a non-flowing stream bed may often find water if energetic enough to dig for it. This knowledge was life-saving among native Americans and first explorers of the semi-arid West.

Changing a stream bed by diversion or rerouting a water course, such as a man-made canal, will often find some water following the old course even when energetic compaction has filled the original channel. This action has been observed by builders when building over such a water course. Water often appeared under the new construction requiring sump pumps for remedy.

Note: *June Rise* refers to peak snow melt-driven stream flows, usually in June.

Harsin Lake, 2020

Maxar Technologies, USDA Farm Service Agency 2020

Satellite view of high water table area incorporating, at left, a modified lake. Smaller areas at right of CR 22.00 appear as separate bodies, possibly interconnected below ground and to the larger lake and the river. Area was modified by gravel mining. East Ranch of the ABSC / ACSC is upper right-*open arrow*- along the angled part of CR 22.75. A leach drainage canal bordering the water bodies drains to the river out of photo at right.

Harsin Lake, Mining

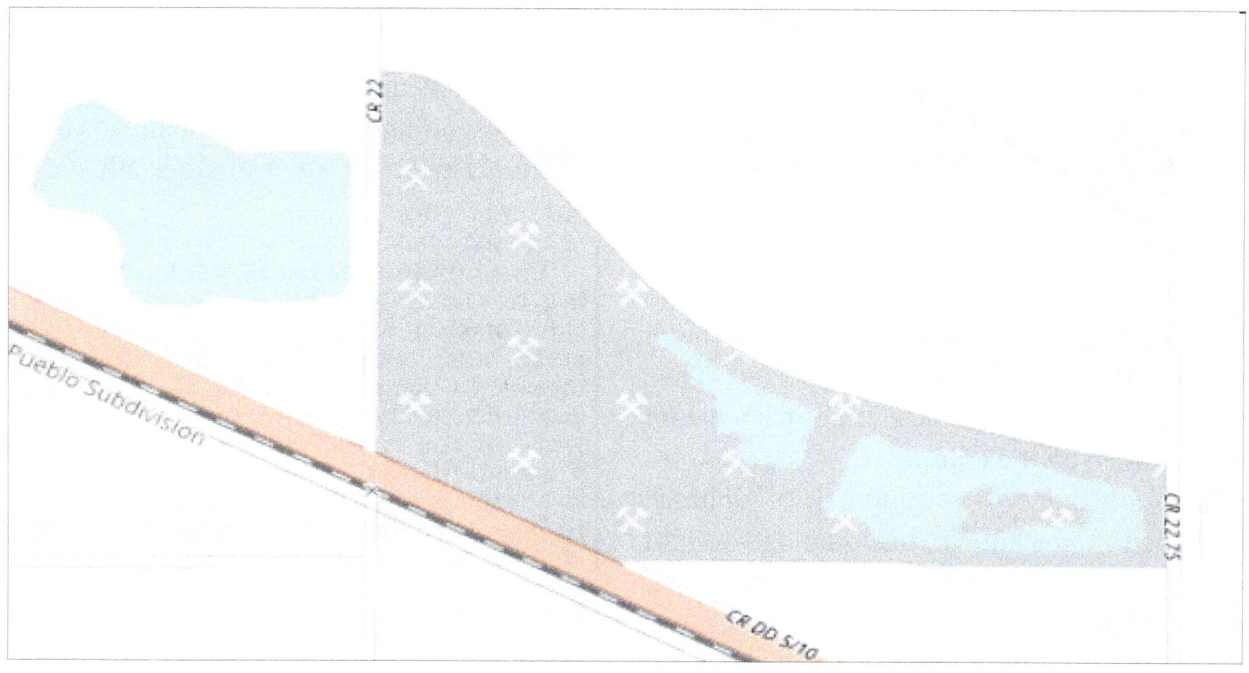

Maxar Technologies, USDA Farm Service Agency 2020.

Map segment does not include detail as in the accompanying satellite view. It does show at left of the illustration the light blue area west of CR 22.00, a water body apparently modified by CR 22.00 and a little by mining. The lake likely is remnant of original Harsin Lake.

Smaller areas of open water appear to the right of CR 22.00 lying inside an extensively mined area indicated by the mining symbols. This entire area was previously farmed-*page 110*. Presence of water represents infiltration from a shallow water table, especially after mining.

Presence of a lake at this site on the earliest maps followed by farming when water was not visible adds to the enigma of water re-emerging as a lake currently.

Colorado Traveling Library Commission

The state legislature and the Colorado Traveling Library Commission (CTLC) once were in the good graces of the railroads who provided freight gratis for CTL books to travel to the towns of Colorado. It is assumed that the service also included return freight.

Two hundred boxes of books were moved this way throughout the state. Management of the system was required to distribute the books, and make exchanges periodically of both books and destinations for certain time periods.

Somewhere in Colorado were two hundred entities, such as libraries, women's clubs, town councils, or dedicated individuals who were receiving and sending agents responsible for these books. A few station agents possibly were involved, schools most likely were, especially if they employed a teacher who was also dedicated to the library sciences.

Apparently, the *Colorado Federation Of Woman's Clubs* came to the rescue, possibly without being fully aware they were being offered the responsibility at the time. Their mention in the news article might have been a liberty taken by the editor.

Size of the *box* or number of volumes contained is not known, but they had weight. Most familiar with books would recognize that an unabridged dictionary will easily weigh over five pounds. The number of other volumes in the box would likely weigh less, but with numbers increases the load. Perhaps this is what caused the railroads to resist free-on-board service. They charged the CTLC by the total weight of 200 boxes. *Enterprise* January 25, 1907

Author assumptions were made interpreting this explanation by the *Enterprise* editor. Reading between the lines can mislead as to fact but may also approximate editor's intent to inform.

> Two hundred boxes of books belonging to the Colorado Traveling Library Commission are scattered over the state, and the commission has no money to bring them back to its headquarters in the capitol building. The work of the commission is virtually at a standstill and unless the State Legislature comes to its aid it will have to be either abandoned entirely or carried on as an auxiliary of the Colorado Federation of Woman's Clubs. The immediate cause of the trouble is the refusal of the railroads of the state to furnish free transportation for the books, as they did before the new bill went into effect. The commission has a bill presented in the Legislature which calls for an appropriation of $6,000 for the next biennial term. This is $4,000 in excess of the money received from the last Legislature, but it is desired to enlarge the work as well as meet the transportation expenses.

Free Reading Room is the name to replace the *Rest Room* in the jargon of local book lovers. Without knowing the details of events between formation of the Woman's Club in 1905 and closing of the room, the following notice appeared in the paper. Difficulty of discouraging magazine-burning miscreants, loungers and snoozing bar patrons from sleeping near stoves was too much to oblige.

Enterprise January 25, 1907

> The Free Reading Room has been temporarily closed, by order of the managing committee.

Note: The terse ad sentence appeared almost two years after formation of the Library Board by Mayor Pollock and Rocky Ford Woman's Club. Possibly another entity or event was referred to in the note of the original 'Rest Room' at 207 South Ninth Street. A 'Reading Room' was also in the southeast front of El Capitan Hotel entered from the lobby. The room was for guests although it probably attracted those off the street who were seeking warmth on a wintry day.

Double-entendre Names-Racket Stores

At least two in Rocky Ford were individually owned businesses vending numerous articles for retail sale. Some might recall the word and business, *racket,* as representing some entered into illegitimately, but legitimacy developed over time with honest transaction.

Found mostly in the South, the first racket store was known in Asheville, NC circa 1887. Origin of the name is not known but may have come from vernacular during late 19th century '*racket*,' a business, profession, or occupation that was considered an easy, profitable livelihood. Such stores certainly were popular and came to be referred to as successful, legitimate enterprises.

The K of P building at 401 North Main Street was site of W.R. Gibson's Racket Store. Gibson's was previously located at 208 North Main Street before Kaplan's opened at that address.

Walmart, Target, Walgreens and similar large chain stores might be considered modern day racket stores because of the cornucopia of articles offered by them.

Rest Rooms

The rest room version described on previous pages as used in Rocky Ford, was functional as a temporary library. Currently, the two words describe many modifications and several other uses.

The modern *rest room* has long been commercialized. In at least one large city in the US, it is a luxurious but temporary rest stop whose first appearance was during the excitement of the Roaring 20s. It is a place for those seeking the ultimate new experience of escape to one of several private pods, get some critical work done inside a sound-proof compartment, or to freshen up in a vintage bathroom with all features of a modern lavatory included.

Some would use the in-house high speed communication such as the internet, with charging stations for personal phones or computers. Whether to take private calls without interruption or simply to take a nap somewhere there is a one of a kind space that supplies the place for it. Most often this modern commercial Rest Room is offered in large cities near rapid transportation, hubs of business traffic, catering to businessmen and women.

Note: Period from 1920 to 1929 is known as the *Roaring '20s* in the United States because of awesome economic and social growth. It was a time of surging economy and an era of mass consumerism, both in the US and many countries of Europe. Stock market collapse in 1929 and resulting financial disarray in the US is generally noted as the end of the *Rollicking Twenties*, referring to beginning of hard times in the US. It was an era of changes.

Rest Room is today a toilet, Mens, Women's, powder room, necessary room, or the Loo. *Reading Room*, likely with a person acting as a guardian, facilitator, or monitor would replace *Rest Room* of the first Library Board in today's usage.

Enterprise August 31, 1893

> Don't go security for the man who lets his gate swing on one hinge.

Ediitor D.W. Barkley used this filler to impart sensible advice to his readers.

Rest Room. Several years before the formation of the Woman's Club of Rocky Ford, interest among several book lovers led to purchase of a *Circulating Library*. Books were replaced as they were worn beyond service but when the library was packed away for lack of permanent storage location, it was eventually forgotten.

Early laws of Colorado provided for formation of library boards and means to raise funds for their work. In 1905, Mayor, Robert M. Pollock and the Woman's Club worked with city council to create a library board. The formative meeting May 2, 1905 resulted in the creation of a '*Rest Room*', colloquialism for the times, which had not entered the interest of the foregoing book lovers of the Circulating Library group. The new Library Board approved magazine purchases, accepted the books of the Circulating Library and placed them in the *Rest Room*.

Location of the Rest Room was the building at 207 South Ninth Street, previously St. Matthews Episcopal Mission next door to the future fire chief's home. Bars in town were in many places and the inebriated and partially so found their way to this convenient quiet place to nap.

Key to this room was placed in the charge of Miss Opha Lantz who daily watched over the library in its new setting until she placed the key into the hands of a neighboring merchant [unidentified] who locked at close of his business day.

Bar patrons and idlers entered when library patrons were not using the facility. They comforted themselves for napping by making beds of the chairs and warming themselves by burning the magazines. Clearly, the Rest Room had to be moved or closed.

Other vacant store front locations appear on Sanborn maps on Main and side streets any one of which could have sheltered the Rest Room but the Ninth and Walnut location was available in 1905. First Church of Christ Scientist occupied in 1909 and later, St. Matthews Episcopal Mission in 1919. Otero County Health Department was the last major occupant before deconstruction.

Today, 207 S Ninth Street is part of Barnes Park, honoring long-time City Engineer Harry Barnes. The fire chief's residence next door at 205, visible to the right, also was razed for the park.

Note: This *Circulating Library* was subscribed from private sources or commercial providers. Books and other reading material such as magazines and newspapers, were borrowed or purchased and replaced when necessary. The library sometimes was physically moved about in school busses or vans (*bookmobiles*) with shelving. State government funded permanent libraries by 1907 about two years after the Rocky Ford Woman's Club instituted the *Rest Room*.

Photo courtesy Rocky Ford Public Library

Crossing the River in normal flow was by horseback or carriage over rocky base of the original ford. During high water one could cross by float, a raft of large cottonwood logs guided along cables. Early *Old Rocky Ford* residents, John Smith and Andy Nichols, c. 1871, applied their abilities to this project beyond their businesses of smithing and operating a boarding house near the ford.

First Bridge at Old Rocky Ford

"The first bridge across the Arkansas River at Rocky Ford was built a mile east of Old Rocky Ford, in 1889 when it was still part of old Bent County. It was a low wooden structure and was washed away during high water about 1900. In 1895, a steel-trussed bridge was built at the old ford. One span and the approaches of this bridge were washed out in the 1921 flood, but replaced, and the bridge was used until the 1940s."   John Doll, 1987

Dates of bridge are 1888 for the wooden bridge, 1894-1895 by two sources for the steel bridge. [*November 10, 1894 was also the completion of the steel bridge on SH 266 toward Holbrook Valley*].

The 1888 wooden bridge lasted to 1894 by one estimate (c. 1900, Doll) until its steel trussed bridge replacement. That 1894-1895 bridge was used into the 1940s after replacement of both approaches and one of its two spans lost in the 1921 flood. Changes in the river course removed the remnants of *Old Rocky Ford* by flood in 1921. One estimation of the ford site after 1921 suggested the crossing was under the end of a corn field after tilling was resumed.

State Highway 71 and Bridge were damaged in 1921 by flood. Among those who lived then and helped to rebuild was Clarence Baker, interviewed for the *Gazette* in 1982. He was one of eight who supplied labor and teams to remove old pilings and bridge remnants near West Ranch of American Beet Sugar Company.

This bridge was predecessor to that built in 1935 of steel and concrete. May 11, 1935 was dedication of State Highway 71 and the bridge. The bridge was replaced again in 1955 after flood and again in a 2019 updating replacement.

Prior travel to the north riverbank was over the wagon road-CR 20.50-across the 1888 wood, later 1894 steel bridge, then west toward the future SH 71. This *long route* crossed the river about two miles west of Dye's Lake, by pioneers' estimation.

The *short route* or *old road* approximated future CR 19.00 toward and over the original rocky crossing and turning west north of the river toward future SH 71. Rudimentary roads in use before dedicated county roads followed farm boundaries through gates and fences. Travel was slowed by farmers' gates in five places along the way before reaching the ford. Some gates were designed to open *"... with the pressure of the carriage wheel on a carefully arranged lever apparatus..."* which was not dependable. Drivers yet had to get down and open the wire by removing *"... cottonwood limbs for latches, ... with varying degrees of inconvenience."* Travelers preferred this route because *"A distance of about two miles is saved over the route by the bridge...."*
Enterprise Dec. 14, 1893.

All inconvenience was removed after January 1, 1894 when the road was allowed by county commissioners. Road Commissioner Hale then had authority to remove obstructing gates and grade the entire road of the new short route to the old crossing.

Bridges Over the Arkansas

Photo AG 282-94. Soil Conservation Service, 10/4/1936. Scale = 1 : 20,000

solid white arrow = CR HH.50
open white arrow = CR 18/SH 71
open black arrow = CR 18.50
solid black arrow = CR JJ.00

black circle = West Ranch
white circle = 1894 Wagon Bridge site
vertical rectangle = 1935 SH 71 bridge
square = approximate site old ford

Note: County roads were not yet lettered and numbered in 1936.

A Walk in the Country

Satellite View of former river channel-*arrows*-under 1894 *Wagon Road Bridge* site-large circle. Flood removed approaches and bridge deck along with the angled northern part of CR 18.50-*dashed lines*-leading to bridge approach. Compare with photo 69 years earlier page 120.

County Road 18.00/State Highway 71 bridge is in rectangle. White north-south line is the former CR 18.50 no longer maintained north of CR HH.50 or designated on maps. County Road JJ.00, shorter white line, is also abandoned east of State Hwy 71 toward former CR 18.50. An irregular border of the field near the river bottom north of the former CR JJ.00 is a farmer's road. The leach channel at lower center remains with discharge into the river bottom. Remaining buildings and structures of West Ranch are in smaller circle.

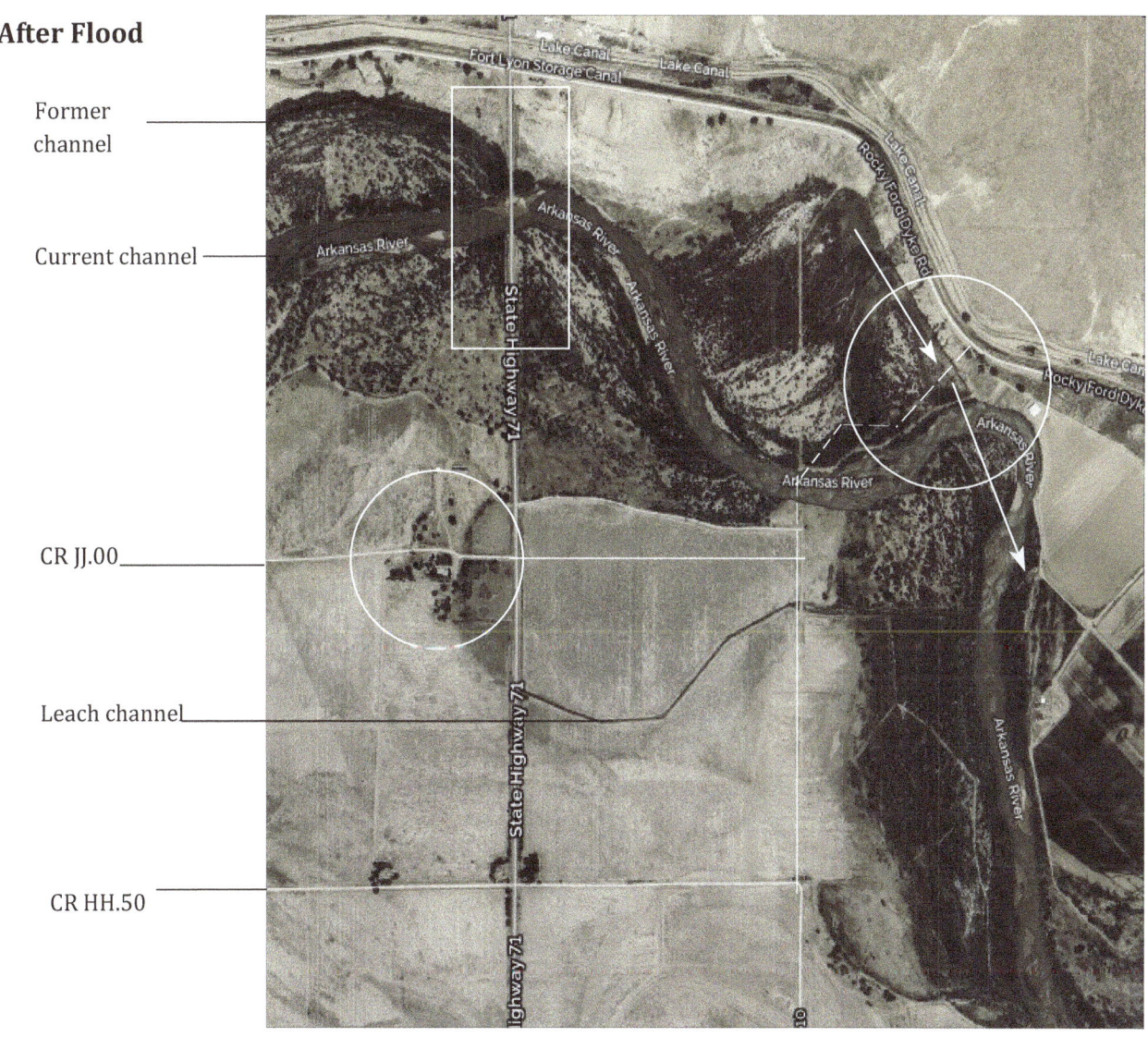

October 2005, Otero Co. Roads, Geographic Information Systems, Geographic Data Technology, Inc. 24timezones.com/mapa/usa/co-otero-/rockyford.php

West Ranch north of CR JJ.00 was flood damaged or removed as needs for stock diminished.

Wagon Road Bridge

Photo attributed to unidentified local photographer

Photograph taken in 1902 of bridge north of Rocky Ford reveals vulnerability to flood damage, evident when the many wooden pilings would catch debris, backing up water and increasing pressure on supports. Low wooden deck would be under water in extreme river volume.

Debris and rubble trapped against pilings, visible upon enlargement at left center, indicates up-stream side of the bridge. Approach from the north bank is visible at far left.

Wagon Road Bridge supports a deck that has an elevated superstructure in the distance. The superstructure is similar in appearance to the bridge on page 125 but differs in being stationary rather than supporting movable sections. This section was built over the main river channel. Foreground shows inside meander of riverbed where current slows and sediment accumulates.

Pioneer description of this bridge was *Wagon Road Bridge* or *Wagon Bridge*, *north of town*, location illustrated on the 1893 USDA map page 128.

Bridge shadow suggests the narrow deck would not accommodate large vehicles or herds in passing. Avoidance of such impedance was achieved in the saying, "*One must stay for another on his way*" was good practice and good bridge etiquette, also requiring some disciplined patience.

State Highway 266 Bridge

Shadows of steel trusses on the water clearly define the number of spans on this bridge connecting the Holbrook Valley with Rocky Ford. Branch of the road to the right travels past the site known as Ryan's Ponds, now Rocky Ford State Wildlife Area, and continues to the Holbrook community.

Soil Conservation Service photo AG-314-05, Oct. 29, 1936, Scale 1:20,000

Branch of the road to the left continues past the southern part of 1927 city dump-*enclosure and* crosses Rocky Ford Dyke Road and Dye Reservoir Road, connecting with County Road GG.55 and CR22.00, north to Sugar City. Bridge was repaired after losing two spans in the 1921 flood. This bridge has now been replaced by steel and concrete.

Bridge Pilings, 1894 Site Three pair of pilings are visible in deposits closing the former river channel. The aspect of this photo is the same as in the photos pp. 120-121. Length of approaches and spans add to c. 600 ft. by PC measurement.

The former river channel was the width approximated by lines. The northern bridge approach was entered from higher ground, upper right, and was the destination of those travelers coming from the west, northwest and east on wagon trails of the era.

Colorado Territory maps show many wagon roads crossing the prairie connecting communities north of the river and east to Kit Carson and Kansas. They followed the route that offered the least resistance and appear as narrow trails taken by cattle in search of food and water.

Horseback and wagon travelers used the trails to link with the Kansas Pacific Railroad entering Colorado to Denver from Kit Carson. Several rail stops east of Denver made travel to eastern Colorado towns and Kansas much faster and easier.

Imagery from 2019 Landsat/Copernicus, Maxar Technologies, USDA Farm Agency, Map Data 2019.

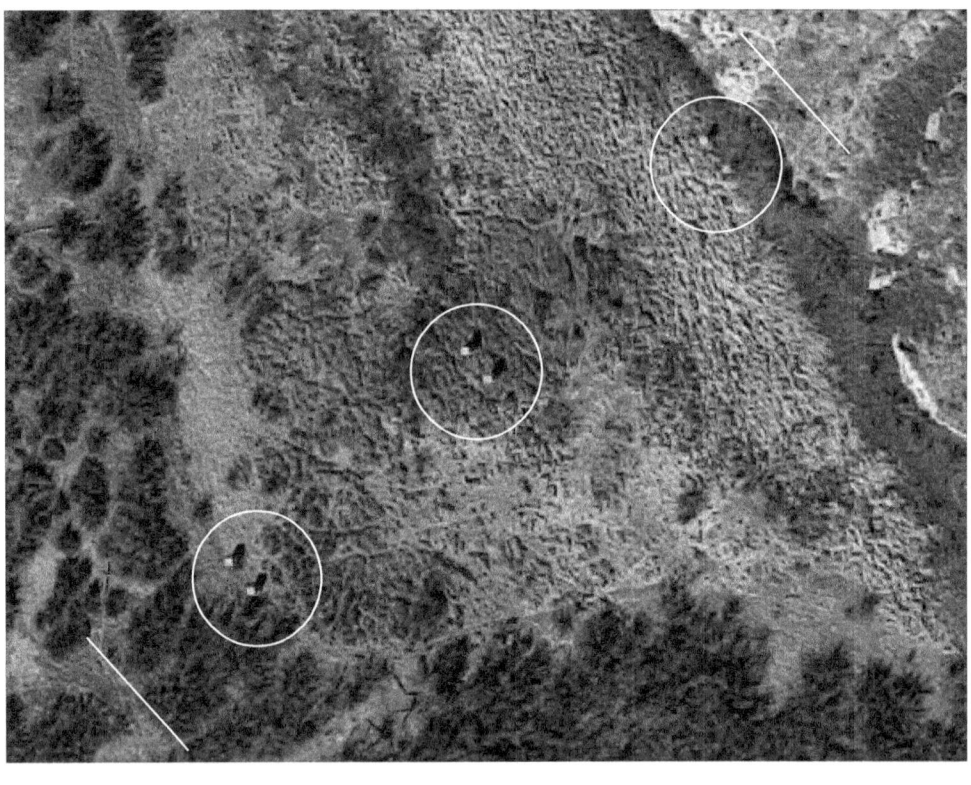

The low wooden bridge of 1888 was washed away June 1894 at this location; later replaced by a two-span steel bridge once on these pilings. The steel-span replacement of c. 1895 withstood time and river until the flood of 1921 when one span and both approaches were lost. The bridge was repaired and withstood time and elements into the 1940s.

Between this site and SH 71 near the West Ranch lay the original rocky bottom of the old ford. A flood in 1955 destroyed the bridge on SH 71. Its replacement lasted until 2019 when a new bridge was built in proactive maintenance.

Bridge Structure
This type of wagon road bridge illustrates a section designed to allow passage of barges with tall loads or superstructure by raising two halves of the deck between the towers. A break at their center allows the deck halves to raise, hinged at the towers, and held up by cables.

Photo from Mazyr, Belarus, 1918 www.bing.com/images

Illustration serves only to show type of superstructure similar *in appearance* to that of the Wagon Road Bridge or Wagon Bridge of page 122 but whose deck was not movable as in this illustration.

Flood Damage in 1894 reported in the *Enterprise* referred to the Rocky Ford Wagon Road bridge. A later bridge toward the Holbrook area on State Highway 266 was not built until November 1894. Several articles tell of damage to farms and livestock losses near the river but no human lives were lost. Events started in May:

> —A splendid rain visited the valley Tuesday night and Wednesday, doing an immense amount of good, starting the range grass and saving farmers much labor in irrigation. This rain, together with the full ditches, almost insures the crops of this season, except of course, the risk from hail. But as lighting never ...kes twice in the same place we may expect to be free from disaster from hail.

May 24, 1894

Lightning did strike again in the form of much rain May 30:

> —Yesterday and last night the Arkansas valley was visited by an old-fashioned eastern rain—a regular ground-soaker and gully-washer. The desires of our ranchmen for water are now satisfied and they are willing for the rain to cease. Excellent grass on the range is now assured. The rainfall has been so great as to cause several washouts on the Santa Fe, stopping all trains last night. The business portion of Pueblo is reported badly flooded. The north end of the Rocky Ford wagon bridge was carried away this morning, with a prospect that the whole structure would go before the rapidly rising flood.

May 31, 1894   [Highlight remains from word search.]

High water was receding until about June 6, 1894 when the water level was down and life and events began to recover.

> The plans and specifications for the repair of the Rocky Ford bridge, as prepared by W H Robinson, were examined and approved, and the clerk ordered to advertise for bids for same. Bids to be filed in clerk's office by noon July 26th, and accompanied by a certified check of $100.

Enterprise, July 19, 1894

> —Road Overseer Hale informs us that he has been obliged to put the county grader aside for the remainder of this year. The unusual number of washouts this season, coupled with the fact that 90 miles of new road has been constructed, seems to have absorbed nearly the entire road fund. The repairing of the approaches to the Rocky Ford river bridge and the Timpas creek and Otero canal bridges has also been a great drain on the fund.—Tribune.

Enterprise, July 19, 1894

Road commissioner Hale had nearly expended his budget for the year and was left with much unfinished road work, but bridge work continued. August 20 commissioners met and posted the following article:

> —The commissioners met last Monday and signed the contract with the Bullen Bridge Co., for the Rocky Ford bridge. Part of the material is on the ground and the work is to be pushed. This will be good news to many as very much inconvenience has resulted from the absence of this important bridge.

Enterprise, August 23, 1894.

Before completion of work, Catlin bridge (Manzanola) was the way to cross the river although some individuals with swagger and bluster "*cooned it across*" on a cable.

Rocky Ford Bridge

Rocky Ford bridge on SH 266 in this undated color-tinted postal card photo shows a steel span construction preceding that of the current bridge.

A three span bridge was over the river on SH 266 that previously had arched steel members over the tops of each section as in an earlier satellite photo of the bridge shadow. Photo could be SH 266 bridge in use before the 1921 flood that was replaced by the three arched span bridge.

Wagon road bridge site near the end of present-day CR 20.50 is also described as the location of a steel replacement for the original wooden one in 1894. It was a two-span bridge as revealed on a previous page satellite photo of the surviving three sets of pilings and therefore does not appear to be the one in this photo.

Bridge over the river on SH 71 has been of concrete and steel without overhead girders, at least since the 1935 structure. Type of previous construction is not known.

bing.com/images/search, CU Williams Photoette post card on ebay

Background visible through the superstructure shows a flume or conduit-*arrow*-downstream over the river. Conduit appears to pipe water across the Arkansas toward the ABSC factory-(see aerial photo following page).

Other similarly named bridge locations are Rocky Ford, Georgia, Rocky Ford, Kansas, Rocky Ford, Oklahoma, Rocky Ford Township, South Dakota, and Rocky Ford, Indiana. Some of these Rocky Fords are near smaller streams but none are near the Arkansas River. They are mentioned here to clarify among similar bridge photos in historical collections.

Wagon Road and Wagon Bridge

Before steel bridges, road from town to the north bank of the Arkansas River and Ordway was by either the *short route*, saving about two miles or the *long route*, vernacular of the time. The former followed approximately the future CR 19.00 past farmers' fields and property lines, through as many as five gates or barbed wire enclosures until reaching the original ford. After crossing on the rocky bottom the road connected to one coming from the east going toward Pueblo. A road turning north to Ordway would be the future SH 71.

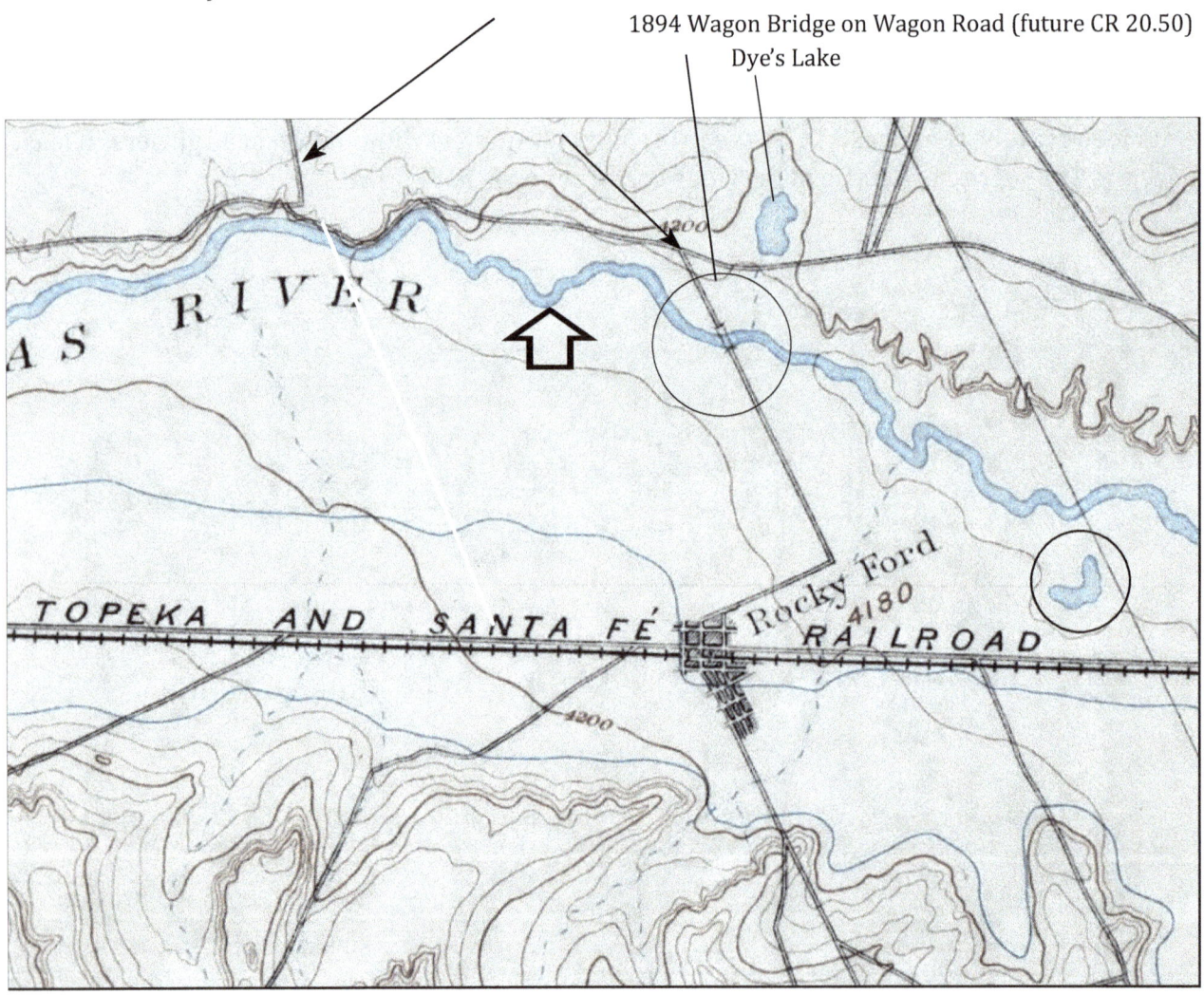

USDA 1893 Recon Map, not to scale bing.com/images/search

Rocky Ford Canal and Catlin Canal are thin blue lines through and south of town, respectively.

The *long route* followed future path of SH 266 to future CR 20.50 north to the wagon bridge-*circle*-to connect with the east-west road toward Pueblo. Early accounts said the roads met about two miles west of Dye's Lake-*at short arrow*. Open arrow is the general location of the original ford. Map precedes US 50, West Ranch, SH 71 and 71 bridge and modern county roads. Future Harsin Lake is in small circle, white line approximates eventual route of SH 71 off future US 50.

Arkansas River Conduit

Color photo page 127 shows the Rocky Ford Bridge spanning the Arkansas River carrying State Highway 266 toward the Holbrook Valley. Visible through the superstructure is a conduit or rather large pipeline carrying water toward the sugar factory. Remnants of the line over land are visible in a series of aerial photos by the Soil conservation Service taken in 1936. Photo this page shows the pipeline remnant path both sides of the river interrupted by area of crossing with remnants of several pilings faintly visible in the water.

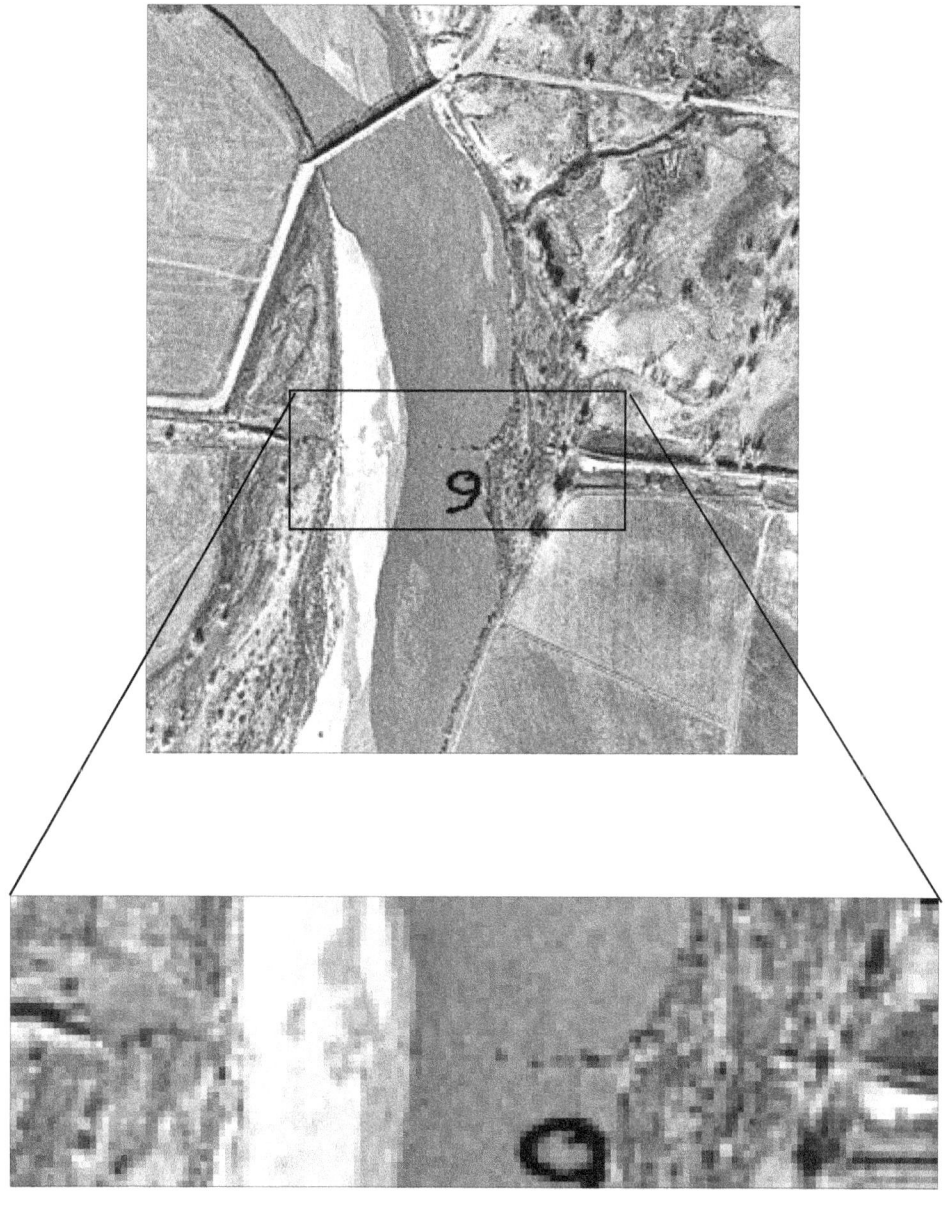

Soil Conservation Service, SCS AG-370-41, November 19, 1936
Numeral was placed by photo analyst to identify prominent objects and locations.

The demise of the conduit, whether by flood, other catastrophe, or loss of need is not known.

Bridge at upper left is identified as *'Bridge over Arkansas River'* placing it among other known Rocky Ford sights. In print and writing the Rocky Ford Bridge has always been known as the one leading to the Holbrook Valley on SH 266 rather than Wagon Road or Wagon Bridge..

Postal Card, 1908   Dates of individual photos not given .   Courtesy *worthpoint.com*

The sugar factory, Central (Railroad) Park, and the high school are included on the card. Rocky Ford High School-in the cantaloup- opened June 20, 1908 indicating recent photos by the October 23, 1908 postmark. Ben Franklin stamp for one cent would take a card anywhere in the U.S..

Part 3: A Random Walk

Developments in the Area

Arkansas Valley Seminary, Caddoa

The small community of Caddoa south of Hasty, Colorado is inhabited by few today but at one time was a significant hub of rail freight entering the southeastern part of the state. Classified today as a ghost town in many referrals, building remnants and foundations remain among few trees. Modern residents live there where memories of thriving business were recorded. As with many early settlements Caddoa was eventually bypassed by pioneering entrepreneurs who took their various activities farther south and west into new territory.

The following information was provided by Ms. Sharon Marcum, once the postmistress at Hasty, Colorado:

"History records that in 1862 a peaceable tribe of Indians, known as the Caddos, was compelled to leave Texas because of their camps being raided by the Confederate forces. This tribe was friendly to the Union so the government undertook to aid them in getting settled in a new location. For this purpose, General Wright selected this site along the Arkansas river just west of Fort Wise [later, Fort Lyon] *and named it Caddoa. The government assured them of protection and built three large stone buildings designed to be the headquarters but for some unknown reason the Indians refused to settle here and moved south along the Canadian river instead.*

In 1863, John W. Prowers, became the owner of the Caddoa and occupied the buildings and used them as his ranch headquarters. The Santa Fe Railway reached Caddoa in the fall of 1873. Until the railroad moved further west it was the shipping point for a vast territory and soon had a hotel and two saloons. In later years, including the 1880s and 90s the town prospered handling heavy tonnage in building material and supplies of settlers moving into the south country. Nobody knows for sure when the stone buildings were torn down and only rough foundations can be seen today."   Sharon Marcum's information courtesy of Jay Warburton.

Apparently among all the activity in Caddoa during the late 1890s Rev. J.C. Horn saw a need and an opportunity. There was slowly diminishing business activity in Caddoa and the area but apparently seminary President Horn saw an opportunity and seized the day to start his enterprise. He listed the advantages of location and low cost but particulars of faculty, catalog of courses, student body and historical church ties were lacking. No church affiliation was mentioned but assumed to be of Christian sect.

Advertising in the *Enterprise* appeared as below but without additional or future information. As with other stories in the news the end isn't always known.

Enterprise
July 28, 1898

Arkansas Valley Seminary,
CADDOA, COLORADO.
On Santa Fe railroad and Arkansas river, 100 miles east of Pueblo.
REV. J. C. HORN, A. M. Pres.
Caddoa is free from the distracting influences of large places. The seminary provides thorough instruction under wholesome discipline, in a healthful locality and where the expenses will be low. For particulars address,   J. C. HORN, Pres., Cadoa, Colo.

A.M.= Master of Arts

Business News

TB Sanitarium on the grounds at Twelfth Street south of the railroad tracks in 1896 once served those with tuberculosis and other upper respiratory ailments. Many who came from the east for the sunshine were supported by friends and relatives who gathered funds for them to travel to Rocky Ford. Tents were set up for them among a grove of trees. Van Antwerp Sanitarium at 401 South Main was the only other sanitarium offering treatment and rehabilitation.

Knaus Barber Shop. Frank Knaus bought his shop from Mr. Britt, then at 305 North Main where Athalie's Dress Shop located in the future. Mr. Knaus then moved to the Reynolds Oil Company Building at 963 Walnut. Fred Knaus, Frank's son learned barbering at this location while John the Chinaman operated his laundry business near the shop.

Fred Knaus remembered ice skating on a fenced pond near Stauffer Packing Plant during his early years. His recall is but one reference to Swink's Artificial Lake. Another early resident recalled a pond several hundred feet long at that same location.

Fred Knaus also recalled ice skating on a pond just east of the fairgrounds. This pond on 1936 aerial maps was shown overgrown with vegetation and trees. The Knaus information was recorded in the *Daily Gazette* during the 75th Anniversary of Rocky Ford, printed June 29, 1962.

Swink Family Residence

Rocky Ford Post Office and Rocky Ford Food Market occupy the tract of land that once held the Swink family residence. The entire block bordered by Chestnut Avenue, Eighth Street, Swink Avenue and Ninth Street was an orchard of several kinds of fruits and vegetables surrounding their home on three sides. Residence would coincide today with street number 401 North Ninth.

Enterprise, May 7, 1896

Enterprise published 23 very dark photos, the first in any early issue with minimal clarity.

Residence was demolished, site selected for the current US Post Office built in 1935-1936.

Business News

Will and B.U. Dye Barn and Livery a two-story-*arrow*- built of adobe soon after the Dyes came to Rocky Ford, circa 1877-*See Doll pages 12, 14.* Approximately 25 ft. x 40 ft., the barn was at this time the only structure in town to accommodate large groups. Livestock were housed on the lower dirt floor and by 1901 there were two cisterns on the adjacent lot for water and feed storage nearby in a small shingle-roofed adobe building. At this time there is no mention or illustration of pens or corrals near liveries. How animals were kept in limited space is not recorded.

Hotel Welcome Home / Rockford Hotel The original frame hotel on this 1895 map was Andy Nichol's *Hotel Welcome Home* in 1878. Now *Rockford Hotel*-above-a contraction of Rocky Ford under new owners. The De Seeley family would soon take it over and build a two-story adobe on the site called De Seeley Hotel. Adjacent the hotel site this map shows a small space between the hotel *Rockford* and the cobbler or shoe store and between the cobbler and blacksmith-original *Swink Feed Store*. Adjacent the feed store were a blacksmith, plumbing and tin shop under one roof, the agricultural equipment of B.U. Dye and Son, a livery, and another blacksmith combined with a wagon shop at the rear. Open space separated the blacksmith and the Dye Livery-*arrow*-at the corner of Eleventh and Railroad.

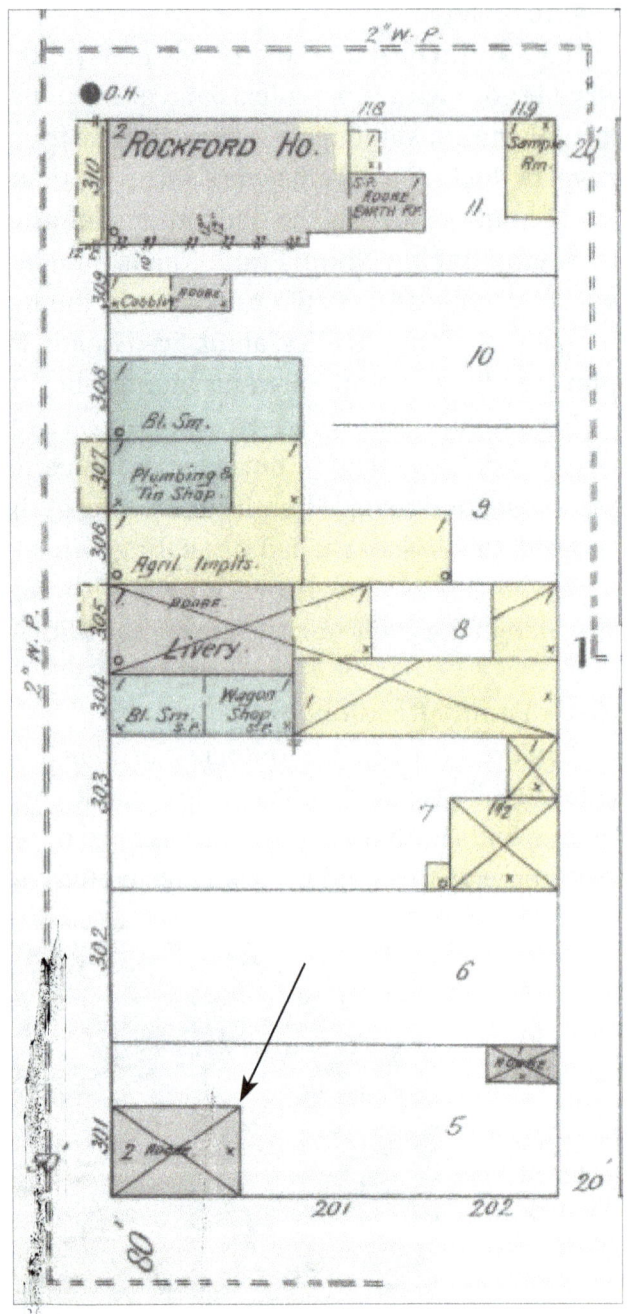

Note: Top is Tenth, bottom is Eleventh Street, original Main Street at left-now Railroad Avenue, future to be Elm to the right.

From the editor:

"Think all you speak, but speak not all you think. Thoughts are your own; your words are so no more."   Enterprise May 22, 1908

Words of wisdom to fill *Enterprise* columns.

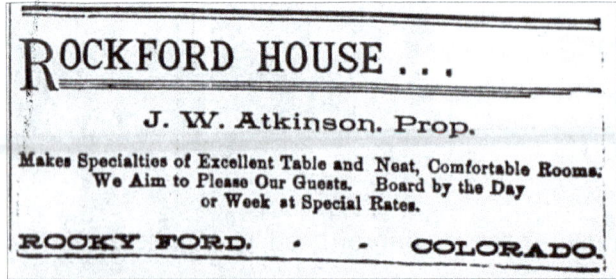

Business News

C.R. Herring Garage preceded Jackson Transfer and Storage at 201 North Ninth Street. Later the Herring garage was moved to Bill and Bob's service site at 902 Walnut.

Higgins Livery was in 1900 at 406-408 North Main purchased by O.E. Wright and transformed into an automobile garage in the era of the automobile, with manager Ed Manny.

Rocky Ford Woman's Club organized in 1897 with a priority to establish a library. This done they petitioned council to do something about men expectorating on the city streets and sidewalks. Council acted very soon after the ladies presented their case and instituted enforced fines. Santa Fe officials soon placed spittoons in their depot, followed by cuspidors in many stores, often supplied with a lid.

Melon Field, Inc., is managed privately south of town on CR 21.00 with one asphalt and one gravel runway. Permission required prior landing. Notation of the several airfields or strips near Rocky Ford is for historical interest. Commercial aviation is based at La Junta Municipal Airport.

Rocky Ford Floral Company, was established in 1913 by Anton Nelson from Denmark. At his death February 22, 1961 long-time associate Alberta Hale took over the business. Years later Ms. Hale's successors saw retail florists operating on Main Street and on Elm Avenue with decline of R. F. Floral's own cut flowers and home-grown nursery stock. Vacant buildings of several glass-covered growing areas burned along with a neighboring barn used for storage.

New Method Laundry-Valley Laundries, Inc. The former was purchased by F.W. Welland from Fred Polhemus June 10, 1912 and operated under that name. In 1925. It was expanded and continued as Valley Laundries, Inc. at 968 Front Street.

Watering Troughs. Horses and mules were able to water at several locations in town, one at South Main and Maple, another was front of the depot. Unfortunately, no photos of them are known. Options for filling with water were by tank wagon haulers and after 1891, by hose or hydrant from established hydrants.

Enterprise July and August, 1898

—The public watering trough has been fitted with an automatic cut-off which regulates the flow of water so that none is allowed to waste. A wooden platform at the gooseneck prevents the forming of mud. The town council has been at considerable expense in providing appliances for the accommodation of the public and it is only fair that some compensation be given when large quantities of water are wanted.

Troughs were removed with advent of motor traffic and fewer draft animals in town. Apparent from the news article some residents were using more water than seemly, possibly filling cisterns and watering lawn and garden. Ditch water was provided for those purposes.

A long tradition has been the water draymen who came to individual homes to fill cisterns. Providers did pay for bulk quantities for home delivery preferred by many because the 'soft water' from some sources was low in mineral and desired for bathing. Ladies also preferred soft water for washing their hair.

Drayman, Mr. Jack Allen of 711 South Fourteenth Street was one who provided soft water in the author's neighborhood during the 1940s and 1950s. His dray was a venerable tank truck.

Business News

Dodd's Commercial College, located in 1902 at 110-112 South Main Street. It was part of a private junior college for women, origin in 1927 Shreveport, Louisiana. Monroe E. Dodd, a pastor and head of Southern Baptist Convention in 1934-1935 was its leader. A radio preacher, he was instrumental in communities across the nation training women in introductory mathematics, commercial bookkeeping and related subjects.

Commercial courses were offered, filling a need in Rocky Ford since high school then was only of three classes until 1903 and the first senior class. Commercial courses were then added. The college in Shreveport closed in 1942 as did sometime later, interest and support of the curriculum in other communities. The longevity of the college in Rocky Ford is not known.

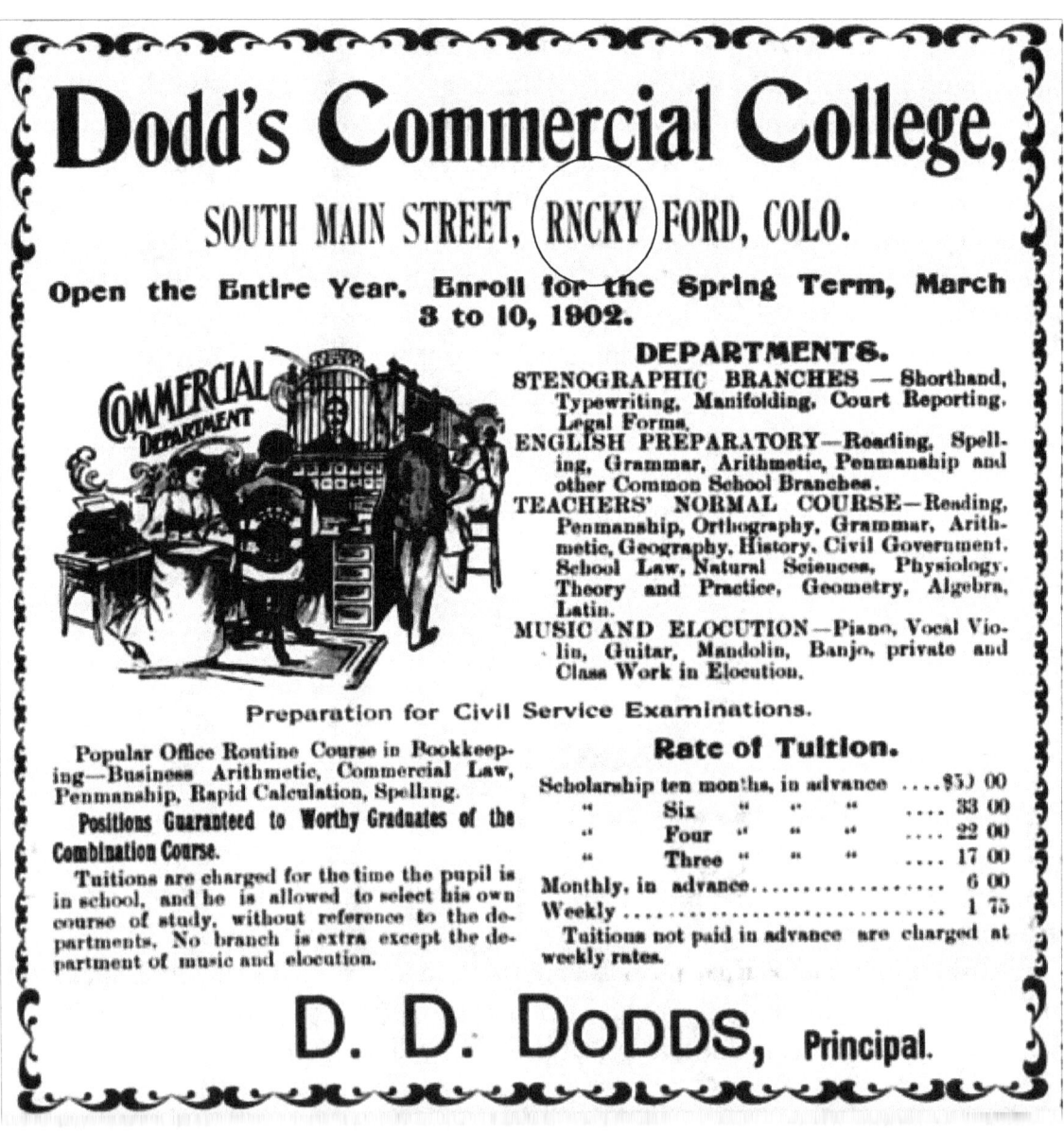

Enterprise, March 7, 1902

Note: South Main Street address number not given.

Business News

Peanut Stand of W.P. Wykle. On May 17, 1899 council received a request from Mr. Wykle to open a peanut stand at the corner of Main Street and Elm Avenue. The request was approved with the stipulation that the stand would be removed at any time an objection to its location be raised.

Site and appearance of the stand may have been captured in the 1900 photo page 279 of *Rocky Ford, Colorado-A Walk Past Local Doors* although that was not considered before publication of the book. It appears as a building on skids that could readily be moved by a team of mules or horses. North Main Street and Elm Avenue intersection was the busy location of the 1895 Hale Building at 301 North Main Street before upper stories were added to other block buildings.

A small temporary structure in the photo, possibly metal-clad, with a door and small window facing Main Street is near a boardwalk across Elm Avenue and is essentially in the street. This may have been the peanut stand on council's agenda. Council's decision anticipated the eventual removal of the stand in view of increasing horse-drawn wheeled traffic. A small gathering at the intersection is unexplained but may have been curiosity and desire to be included in the photo.

Note: Mrs. Mandana Wykle worked as a cook, listed in the *Rocky Ford City Directory* for 1914-1915 while living at 301 North Fourth Street. Mr. W.P. Wykle may have been related though there is no corroborating information. Roasted and salted peanuts are familiar food items but to many, boiled, salted and variously flavored ones are a desirable alternative. Perhaps this fact made the mundane idea of a peanut stand more palatable and attractive to the public.

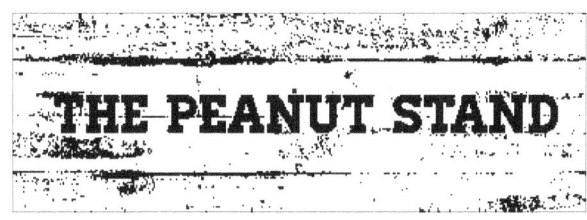 

Illustrations from *stock.adobe.com*

Fillers

Newspaper fillers are all the extras used to fill in the blank spaces. Examples are endless and include such things as quotations, articles, crossword puzzles, recipes, unusual facts, cartoons and even the three insets here. When the news didn't quite complete a column the editor would often include one or more two liners-jokes-or limericks. For the August 31, 1893 issue Editor D.W. Barkley placed this interesting intellect twister in one of the empty spaces:

> SNUG & RAW WAS I ERE I SAW WAR & GUNS.
> **The Peculiar Thing**.......
> About the above sentence is that it reads backwards precisely the same as forwards.

Business News, Fads and Fashions of 1910s

Clothing and fashions in the 1910's were changing. Women wore their hair up in turbans and buns, strange to us now, but then it was fashionable. Men wore suits, if they could afford them, and women wore dresses or long trench coat-like outer garments. The zipper was invented by Gideon Sunback that simplified fasteners and enclosures. People could take off their wraps quicker by operating a zipper rather than unbuttoning several large buttons,, a very popular development in the day.

Editor D.W. Barkley was known for his wry humor often in the news. Here, he offered the same advice to girls and boys in town when July 14, 1898, this ad appeared in his paper. The implication being that endless chewing would not lessen with time nor mollify the disgust some equated to this habit among the young, especially girls. Mores of the time favored the uplifting pulchritude of girls and women rather than the uninhibited, sometimes crass actions of boys.

> —The tax on chewing gum must be paid in advance. It can't be worked out with the maxillary muscles.

Note: The first gum marketed in the United States was in the 1800s. John Bacon Curtis was first with the idea of making and selling spruce natural gum for chewing. People chewed gum in this most natural form in history hundreds of years ago. Different chewing gums in the past included resin and latex from certain trees, sweet grasses and leaves.

Larmore Brick Kiln Brothers L.W. and G.H. Larmore fired bricks for early 1900s buildings. Their business has been referred to only vaguely as to location. Fortunately, Rocky Ford school children placed their yard location in the book *Rocky Ford as the School Children See It*. Business was located at Sixth Street and Maple Avenue. This area has been residential for many years. Likely with other changes this caused the end of business and its movement.

Mexican Laborers first brought to town to cultivate beets were to some the cause of job loss. Many locals were not willing to take those jobs that field labor represented and yet blamed the newcomers for loss of them. Hotel managers, the Bettermans, took them in and housed them on the lower floor of the St. James Hotel guarded by shotgun-toting Mrs. Betterman at the door.

Commercial Hotel. This two-story hotel was of adobe on Sanborn map of 1895. It stood at 310-312 North Main before Bruse Variety Store at 312 and the future Ichi Ban restaurant at 310, (formerly at 202 N Main). Many years after these businesses the 310 North Main site was location of the first Safeway store. North Main at 312 remained unoccupied and became Safeway parking lot. South to the end of the block were an unknown office-tailor-jewelry store combination and telegraph office shared with a confectionery, millinery shop, undertaker and lunch shop, with a hardware at 300 North Main. Buildings on this block were roofed with slate or tin.

Note: Martin General Store at 304 North Main razed for First National Bank drive-thru, 2022.

Central Hotel was the upper story of the brick building that later housed Kaplan's at 208 North Main Street. Wooden framing covered the front with two store fronts on the ground floor. South store front housed a saloon, the north store front was a lunchroom on the 1895 map.

A second story fire escape was later provided at the rear of the hotel. South to the end of the block continuing from 208 were a lunchroom, saloon, cobbler and barber, two drug stores and a general store at 200 North Main Street. All buildings were destroyed in the fire of September, 1898.

Business News

Wilson Hotel, active during 1901 in Recker's building on its Front Street side, apparently operated only a short time since hotel name was not noted in later Sanborn maps. It offered a restaurant on the ground floor, rooms on the upper story. The Wilson apparently was the first hotel to occupy this location in then new 1897 Recker's Hall building. Later, National Hotel and Pacific House were at this Front Street address.

Old Stone Foundation. North Main at 511-513-515 on the Sanborn Map of 1901 was location of this structure. Foundation was also present on the map of 1906 but not present on the first 1895 map. Original town plat of William Matthews in 1876 and later 1887 re-plat do not show the structure. It appeared after 1895 but building plans for the site apparently may not have materialized until after 1906. Its use constitutes a mystery.

Cartographers mapped buildings as businesses were appearing along Main Street, Swink Road, and Elm Avenue. They also included buildings in progress. Nothing is given of origin or intended use of this foundation. Cartographers indicated that it was truly stone by recording it so in two successive city maps. They certainly would have noted adobe, a common construction material for the time, or concrete.

Constructors often used limestone block from local sources or from western Kansas when laying foundations. The latter is agreeable with the cartographers' *stone* description. Emphasis on *old stone foundation* by the cartographers who drew the map, possibly were indicating a remnant of an incomplete early enterprise. Dimensions of the foundation were regular, 40 ft. by 80 ft. with 90 degree corners. The undisclosed height, width, or depth in the ground of the structure might indicate that it was a footer or base for a foundation, but isn't noted.

Presence of the large boarding house at 519 North Main Street, the Berkeley, was noted on the 1901 map. Cartographers also noted a 6 ft. board fence from front to alley south of the foundation.

Years later the Plews Ford Motor Company would occupy this North Main site after the advent of automobiles. This business could not have been so forward in planning a future there years before the oncoming automobile. There is no indication of intended use for this structure before then but perhaps it was fortuitous and consistent with building plans to have it incorporated into the future Plews building. Original purpose for the stone foundation was not discovered.

Patterson Hollow is a shallow valley NW of Rocky Ford between CR 15.00 on the west, CR 17.00 on the east and north of CR HH.50 where it junctions with CR 16.00. Relationship to Patterson Valley, west of Rocky Ford on State Highway 202 is not known.

King's Arroyo Bridge, close to east La Junta was over a tributary to the Arkansas. Nearest other crossings were a ford known as *Valle Inpredodo (sic)* [Pedregoso] between Rocky Ford and Swink. Spanish Pedregoso translation = stony, rocky, gravelly, or a *slab of stone*.

King's Ferry, earlier **Knight's Ferry** was the La Junta crossing at King's Arroyo Bridge apparently using a floating craft of some kind.

The bridge was to replace the ferry in 1893 when Rocky Ford contractor, W.B. Gobin was an unsuccessful bidder on the project. He was late in placing a deposit securing his bid-the lowest-but was eliminated by the [County] Clerk's office because the bid had not accompanied the deposit, which turned out not required in the specifications. Though no further explanation was given in the news Mr. Gobin was apparently unwilling to dispute the process.

Business News

Iris and Isis Theaters were on opposite sides of South Main Street in the 300 block. One preceded Stauffer's and Rhoades Food Center at that site. The theater may have been in the Saint James or one of the later-named hotels. The other was on the west side of that block, exact location unknown. Both existed from 1906 to 1909 but nothing is known of them or the type of theater. Possibly, because of dates of existence, they were not movie theaters, but with a stage offering discussion, readings, oratory, plays or room for society and club meetings.

Note: Greek goddess of the Iliad, Iris; Egyptian goddess of fertility, Isis, were theater name translations.

Enterprise, September 7, 1893

Editor Barkley waxed poetic following the annual Watermelon Day festival.

WATERMELON DAY!

ROCKY FORD'S FAMOUS FESTIVAL.

Delighted Thousands Dispose of Tons of Luscious Melons.

Should you ask me, whence these melons?
Whence these ruby hearted monsters,
With their swelling gen'rous roundness,
With their juice like heavenly nectar,
With their seeds of ebon blackness,
With their rinds so smoothly polished,
With their tints of mottled greenness,
And their luscious, toothsome sweetness,
Than of honey, three times sweeter?
I should answer, I should tell you,
Rocky Ford alone doth grow them.
Here come thousands in September,
To the Ford's most juicy banquet;
Laid for statesmen and for hobo,
For the merchant, lawyer, clerk,
For the lady and her maid,
And for all mankind in general.
All do eat our nectar melons,
To the terror of the stomach,
Then homeward goeth heavy laden,
With a melon on each shoulder,
And for the coming twelve-month,
All do sound the hearty praises
Of this glorious ROCKY FORD,
Known through all the State and Nation.

Kitch Feed Lot / ABSC Factory Corrals-now Ribeye Feeders

Intersection CR GG.00 and CR 19.00 at 29998 CR 19.00, Rocky Ford, Colorado 81067
Soil Conservation Service photo AG-282-96, Oct. 4, 1936.   Scale=1:20,000

Sixteen pens-*above left*-are empty. Concentration of manure and wet areas appear dark, as well as feed bunkers at the edges of each pen. Factory storage tank-now removed-at county road 19-*arrow*- intersection with CR GG.00 stood near the factory lime dump. Number of pens is increased currently [2020].

In magnification, some hay fields show recent cutting or are awaiting baling or stacking. Dark fields appear unharvested. Enlargement reveals wheat or corn shocks in rows in the fields at upper left and upper right corners. A leach lateral canal angles across the upper right of the photograph and Rocky Ford Canal across the lower left corner.

Holbrook Lake Pavilion and Arkansas Valley Dance Club

Though not a building sited in Rocky Ford, this structure afforded many in the towns of the Arkansas Valley memories of weekend band concerts and venue for public recreational dancing. Information of the dance club provided only the name and possibly was without organization but for interest in dancing.

A search for a photo of this building revealed this lone aerial exposure. The structure was demolished several years after the photo and long after abandonment of the rail spur on the left. Pavilion stood in the current parking area of the state facility developed for boating, fishing and swimming.

One end of the dance floor was separated by a low partition where a bandstand accommodated musicians. The opposite end was an area of tables and chairs.

Photo AG-314-23, Soil Conservation SVC, 10-29-1936, scale 1:20,000.

Long sides were open in summer by hinged wooden covers. Patrons outside could view and listen to the music. The dance floor was sheltered by a double hip roof and the building sat in an open area near the lakeshore. A faint tree line to the west was shelter for white clapboard outhouses for Men and Women near the rail grading.

A bathhouse and small refreshment shack were among the trees near the top center of the photo. A clearing among the trees at one time was site of a makeshift arena where the 1940 Colorado A & M NCAA wrestling champion Gene Grenard and World Heavyweight Champion Everett Marshall, both of La Junta, Colorado entertained onlookers with impromptu bouts. [Mr. Marshall's title, June 29, 1936, preceded time of this photo by 4 months].

Rail cars from Pueblo steel mills, in war-time, delivered furnace slag to the northwest shore of the lake. This spur line, now defunct, continued through an area called *Hays* coincident with State Highway 266 as it turned eastward to Shelton, Randall, Catherine, Fenton and Cheraw. The gray-blue slag chunks were formed with rounded bottoms shaped by the cauldrons which held them. They have since crumbled but the rail grade remains along County Road BB.25.

Note: Swink-Holly RR spur, subsidiary of AT & SF RR, went to Shelton, Holbrook Center, Fenton and Cheraw.

Otero County Interurban Light and Power Company (OCIL & P Co.)

Editor of the Enterprise announced the activities of this new corporation and proposal from G. W. Swink, who along with the named in the article, were offering stock to interest investors.

Developments were inconclusive as far as continuing the trolley line when emphasis in 1902 was on the proposed new towns of Shelton, Holbrook Center, and Cheraw. An energetic start, possibly unrealized at the time, was begun by A.W. Shelton, prominent land-owner and farmer north of Holbrook Lake. He had done early polling on his own among the farmers of the area and found favorable sentiment to expand crop production. There was land and plenty of water.

Editor's comment-*below*-implied production capabilities and possibilities by a comparison to wealth of Solomon. *Enterprise*, December 16, 1897.

> **A New Trolly Line.**
>
> The Otero County Interurban Light and Power company has been incorporated. The promoters are: Senator Swink, W. B. Gobin, Rocky Ford; H. P. Dye and J. W. Beaty, Manzanola; F. W. Wieland, Fowler, and Charles F. Lacombe, Denver.
>
> The purpose of the corporation is to build an electric railway and to furnish power to a number of towns along the route of the railway. It is intended to do both a passenger and freight business.
>
> The company is incorporated for $1,000,000.
>
> Further particulars next week.

Enterprise, June 6, 1902

> - A. W. Shelton of Holbrook has recently been making a house-to-house canvass of that prosperous section of Otero county. His object has been to learn the value of farm products raised during the past year. He has gathered detailed statements of each farmer's crop and the showing is most gratifying. We have always had the impression that the Holbrook country was rapidly advancing in material prosperity but the statistics gathered causes us to repeat the remark which the queen of Sheba made about Solomon's glory.

Two railroads, Santa Fe and Arkansas Valley RR were planning extensions from Lamar and from Swink, respectively. There was benefit also to be realized in the Arkansas Valley from a future traction line, an opportunity recognized by G.W. Swink and his promoters when towns with sugar factories were new or to be developed. Their move was to stay ahead of events and their planning of this new venture put them in speculation of success, and *out on a limb*.

The traction line would be a separate entity, using its own rails and electric energy provided by local generators and suppliers. This would ensure independence from established commercial rails traveling the length of the Arkansas Valley. Service was designed to include all smaller areas not benefitting from passenger or freight service by established lines (Fenton, Laguna, Hays, Randall, Catherine, Orr, and Castiel in near vicinity).

The June article's final sentence, *'further particulars'* did not reach print in the next three weekly issues until June 27, 1902-see article page 147. It was advantageous to omit report of non-progress, but there was a little. The energy and emphasis surfaced nine weeks later, August 15, 1902, to set in motion this new project, Arkansas Valley Traction Company.

Note: Queen of Sheba found King Solomon's wisdom and prosperity exceeded his fame (1 Kings 10:1-13).

Shelton and Holbrook Center

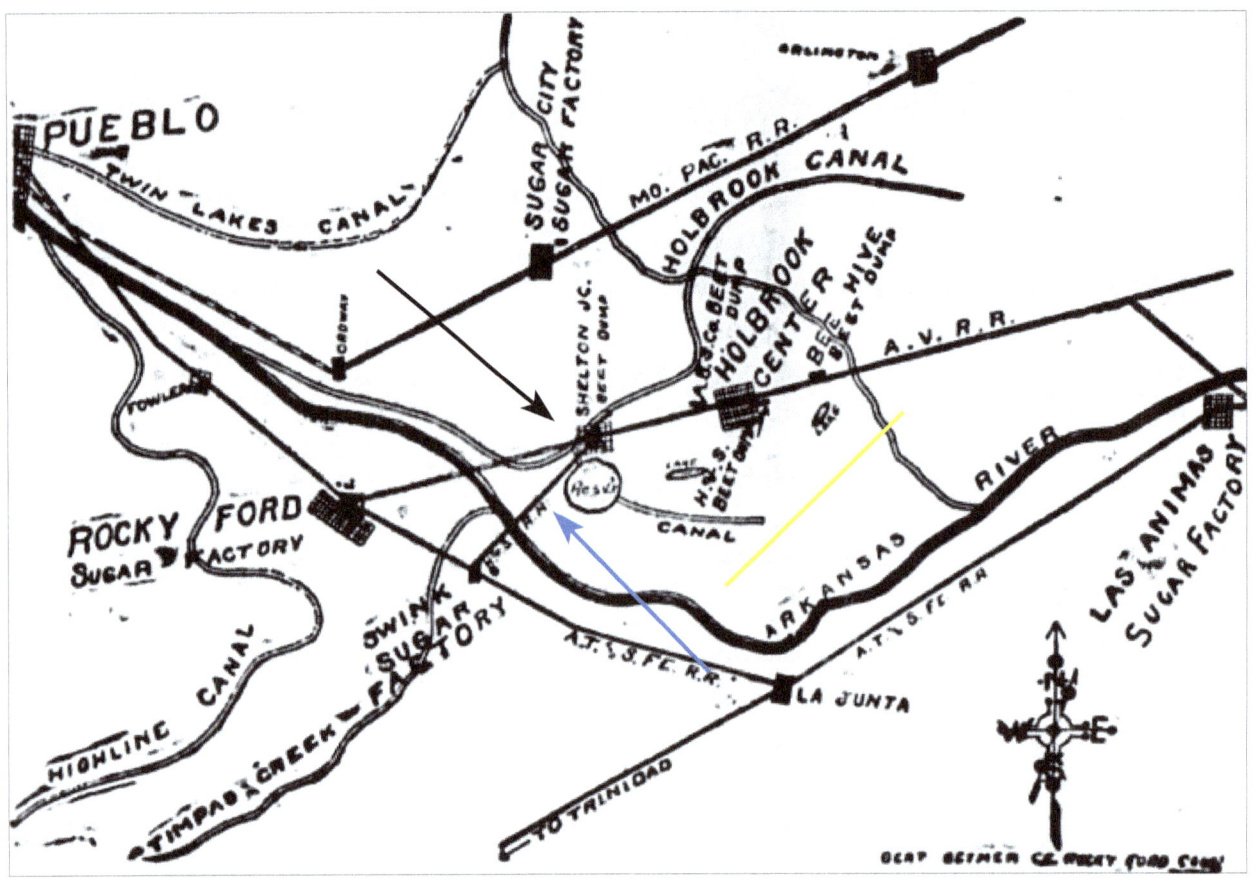

Hand-drawn Realtor's map of features in area surrounding these new communities. Not to scale.

The words of the *Enterprise* describe both map and *"Valuable Improvements"* in the Arkansas Valley-page 145.

Valuable Improvements in the Arkansas Valley

"*The above* [preceding] *map is the first that has been published showing the two new railroads in this portion of the valley, Arkansas Valley Railroad and Holly and Swink RR* [blue arrow]. [*Both subsidiary to Atcheson, Topeka and Santa Fe Railroad*]. *It also shows the location of two new sugar factories–at Swink and Las Animas (the latter under construction.) The location of the new town of Shelton is seen* [black arrow] *and in the center is the new town of Holbrook Center. For the use of the map we are indebted to Arthur* [S.] *Beymer,* [411 North Main Street] *who is agent for sale of lots in Holbrook Center.*" Rocky Ford *Enterprise*, V. 20, No. 16, September 14, 1906, Ed. 02

Shelton and Holbrook Center were featured on the map which also revealed the omission of the site chosen for the new town of Cheraw east of Holbrook Center on the Arkansas Valley Railroad. Holbrook Lake is shown at center as a small circle labeled 'reservoir.'

Cheraw was platted November 3, 1906 about 14 miles east of Rocky Ford and 10 miles north of La Junta. A town lot sale was held December 20, 1906 for passengers of a five-car train of prospective investors from Pueblo, Holly, and Trinidad via Rocky Ford. Santa Fe officials brought them through on special rates expecting to benefit from more development along their line.

Mr. Wiley, General Manager of the Swink and Holly sugar factories, was honored by the name *Cheraw,* for his home city in South Carolina, Cheraw, an Indian word, 'clear' or 'sparkling water.'

Prior the locations of all three of these towns there had been for several years an increasing population of farmers and ranchers, living in the region building churches, schools, businesses and other important assets. In so doing they created a community of friends, relatives and like-minded people willing to assist one another in their common interests.

Rivalry existed among these communities comparing schools, churches, wells, or size by suggestion of influential area residents, land offices and Realtors with their interested potential investors. Developers of Shelton and Holbrook Center possibly saw benefit of convenient map omission of Cheraw which was not their focus.

Late in 1906 investor Paul E. Kennedy with A.W. Shelton, holders of 2000 acres in the Holbrook area, sensing opportunity decided to offer 400 lots on 40 acres for sale at $50 each. Their plan was to sell all 400 lots before a grand opening at the town site.

At the lot sale early in May, 1907 all lots were sold and the opening for Shelton was set for May 22, 1907. The general public in Rocky Ford and people from La Junta and Swink came free of charge on six cars of the Santa Fe Railroad. A lunch was served by the town-site company and soon the Rocky Ford Concert Band drew the crowd to a large tent where a random drawing of lot cards from one basket were matched with random-drawn names from another basket.

In the next hour lot owners viewed their purchases before the train returned them home. A new depot, artesian well, and water tank were completed by October, 1907 and plans were in place to construct the Arkansas Valley Traction Company (streetcar or trolley line) for transportation among Holbrook community and valley towns. The enterprise was in care of G.W. Swink who offered stock certificates.

Note: Rails were Arkansas Valley RR, Holly & Swink RR, to Shelton, Holbrook Center, Cheraw, Las Animas Sugar Factory. Holbrook Center Post Office opened June 1906, closed c. January 1907. Cheraw Post Office opened September 1910. Town was incorporated 1916.

Rails in Southeastern Colorado

Arkansas Valley Railway (AV) was built from Kit Carson, (shortened to *Carson*), on the Kansas Pacific Railroad (KP) rails, to the settlement of West Las Animas. The line opened in October 1873 controlled by the Union Pacific Railroad (UP). The AV continued construction and reached Swink by 1875. The line was abandoned in 1877, the first large abandonment in Colorado involving 80 miles of track.

Atchison Topeka and Santa Fe Railway (AT&SF) mainline was the first line from the Kansas-Colorado State line to Granada built by the Colorado & New Mexico Railroad Company (C&NM), and was opened on July 4, 1873. The next segment to be constructed in 1875 was from Granada to Rocky Ford by the Pueblo & Arkansas Valley Railroad Company (P&AV). The P&AV absorbed the C&NM in 1875 and continued on to Pueblo by 1876 and also to Trinidad from La Junta in 1878. The P&AV leased the line to the AT&SF until 1900 when it reverted to the AT&SF. The line is still in use today along with the daily Amtrak Super Chief passenger train.

Grand Valley (GV), branch rail line of the AT&SF, was 5.9-miles long from Newdale on the mainline to Hawley in 1907. The line was abandoned in 1966 and removed in 1970.

Hauck, or Houck, was the town name preceding Hawley, on the Grand Valley line (GV) west of La Junta. Hawley originally incorporated a beet dump adjacent and north of the Grand Valley School. Hawley, as the proposed town, was named for Floyd Hawley of the American Crystal Sugar Company (American Beet Sugar Company before 1934) with a railroad station on AT&SF, (GV).

Note: Some maps show both West Las Animas and Las Animas City as separate towns. The former grew when voters rejected partial finance of the KP to set rails to Las Animas City. The KP established West Las Animas about 4 miles west and the town grew as Las Animas while City of Las Animas businesses moved and the site was abandoned.

Railroad information from:
Scott, G.R., Louden, R.H., Brunstein, F.C., and Quesenberry, C. A., 2008, Historic Trail Map of the La Junta 1° × 2° quadrangle, southeastern Colorado and western Kansas: US Geological Survey Scientific Investigations Map 2923, scale 1:250,000; 56-page pamphlet.

From Sanborn Map, 1886, West Las Animas, CO.

Fates of towns were often determined by rail agents unaffected by nor living on the route.

The Arkansas Valley Traction Company

Enterprise, December 16, 1897 article on page 143 identified the beginning of potential and actual speed bumps for creation of the trolley line, *financing*. This was a large undertaking requiring much planning to clear the right-of-way of these new rails with all land owners and towns to be served. Supporting services of electricity generation was another requiring generating plants.

Incorporation target of $1,000,000 represented numerous stock investments to be subscribed, Events were to show that several impediments would be encountered toward this goal.

Location and construction of a plant for electrical power generation had to be considered. Some possibilities were electricity generation from among power plants in towns along the line but a completely independent service would require its own generating plant.

Stations or depots were necessary to accommodate passenger traffic and freight. A maintenance shop or facilities for service of several trolley cars potentially to be in service was another large project.

All depended upon obtaining the 'franchise right-of-way' before anything could begin. Subsequent editions of the news revealed more information of the project.

> G. W. Swink, of Rocky Ford, president of the executive committee of the Arkansas Valley Traction Company, J. E. Gauger and E. S. Alnutt, were La Junta visitors last Wednesday for the purpose of attending a meeting of the directors. Preliminary arrangements for the floating of the capital stock of this company were completed at this meeting.

La Junta Tribune, September 28, 1907

Note: A third rail carrying electric energy was proposed at first. As planning proceeded steam power was considered along with gasoline powered engines and even the possibility of '*unknown or undiscovered devices.*'

> The people interested in the Arkansas Valley trolley line are working diligently on their scheme. The first business is to get the franchises for the road. This is understood to have been secured so far as Otero county is concerned, but action on the part of the different municipalities, Fowler, Manzanola, Rocky Ford and La Junta, has yet to be secured. Application to the corporate bodies of these towns has been made. The question of right of way is also being considered, as consent of all fronting property holders must be obtained. The expectation is that beet hauling will be one of the important services of the road and so the line must pass near the sugar factory. The present proposition is to enter the town near the west end of Swink avenue and run to Main street, where the road will divide north and south and branch off into Holbrook and Fairmount, to unite again at La Junta. But this is largely preliminary speculation. No details will be formulated until the franchises are obtained.

Enterprise, June 27, 1902

At last published news, financing was being provided by sale of bonds. At least one wealthy speculator was mentioned from out of town.

Construction was to begin January, 1908, according to the *La Junta Tribune,* Oct. 26, 1908 but that was never to be realized. It seems the prospect of shaky investment returns cooled the ardor of the moneyed men who were getting cold feet in the frenzy of speculation.

Bold Venture: Arkansas Valley Traction Co.

Courtesy *worthpoint.com*

Enterprise, August 15, 1902

> Hon. G. W. Swink is a man of abundant influence and energy and by putting the force of his personality into the valley trolley line he can make it go. By so doing he will add greatly to his past immense services for the development of the Arkansas valley.

Stock was presented to any potentially interested investor to finance the development of convenient and speedy transportation to the new town of Shelton and others in the Valley. It was often referred to as the *Swink Trolley Line*, electrically-powered and independent of existing steam powered railways. The line would serve several valley communities with sugar factories.

The facsimile stock certificate is of one never sold. A sale would have been registered by an embossed serrated foil seal at lower left. Many became souvenirs with failure to raise funds although the effort expended might have been successful had Shelton development continued.

Note: A traction trolley, tram, streetcar, tramcar, or trolley bus operated electrically with overhead wire or third-rail contact using power from a generating plant.

Holbrook Center never developed as a town but retained permanence as a community of agriculturally prominent farms. Business activity shifted eastward to Cheraw of the Holbrook Valley but social interaction remains in the area.

Towns were planned on the Great Plains of Colorado for several reasons. But they were not like ones of the mountains and high valleys started in places where minerals, gold, silver and timber were found. Plains towns were started because of agriculture nurtured by developers interested in land sales. Railroads contributed to platting many would-be towns so that land along the rails could be sold for generation of profit in increased freight and passenger business.

Farming and ranching out on the plains was very different from the same ventures back in the eastern states. The Great Plains were windy, mostly dry, baked by the sun in summer, frozen by deep snows and high winds in the winters. Many settlements failed to overcome those rigors.

Towns that were able to survive learned to adapt agricultural methods to their environment. Most important was use of irrigation where water was always a limited asset. Communities not able to get enough or apply it judiciously would soon fail. Poor farming methods in general contributed to abandonment of claims and exit of many families. Economic depression, drought, insects and dust storms were other hazards to survival that were periodic but devastating.

Life and Death Cycle of an Agricultural Town can best be described using the *Endicott AGToL Scale* [Agricultural Ghost Town Life Scale developed by the High Plains Ghost Town Preservation Project]. True of deserted towns, the phases of the scale also developed for Shelton:
1. *Uncertain establishment*: Town builders or railroad create new town by having a plat surveyed and sometimes a post office established. Motivation was real estate or social improvement
2. *Generation of interest*: Town grows by attracting property buyers; services are established.
3. *Focal event*: Something occurs that is ultimately responsible for halting phase 2 and beginning phase 4. For Shelton this involved economic downturn with *"... extremely dry and unfavorable weather,"* resulting in loss of confidence to proceed.
4. *Degeneration*: Population vacates region and services discontinue. These events may take place immediately or over a long time. For declining Shelton, limited rail service continued briefly.
5. *Nadir*: Town declines to status directly opposite of its peak. Site is neglected in decay.
6. *Recovery*. Removal of structures and other modifications to return the site as much as possible to that existing before the *establishment phase*.

Today there is no visible evidence of the sites of Shelton or Holbrook Center. Declining references to Shelton appear in the *Enterprise* until about 1912 after which there was little to report but social activities of a few area residents. Holbrook Center lost '*Center*' in its name and Holbrook Valley activity devolved to Cheraw after interest in Shelton diminished.

The economic slump of 1907 and subsequent years caused investors to regard as unstable the times for town-building. Population did not increase to support planned businesses and services. Railroads, losing the hoped-for business, eventually removed rails, sidings, depot, water tank, and beet dump. The partially-cultivated land was reclaimed by prairie and Shelton, the town site, was finally removed from county maps in August 1975.

Note: Shelton remained on a hand-drawn map, back cover of the 1925 book, *Rocky Ford As the School Children See It*.

Shelton Disappearance

Prairie land north of Holbrook Lake today is generally flat, dry, and treeless with nothing above ground surface that would indicate what once was a very promising new community. Publication of Shelton in the *Enterprise* first appeared May 5, 1906 describing the town survey.

The A.W. Shelton family, since about 1890 owned 2000 acres of Holbrook land for farming and ranching. When the times were good economically and with opportunity luring the investment of time and resources Mr. Shelton proposed town-building with Realtor partner Paul E. Kennedy.

Holbrook region was productive for several farm families drawn together by joint interests, family ties and close friendly neighbors. There was interest also among them to develop a town they referred to as Holbrook Center a short distance east of Shelton. It was platted and appeared on the same map drawn by Realtor Arthur S. Beymer-page 144.

Whether competition to be first or larger, such sentiment was not apparent in the news but the time was right for the Sheltons to develop the 40 acres they had chosen for the town. Additional acres were opted by investors, including a colony of Amish families from Kansas City.

Farming north of the lake and the Holbrook Canal was not supported by abundant water although the soil was deemed rich enough. The Shelton's water, while adequate for ranching needs, was supplied by an artesian well at first. The well was not a flowing one. It had not pressure enough to push water out of the casing to the surface. While the head did not flow it maintained a constant 12 foot level below surface. Sustained pumping for 20 days did not lower the well head (level of water that arose in the well). Later, a large cistern was filled from Holbrook Canal with water delivered in ditches to fields by a powerful pump.

Arkansas Valley Railroad (AVRR, 1900-1907) built to the site from Lamar and the Swink and Holly Railroad (1906-1907) brought people from closer towns. Beet dumps, sidings, a depot, cantaloupe sheds and a water tank were in place with more construction planned. There was to be the Arkansas Valley Traction Company (trolley or streetcar) operating from Shelton to and from valley towns but shares of stock sold by G.W. Swink were not enough to support the venture.

A drawing at the platted site in May, 1907 attracted several train car loads of valley people as well as many locals who drove their own conveyances to the site. The first 400 lots were sold before business was concluded and the town opening was set for Wednesday, May 22, 1907.

Residences or population numbers were not publicized in the local news beyond note of a few un-named small businesses. Original Shelton merchants first traveled from valley towns thus reserving a personal household move while hoping for increased town development.

As time passed and infrequently at first but steadily gaining in number were news articles about taxes, financing, withdrawal of plans, slowly contributing to loss of interest in Shelton. The year 1907 was a dry one and also of decreased economic activity (see *Panic of 1907* page 151). Failure of the Rocky Ford State Bank holding some notes and representing the loss of one of the town's financing entities contributed greatly to loss of confidence (*Enterprise* article following).

Eventually improvements of the AVRR such as beet dumps, depot, water tank, siding and track were taken up as also with the Swink-Holly line. Similar loss of confidence to develop Holbrook Center also cleared the way for development of Cheraw as focus of activity in Holbrook Valley.

Note: Holly railroad tracks were subsidiary to AT & SF RR

Panic of 1907

A financial crisis of about six weeks involved large banks in New York City and others across the nation October into November. It began with losses in failed enterprises leading to bankruptcy of two large brokerage firms. But the panic really had begun when an earthquake in 1906 San Francisco caused so much devastation the city drew gold out of many of the world's financial centers to rebuild. Less cash fluidity added to recession beginning June 1907. Reaction occurred across the nation that continued until Rocky Ford business community was involved.

> The Shelton Realty Co. is notifying owners of lots that the town site was assessed as acreage last year and that if 20 cents per lot is sent in the company will pay this year's taxes. Lot owners would be much pleased if this condition would continue indefinitely.

Enterprise, June 5, 1908

Enterprise, February 14, 1908

> **"Hard Times."**
> It must be admitted that after a period of prosperity which has been unequaled both in duration and degree, the country is now experiencing an industrial and financial depression which comes near to being genuine "hard times." In a great many places large numbers of men are unemployed.

Shelton Afterword

Though progress of Shelton was often written in the *Enterprise*, and some in the La Junta *Tribune-Democrat*, there is nothing of the town's ultimate demise. Rocky Ford history in Doll, *The Story of Early Rocky Ford* did not mention Shelton or other communities in the Holbrook Valley. Apparently no application was made for a Shelton post office and there are no photos of buildings or structures contracted by the railroads for Shelton. Facilities were built and after the ardor of town-building waned they were moved to other locations or de-constructed.

Author Frances Bollacker Keck published a paragraph about the town in *A History of Otero and Crowley Counties Colorado.* Several other authors, in their books of ghost towns of the state, including one specifically about the eastern plains, did not include Shelton and several other towns for lack of space and other constraints. Over 1500 Colorado town sites are known to have existed, most in the mountainous counties, but a much fewer 640 of those have any remainder. Should there be any remnant of Shelton it might be below ground in Mr. Shelton's well casing of 1907.

Many towns, abandoned for any of several reasons, are remembered because their site appears on a map. School children of Rocky Ford mapped Shelton on the back cover of their 1925 book, *Rocky Ford As the School Children See It.* Shelton was on the Otero County map until officials finally removed the name 50 years later in 1975. Some topographic maps retain Shelton as a rail-side site of an event relating to the railroad-see map page 152. Another rail site example is east of Rocky Ford where *Krammes* does not involve a town but commemorates a rail worker.

Shelton at Holbrook Lake

Once planned and under construction, but never finished, Shelton is located on this *Topo* map of Colorado as a rail site. A side track is in place to accommodate a beet dump, depot and freight of the town's businesses. The map was designed to be continually updated with all recent discoveries or changes in the countryside.

Rails at the Lake

Immediately north of Holbrook Lake is the rail line from Lamar crossing the Fort Lyon Storage and Holbrook Lake Canals. The rails then turn south along the western edge of the lake all the way into Swink to reconnect with the Santa Fe main line.

Shelton's Main Street was designed to end at the lake shore where a marina and water sports area were to be developed. Water levels during irrigation needs would, as for Dye Reservoir and other area lakes, periodically lower until improvements would be in the mud of the lake bottom. The best of planning did not consider the increasing use of water for the available supply.

Topozone.com/colorado/otero-co/

Note: Heavy double lines east of the reservoir are part of an extensive drainage system bordered by levees both sides of the canal designed to empty into area reservoirs or the river.
During development of Shelton the rail line from Lamar was known as the Arkansas Valley Railroad. The line would eventually revert to Santa Fe Railway. Failure of Shelton was soon followed by removal of all track installations.

A Town not Mapped

Naming, spelling and pronunciation for another new town left off the realtor's map was at odds with some area residents. Hard pronunciation of "C" resulted in the "K" sound but eventually devolved to the "Sh" sound of *Cheraw*.

Enterprise January 4, 1907

Cheraw's advantage over proposed Shelton and Holbrook Center was because of an earlier established beginning on November 3, 1906.

> The name of the new town on the new Arkansas Valley Railway is spelled with a "C," but is pronounced "Ke-raw," and it is probably pronounced right, but things never stay raw very long along the Arkansas Valley.

Ocher Mountain, south of Rocky Ford, was discovered by W.A. "Gus" Hansbrough c. 1886. J. W. Stailey of the *Garden City Sentinel,* invited guest, toured the new town of Rocky Ford and later offered his observations upon returning to Kansas to report what he saw. His tour description, too long to be printed here, was reprinted in the *Bent County Register* of Lamar July 9, 1887.

Journalists and businessmen from around the Arkansas Valley were invited to view the new and active town along the Arkansas. Such a tour was always an enlightening and invigorating experience for those whose business was investment and growth. Encouragement was thereafter offered to the new settlement's residents and much praise added for their accomplishments.

The *mountain* site, a mile south of town near the Catlin Canal, isn't known exactly but may be presumed to be one of three former mining sites on low bluffs or hills. Ocher was being removed from a tunnel, suggesting a burrow into a rise or mound rather than a pit excavation.

A map search reveals no tunnel in the areas described. It is reasonable to find that continued mining would have exhausted a tunnel, resulting in surface mining. An 1893 USDA. map shows three areas of mining activity but doesn't differentiate between tunnel or surface mining.

Neither was there an actual *mountain*, as in a very high prominence but '*hill*' was used by Editor Stailey to describe the site. He was taken there with others during a tour of area developments just before the plat of April 12, 1887 [*legally accepted and registered with the Bent County Court August 10, 1887 with incorporation papers filed in Denver August 19, 1887*].

Ocher is a yellow or red-brown clay colored by iron oxide, valued for use as paint pigment. Before it was mined in earnest, samples were sent to assay laboratories in St. Louis, Chicago, Kansas City and Denver to determine its quality. The material was tested locally as a paint by pulverizing some chunks of it and mixing with boiled oil-possibly linseed. It proved a dense, solid cover for priming and an excellent paint base with an added color for a second coat.

In the same area an excellent clay was mined for brick-making which when fired filled the requirements of contractors building the earliest brick buildings in town. North, approximately three miles from this clay and ocher site across the river, was a stone quarry. Stone was reported in abundance by Mr. Stailey but location of it was not identified. Map position of possible mining sites accompany on pp. 154 and 155. Little description of them was offered in printed history.

Note: Ocher is feminine meaning *pale yellow*. The name has been rarely used since the 1800s, and not at all in recent history. The mineral ocher is similar to sienna, another clay colored with iron oxide.

Speculation by this author is that a quarry once existed on the north side of the river north of the SH 266 bridge. This area is within range of description and was the site chosen May 11, 1927 for an open dump. Prior the use as a dump, a quarry could have operated there up to forty years from the town plat date in 1887. Quarrying for that time would have removed the best stone, contributing to future abandonment, leaving a significant excavation. Mr. Stailey could not know that the bridge now on SH 266 near the site would not be built until November 10, 1894. He would have known of the wagon bridge east of the old ford near CR 20.50 as the river crossing access to the quarry.

Note: My speculation is that clay and ocher deposits were depleted after time and much mining. Local papers, Rocky Ford *Enterprise, La Junta Tribune, Ordway New Era, Bent County Register*, and *Lamar Register* printed no details. One quarry-type not identified-was mapped on the north side of the river within the mileage given by Mr. Stailey. Stone was known to have been quarried and shipped to Rocky Ford from sites in western Kansas and canyons of southern Colorado south of La Junta. Stone of Timpas Creek was also mined by individuals for sheds and house foundations.

Ocher Mountain-*postulated*

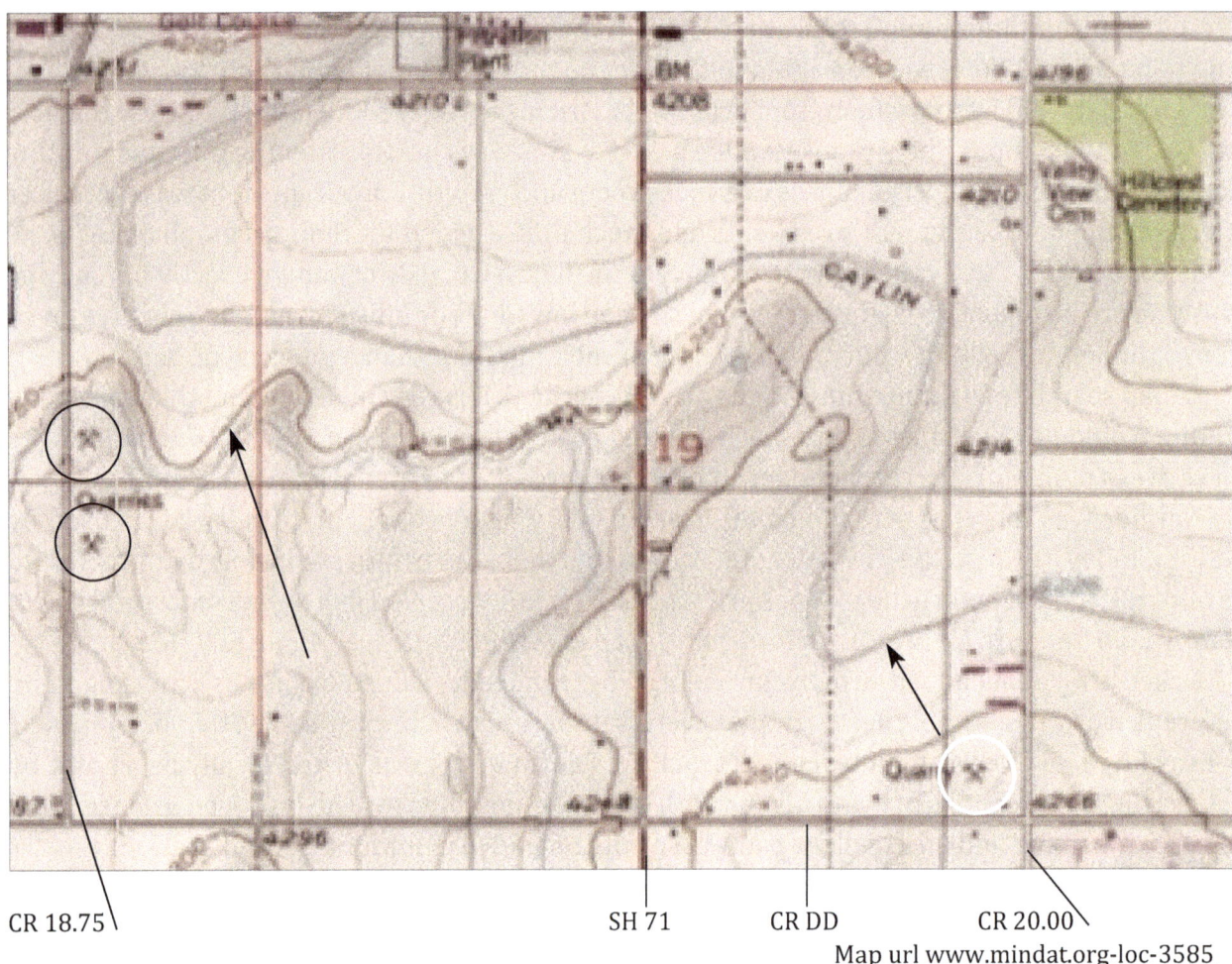

CR 18.75   SH 71   CR DD   CR 20.00

Map url www.mindat.org-loc-3585

Historical mining data for the state includes quarry sites in Otero County south of Rocky Ford. On this map three are identified. Though quarries are sites identified with some type of stone, the hammer and pick symbol by conventional use came to indicate mining in general, including gravel.

Catlin Canal was established in 1884 three years prior J.W. Stailey's visit in July, 1887 and his tour description. Otero Canal was not developed until 1890 well after the discovery of Ocher Mountain in 1886 and was excavated at the base of an undulating, low peneplane-*long arrow*-at about 4250 ft. elevation. Mines were at elevation 4270-4290 ft..

Accepting *'just one mile south of town'* [1.12 mi.] the mine at lower right is more likely site of the tunnel and ocher deposit. Distance from the Catlin, *'a few rods,'*-*short arrow*-would also include the two sites at left center though they are much less than a mile from town. All three sites are at elevation, nominally agreeing with the description that ocher was *found on three sides of a hill.*

Note: Plausible locations of the ocher deposit are indicated on the peneplane. Original description of the find said the mineral was *'... free and clean of any impurities ... practically inexhaustible...found on three sides of a hill ... a few rods from the Catlin ditch ...just one mile south of town.'* Rod = 5.5 yds, 16.5 ft., or about 5 m.
Peneplane = Land eroded almost to a level plain. It is the ancient riverbank farthest from the current riverbed.

Stone Quarry This quarry-*square*- may be the one referred by J.W. Stailey northeast of town across the river. It appears as the only one on a Topo Map of Otero County north of the river and is within the distance stated, about three miles from the ocher mountain tunnel.

State Highway 266 bridge-*circle*-would be a short distance from the mine across the river but would not be in place until November 10, 1894, eight years after discovery of *ocher mountain.*

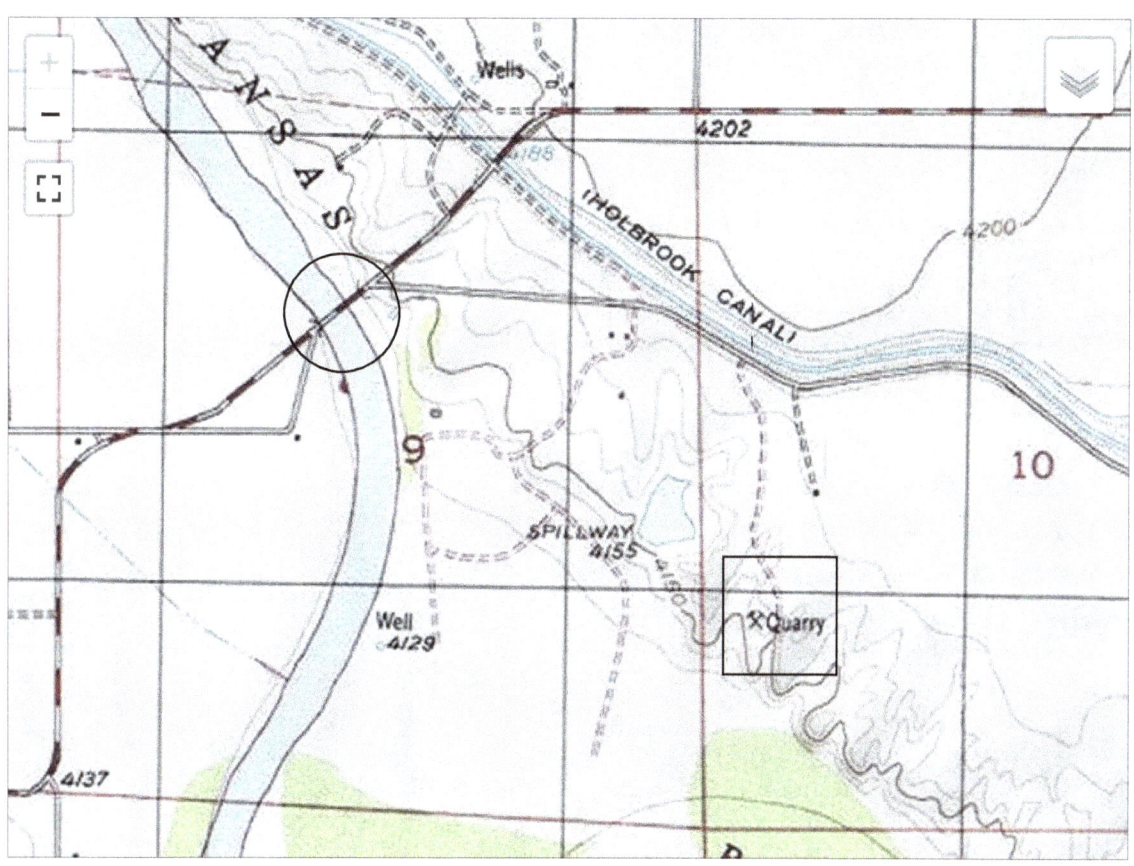

TopoZone.com/colorado/otero-co/

The bridge is noted here only for reference.

Access to the quarry would have been across the wagon road bridge farther west, estimated two miles beyond Dye's Lake by early residents; see also *Wagon Road and Wagon Road Bridge* pages 122 and 128.

Note: December 13, 1894 *Enterprise* informed of a coal seam of low quality discovered on the north side of the river after the spring flood that year. Location was not given. The cost and effort of mining and hauling to town was not economical, though the coal was 'stove tested' and acceptable for heating. The seam was small and pursuit of mining it was discontinued. The area is not apparent today probably because of several course changes since the 1894 flood and passing of many years since discovery. Poor quality coal was mined near Bloom, Colorado south of Rocky Ford on US 350 and the route of the Santa Fe Trail. Coal to Rocky Ford continued by rail from mines in the Trinidad region.

Ocher Mountain Discoverer Gus Hansbrough

Gus Hansbrough moved to Rocky Ford from Kansas in 1887, noted May 5 by the *Enterprise*. He was an active businessman; some of his activities were published:

> A. H. Martin and Gus Hansbrough, of Rocky Ford, have a contract to fence 8,000 acres of state land north of Las Animas for T. C. Henry. He will sow 4,000 acres of oats.

February 28, 1888

> —Gus Hansbrough, one of the Rocky Ford pioneers, has been mining in the Cripple Creek country for a number of years. He is now on a visit among many old friends here and will remain several weeks.

August 18, 1898

> State vs. Gus Hansbrough and H. Buckley—Violation of city ordinances, Rocky Ford; set for trial October 14.

October 12, 1898

[Nature of offence not given in the news].

> People vs. Gus Hansbrough and H. Buckley—Appeal from justice court; dismissed on motion of district attorney.

March 18, 1899

> Gus Hansbrough left last Tuesday night for Sheridan Lake to attend an "old-timers' reunion," which took place there Wednesday. Mr. Hansbrough came to Colorado in 1863, and has been a resident of this state ever since.

August 25, 1906

Gus Hansbrough was written about in *Enterprise* news at least these five times since the announcement of his ocher mountain discovery in 1886. Unfortunately, details of his find were not later seen in the news and except for the eye witnessed report of J. W. Stailey and site visit we would know very little.

W.A. Hansbrough was known by Editor J.W. Stailey of the *Garden City Sentinel* as a former resident of Leavenworth and Abilene, Kansas. By these articles he appears to have been bold and industrious but his remunerative ocher mine eventually became a diminished and depleted one.

Traction Engine Coffee, 1887

This brand name was not known to have been applied to coffee at the 1902 Arkansas Valley Fair but the method of making it was novel in the time of G.W. Swink at the 1887 Fair. Free dinners were discontinued in 1887 because of the large number of visitors arriving in the first year of special trains for the Fair. A *committee of public comfort* stepped up, employed their hospitality toward visitors and provided what they were able; specially prepared coffee as a welcome favor.

G.W. Swink's words, reprinted in the September 1, 1916 *Enterprise,* described how a very large number of Fair visitors were served on Watermelon Day 1887. Though he passed from this life in 1910 Mr. Swink's words are preserved. Coffee-making for crowds of 1887 was also employed for the 1902 Fair when Frank Gilmore, with Mark Denson and the aid of his traction engine, repeated the process.

Traction engines were invented more than 50 years prior and were of many shapes and sizes. Some were gasoline powered, others by wood or coal, some were stationary, some self-propelled but they all were very large and heavy. Not the least of their notoriety were the sounds and volume of noise they produced when operating. They easily drew an interested crowd.

Some may know the traction engine as a steam engine, separate from the engine that ran on rails and pulled cars. The former were all-purpose mobile or stationary devices that could provide power for operating farm machinery, saw mills, pulling wagons, or many other chores that were designed and adapted for use of the machine's horsepower. Today's version is the tractor.

Tables set up for Watermelon Day were arranged among the trees of Mr. Swink's still young Timber Claim, awarded by the government on November 3, 1887. Trees, now 15 years old in 1902, were large enough to provide comfortable shade during the hot summer of August and September.

Very close to the tables among the trees but outside the grove was Mark Denson's traction engine. It must have been a novelty for many who were seeing one perhaps for the first time. Many versions had been developed beginning with the first about 1850. They all had in common size, bulk, weight, and noise, much of what made them an exciting sight and presence. They all produced steam and had whistles for alarms, signaling, or for calling assembly.

Charles Recker, known for preparing food for large numbers, was a bakery and restaurant owner with experience and his charge was 15 cents. The menu included beef, pork, mutton, bread and pickles and the food was reported *"wholesale cooking ... well done"* by the *Enterprise*.

Coffee was much in demand and it was produced on location in volume and rapidly. The *Enterprise* editor, D.W. Barkley, published the process August 8, 1902:

> *"A pipe from the boiler led to a barrel in which the coffee was made by steam–the best known process. Three 50 gallon barrels of coffee were required to go with the barbequed meats and the universal verdict that the coffee was of a high grade. A mixed Mocha and Java of the 25 cents per pound quality was used and the result–the eminent satisfaction of the public–justified the wisdom of Mr. Recker's selection for that contract."*

Public meals during the Fair and novel coffee-making in quantity did not survive the years.

Note: Recker's Bakery and Restaurant on Ninth Street was opposite Otero Co. Health Depart., 207 South Ninth Street.

Traction Engines in Rocky Ford History

Construction of the American Beet Sugar Company (ABSC) factory was preceded by preparation of the site chosen for the several buildings. Because the ground in part of the area was '*seepy*' Mr. S.W. Sinsheimer of the sugar company supervised initial ground work, described in *Doll*, prior to construction beginning fall of 1899. First activity provided site fencing and permanent housing for workers.

Dr. Portus arrived with the Ames Construction Company of Oxnard, California early March 1900. This company was chosen by the factory because of their previous work of the same type needed for the new factory. First attention to site preparation, described by author John Doll is in *The Story of Early Rocky Ford (Rocky Ford Colorado)*, Rocky Ford Archaeological Society, 1987.

> "The American Beet Sugar Company reclaimed much of the seep land and built houses on it for their employees. During the reclaiming process, they brought two large steam cable tractors and a plow to work the swampy areas. One engine was placed on each side of a swamp and fastened to the plow by a cable. In operation, the cable spool under the engines would first reel in the cable, pulling the plow across the boggy area. During this cycle, the other engine would release its spool so the plow could move freely in its direction. The plow was built with four plows [shares] in each gang on a frame that was inclined, so when it was pulled by one engine, the gang facing that engine would be pulled into plowing position and the other gang would be lifted free of the ground. With the cable plows it was possible to turn a soggy path about eight feet wide with each pass across the swamp. The soil was exposed to the air and sweetened with lime to help bring it back into profitable use."

People in 1902 would have known of steam tractors, steam cable tractors, steam engines, agricultural tractors, and traction engines. Mark Denson's engine apparently was known locally before the factory-employed machine appeared in 1899. And, his engine would have been familiar to many since his coffee-making demonstration during the 1887 Fair.

An *Enterprise* article, April 6, 1900, two years before the 1902 Fair and coffee-making, described G.W. Swink's employment of a traction engine to compact soil in the bottom of his leaking lake off Maple Avenue east of 15th Street adjacent the railroad:

> "Senator Swink's lake near the [Santa Fe] *stockyards is being treated for seepage. A traction engine is meandering over the bottom of the lake, hour after hour, in order to pack the earth more solidly.*"

Mark Denson's machine was probably the one compacting the lake bottom since both men were acquainted, well-known businessmen of town.

Note: If additional methods of interrupting seepage from his lake were employed, they were not discussed in the news. The addition of clay is another method in which the mineral, swelling in the soil of the bottom, seals off much loss. Because the longevity of Swink's Artificial Lake was affected by this loss the lake's demise may have been for this in addition to other reasons mentioned elsewhere in this narrative.

A Random Walk

Pacific House

Denver 1860, part of Kansas Territory until statehood in 1876 was location of Pacific House Hotel and Denver Theater, Blake Street, c. 1861-1877.

Photo courtesy *Pinterest*

Pacific House in Denver -*left center*- has been mistaken by at least one contributor to *Pinterest* online as Pacific House in Rocky Ford. There is similarity at first inspection until surrounding neighborhood is noted. Both were hotels in similar large buildings.

Recker's Hall on Main Street in Rocky Ford was the building housing the hotel facing Railroad Park with the hotel entrance at 920 Front Street. There is similarity in size but little of overall appearance between the two hotels.

Denver Theater is right center, above, with its marquee at top of the facade. Size of Denver in 1860 shows in the background much larger than a similar photo of Rocky Ford before its incorporation August, 1887. Other 'Rocky Fords' in the US have similarly been mis-identified by shared street names, bridges over nearby rivers, or buildings.

DENVER HOUSE.

HE PROPRIETORS of the above House would respectfully call the attention of the Travelling Public to their large and commodious House, on BLAKE STREET. Denver City, K. T., which is now open for the reception of Travellers.
A. J. WILLIAMS & Co.
Denver City, May 11, 1859.

Ad for a similar hostelry in Denver. Note the absent 'T".

Rocky Mountain News, June 18, 1859

Home Remedy

Home medicine has been practiced throughout history. At least one Rocky Ford citizen displayed some knowledge of it in questionable treatment of whooping cough, also known as pertussis. A vaccine would be ready by 1914 that would be 80 per cent effective among children, but 20 years late for this one child..

Whooping cough was epidemic locally in 1894 and 1895 among school children in town. Worried parents tried to isolate hoping to prevent the most serious illness, which could progress to mortality. Medical doctors in town may have been consulted, not indicated in the article, but if they were the likely treatment would have been quarantine at home, bed rest, and cough medicine. Maybe even hot chicken soup, good for soothing sore throats and providing nutrition after much energy spent in coughing.

Enterprise December 20, 1894

Families might prescribe honey mixed with lemon or a teaspoon of whiskey and honey to ease the coughing reaction. Some swallowed a glob of aromatic menthol-flavored petroleum jelly, then afterward soothe an upset stomach.

> —A novel remedy for the cure of a very sick child was tried with success in Rocky Ford a few days since. The two year old child of Mr. and Mrs J. J. Elser was dangerously ill with whooping cough and severe inflamation. Mrs. B. U. Dye prescribed for it as follows: Two cats were killed and taken to the room where the child was sick. The skins were removed hastily and placed on the child's throat and breast when quite warm with animal heat. In a very brief time the inner side of the skins became covered with a greenish color and emitted a very bad odor. The babe at once began to recover and was soon out of danger.

Five concoctions were prepared and offered in the news specifically for cough treatment: *Chamberlain's Cough Remedy, Begg's Cherry Cough Syrup, Ayer's Cherry Pectoral, Dr. King's New Discovery,* and *One Minute Cough Cure* developed by local druggist Dr. E.W. Kearby at his pharmacy 202 North Main Street. Most cough remedies were syrup rather than drops although there were some available; the first, *Smith Brothers* in 1852, *Smith Brothers Menthol* in 1922.

There were varied ingredients among preparations. Historically, many cough syrups in the 19th and early 20th century contained combinations of alcohol, cannabis, chloroform, heroin or morphine. Cherry was a popular flavoring. The common ingredient of all, alcohol as a cough suppressant, remains an ingredient today.

As the news reached readers of the *Enterprise* who viewed the whooping cough treatment of the two-year-old child, some were indignant, incensed, even outraged at the act. One matron, noted pillar of community, wrote to the editor to express her shock and indignation at this display and horrid example of charlatanism and quackery.

Sympathy for the parents wasn't mentioned in her complaint, nor the condition of the dangerously ill child. Neither did the lady pause over treatment and demise of the two cats, decried by animal lovers. But, *the child was on the mend.* An interview with Mrs. Dye might have been fruitful in finding the extent of her knowledge of home medicine for other illnesses.

Barton

A list of notable ghost towns of Colorado does not include the *Barton* mentioned in the accompanying article or any in Otero County. Barton is listed for Prowers County on the Atcheson, Topeka and Santa Fe between Granada and Amity. The site was a railroad post office in operation from 1895 to 1917.

A 1902 map of the area locates a station named Heron as the rail site and Barton as the post office but no indication Barton was more than a named site. Structure remnants do not exist in the area. The number of area farmers and ranchers was the reason for the railroad post office to exist, precluding development of a town or concentration of buildings.

Origin of Barton in Otero County stems from H.V. Barton, prominent farmer with extensive lands near Timpas Creek, north of Catlin Canal. The intersection on which H.A. Whitsett built his store (later Hawley) was prominently known then as Barton Corner.

Land purchased by H.A. Whitsett was a speculative venture but his expenditure for stone blocks and construction of a large country store showed substantial material planning.

Enterprise, June 7, 1907

> **The New Town of "Barton"**
>
> H. A. Whitsett has bought a ten acre tract bordering on the corner of the cross roads of the Barton corner, five miles south of town. He has bought of the Rocky Ford Cement Stone Co., one thousand blocks of stone with which he is building a large country store, locating it on the corner. He will stock it with goods suited to the country trade. From this corner one road makes an air line to Rocky Ford and another an air line to La Junta. The other two roads lead out into well settled country districts with many comfortable homes and well developed ranches. It is expected that when the Santa Fe spur line of railroad, now contracted for, is built, a beet dump, will be located near the corners. That customary advance guard of a new town settlement—a blacksmith shop, is already provided for. There is a school house on the ground. So it is that the new town of "Barton" looms up as another of the active centers of suburban industry in this part of the Arkansas Valley.

A school named Barton was already on the acreage and a Santa Fe rail spur was under contract. Construction of a beet dump, hiring a blacksmith for a shop and other businesses of a small town were being considered.

Until the 1970s remnants of the railroad grade and crossing were visible immediately south of Hawley store. Cement stone blocks in the article appear in the walls of the store extant at crossroads corresponding to those in the article, one road leading to Rocky Ford, another to La Junta, the other two to the '*well settled country districts*' described in the article. Descriptions of location, school and store substantially identify the Colorado SH 71 intersection with SH 10, the location of the Hawley Store and former Grand Valley School nearby. (SH 10 would eventually be graded to Walsenburg, continuing beyond '*well settled country districts*').

Barton was changed to Hawley many years ago after planning and construction for the new town lost traction. There was no post office or known plat of the proposed town in the article.

Note: Railroad post offices were sidings established and named by the railroad where concentration of settlement required so. Essentially, they were message drops and pick-up stations, not necessarily from a depot. Later established US Post Offices offered stamped mail, registered letters, and insured package delivery.

Editor's use of '*air line*' in the article most probably means *as the crow flies*, or the *shortest distance is a straight line*.

Floyd Hawley; Meador; Hawley Store

Hauck, or Houck, was a previous name for the proposed *Barton* eventually to be Hawley on the Grand Valley Line (GVL) west of La Junta. Rails to Hawley from Newdale, begun 1908, were abandoned 1966 and removed by 1970. The line originally incorporated a beet dump adjacent and north of the Grand Valley School. Proposed town was to have a station at Hawley influenced by and named for Floyd Hawley of the American Beet Sugar Company (American Crytstal Sugar Company after 1934).

Construction of the store was documented in the *Enterprise* June 7, 1907. Though known as *a large country store*, it was probably then referred to as the store at Barton Corner or Barton Store. Although owned by the builder, H.A. Whitsett, his name was never applied.

A notice in the news, well after the 1907 article about the new town Barton, names were printed of new store owners. Efforts for town-building failed and rails for the beet dump were discontinued that were also to have continued to Omar, south of Fowler. The completed beet dump was used a while and eventually removed, with tracks, back to Newdale siding.

> Will Ritchie and father-in-law, P. L. Callahan, this week purchased the Meador store at Hawley, and the former will move down from Denver and take charge at once.

Enterprise, March 22, 1912

Enterprise, August 4, 1916

> **OBITUARIES**
> **J. D. MEADOR**
> At Burlington, N. C., on Saturday last J. D. Meador passed away at the age of 62 years.
> Mr. Meador was formerly a resident of this city and later was proprietor of the store at Hawley now owned by Ritchie & Callahan. He was the father of Mrs. Wallace Best, now living in La Junta, and had many friends in this section of the Arkansas Valley.

The long history of predecessors and the extant Hawley Store, 115 years (to 2022), may qualify it for national historical preservation efforts, or, maybe only for preservation of a local well-known landmark, referred to in many historical events.

Charley and Elma Black were probably the last owner/proprietors of Hawley Store, recalled by many in the late 1940s and 1950s. Memory of the store for this elementary school student during W W I I is one of visiting the store from work in my uncle's fields to the west. Cold drinks were available from a cooler inside where the cement stone block walls kept the place in moderate temperature..

Note: Orlo M. Barton, early-day resident of Pueblo, Colorado was born in Wisconsin in 1856, Barton and wife Laura moved to Pueblo in 1886 where he farmed and operated a mercantile business for many years before establishing a farm in Rocky Ford, Colorado. Relationship to H.V. Barton-page 161-not known.
In the 1930s Grand Valley School principal roomed on the upper floor of the store where later other teachers would live, conveniently a short walk to the school. More fuel stops for automobiles and the short drive to town for groceries and services eventually reduced need for the store.

Hawley Store

Aerial photo of Colorado State Highway 10-*horizontal*-and Colorado State Highway 71-*vertical*-with Santa Fe spur line, diagonal. Rail cars, some crossing SH 10 near the Hawley store are moving toward the beet dump. Grand Valley School, right center-*circle*-casts shadow near large trees. Rails from near Newdale, passed Timpas Creek and Roberta southwest to Barton Corner (Hawley). Rails were planned but never completed to Omar south of Fowler. Catlin Canal courses at lower right.

Photo of Hawley Store shows sculpted cement stone blocks in ground level, as now appear. Upper framed story and side additions were added years later. Because of its location the store has endured automobile collision on its long west side.

US Soil Conservation Service aerial photo, October 28, 1936.

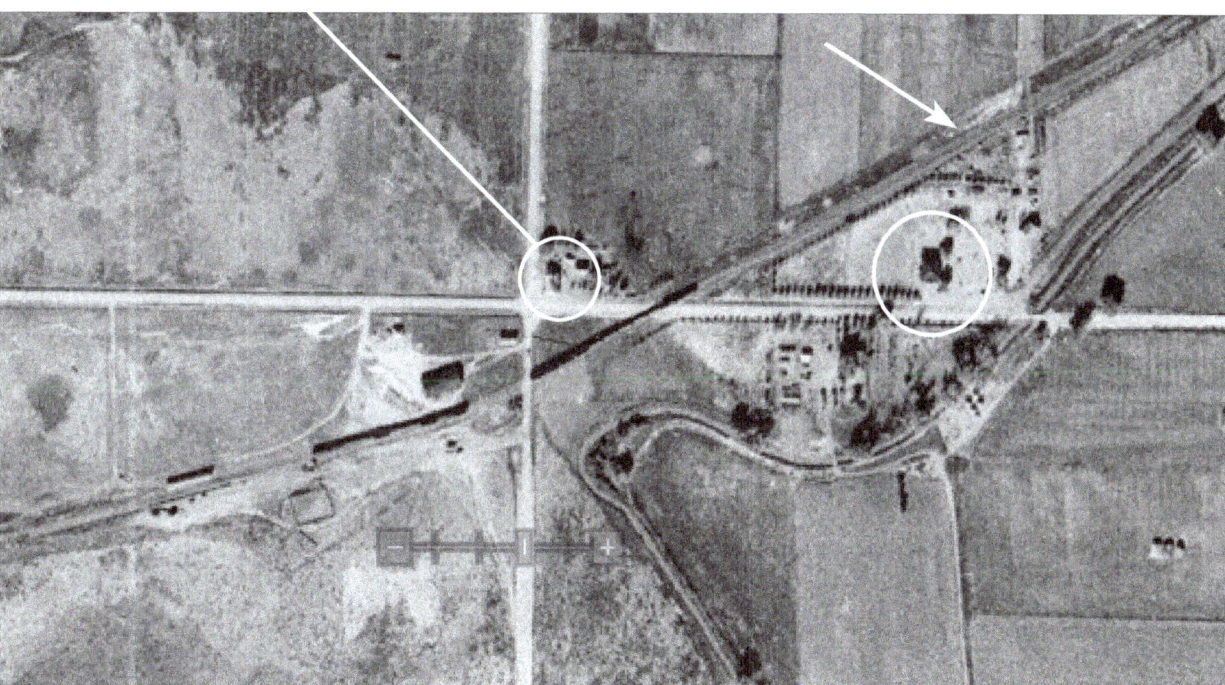

Large circle=Grand Valley School; Arrow=beet dump

A November 20, 1936 photo of this same area a month later shows approximately 30 rail cars along tracks at lower left indicating much beet transport activity.

Note: Before Hawley, the store was known briefly as Meador Store from buyers Will Ritchie and P.L. Callahan relocating from Denver.

Best=Barton=Grand Valley School

Schools were mentioned frequently in the *Enterprise* telling of the activities of students and staff. During hours school was not in session other organizations used their space for many kinds of activities, religious, political, private social and community social.

A succession of school names, in this instance relating to Grand Valley, has been printed in the *Enterprise* over many years. This was before the name *Grand Valley* when the school began with the few children of a rancher or farmer, including newcomers and those of neighbors, and eventually of the region. Common to application of school names was simply the attachment of family name in whose home the school was established.

For community Grand Valley, numerous articles were printed about *Best School* preceding another series of news items about *Barton* School, functioning before the proposed building of the town of Barton. One *Enterprise* article placed news of Best School in the same paragraph with Grand Valley School House May 13, 1897.

Because of numerous publications in the *Enterprise* it seems Best School was the first name of the school, named for the family, *Best*. Not evident in school history is the name transition from Best School to Barton School. The Bartons and Bests were prominent in the area with Alexander Best and holdings six miles southwest of Swink. This placed his ranch northeast of the proposed town of Barton, the town advertised June, 1907.

The O.M. Barton family ranched four miles south of Rocky Ford, placing them about one mile north of proposed town of Barton. Close neighbors, as they were, fostered frequent interaction but how the school names were changed is guesswork. Both names were temporary before and after the Otero County School District No. 1 was established in 1889.

Some preferences may have acted in the region over what or for whom to name schools, names likely used interchangeably. I draw an analogy of The Country School built on Washington Road in Rocky Ford with The Old School or the Boardwalk School named for walkways built to it by volunteers. For nine years no official name was applied until school children, presented with the opportunity, decided the name to be Washington School.

Naming the school near the intersection of SH 71 and SH 10, once the Best or Barton School was simplified unknowingly by teacher Irene Egbert circa 1895 when her first view coming to the area prompted her to say, *"My, isn't this a grand valley!"* Her comment was remembered and later applied to the school and has also been applied to the Valley ever since.

Mrs. Egbert began teaching at Grand Valley circa 1895 and was chosen by School Board election to serve as Treasurer, six years after formation of Otero County School District No. 1.

In the news: "Last summer [1909] School District No, 1, known as the 'Grand Valley School District,' was divided, the northern portion being numbered School District No. 29." *Enterprise*, December 23, 1910.
After the division the voters approved a new schoolhouse (third Grand Valley School) June 10, 1910, which was the school that burned winter 1933.

Note: Substantial factual information contributing to this article derives from publication in 1956 and following, information about country schools near Rocky Ford, particularly, Grand Valley School. Information compiled by Joyce (Bitter) Clute, Ruth (Muth) Grenard and Donna L. (Burchett) Abert was printed in the *Rocky Ford Daily Gazette*.

Barton School = Grand Valley School

Barton history began April 19, 1889 when a special election was conducted at the Alexander Best Ranch, six miles southwest of Swink. Colorado Governor, Alva Adams had signed the document creating Otero County March 25, 1889. Decisions of the special election renamed the school district Otero County School District No. 1, also known as 'the Hendrix District' for the first president of the new school board, Thomas N. Hendrix.

All business of the special election was completed May 22 and preparations were made to re-define the district from Bent County School District 15 to Otero County School District No. 1, its new designation. (Parts of Bent and Las Animas Counties were sectioned for creation of Otero County in 1889).

One of the first items of business was replacement of the original frame school built in 1887 (Best School). A brick building-the second school-was built 1896-1897 of one room (Barton). It was soon inadequate for the number of students moving into the district.

A third school was built and by 1910 Grand Valley District 29 was formed with Barton then known as Grand Valley in the reorganization. Fire destroyed this third school when its furnace was improperly banked one winter night in 1933. Temporarily, classes were held in a neighboring home until a new school was built for the September, 1933 start of school year.

Grand Valley School building number four stands today, a two-story brick that served until reorganization of the district in 1959. The building now houses a child development center.

Otero Junior College Child Development Service

Note: Banking is recharging a stove or furnace, with coal in this case, to keep a hot ember bed throughout the night. Last tended before retiring, coals are pushed to the rear of the firebox with the embers tapered down toward the front of the firebox. A new layer of coal is added leaving some embers exposed in the front, allowing more coal to be added to 'bank' for the night. Exposed embers at front of the bank burn off volatile coal gases that could cause an explosion (blow back}, the probable cause of the fire that burned the third school building.

The Editor Deplores *Knockers*, Kickers and *Croakers*

To most, these words, like many, can have several meanings. Its frequent use in the archived *Enterprise* editions favors one in particular. The not fully enlightened naive person might draw smiles from his other informed neighbors when trying to explain an incomplete understanding of these words' definition.

We had not used our language long before hearing in some discussion, "*Don't knock it.*" In other words, don't discard or dismiss the premise before you understand it. If the subject is an automobile with a serious engine *knock*, that is something not to be avoided. Many remember street salesmen, otherwise known as door-to-door men, who would *knock* on doors in past years.

Webster's New World College Dictionary defines knocker three ways, among them number two, the editor's favorite peeve:
1. door knocker.
2. person who continually finds fault; as a critic, disparager, denigrator, depreciator, belittler, attacker, censurer.
3. woman's breast.

Enterprise, July 15, 1910

> There is, however, a wide gulf between legitimate dissatisfaction and that which consumes the chronic complainer, the disreputable knocker, and the everlasting kicker.
>
> Life is made up of affirmatives and negatives. One without the other is incomplete. The two properly blended are part of the composition of success.

Enterprise, October 1, 1915

Respecting number three, street jargon of the 1950s made the comparison to two protruding adornments on the front bumper of the Cadillac.

However one looks at the word Will R. Monkman, *Enterprise* editor, intended the second meaning when he wrote the accompanying articles. He often wrote short filler paragraphs throughout his paper's editions castigating openly pessimistic or cynical persons, no matter the subject, as these articles attest.

> If there is one person that makes us tired it is the habitual knocker. He is the foe of co-operation and organization of any kind. If he is a farmer and even so small a thing as a cantaloupe association is to be launched, he opposes every move made which will fail to put him in as an officer. If he does not land an office he will either withdraw from the organization or ever afterwards appear at their meeting and with long winded harangues oppose every measure which is proposed by the members for their own good. This class of knocker is not patent to the farmers; you will find them in all stations and walks of life. You will find them constantly criticising the officials and government of the town in which they reside; you will hear them hurling anathemas at the county, state and government officials They pose as reformers but in reality their rule would be ruin, and they propose to ruin if they can't rule. This sort of a knocker would be a dangerous man if he had much of a following, but fortunately he don't often have. However, this kind of a knocker is a very disagreeable person and fortunate is that community from which such persons are absent

Postscript

Many former citizens could be lionized here. Two who were among the authors of Rocky Ford history are included as well as those who were not but lived part of the history of the city.

Blanche Bulifant McFarland

There is surprisingly little information among the editions of the *Enterprise* about this lady. She was born in York, York County, South Carolina. Whatever turn her life experiences took, she was eventually to become a teacher, educator and administrator in Rocky Ford School District 4. She served concurrently as *Principal of Lincoln School* and *Supervisor of the Social Subjects* for the school district.

She married Alfred Jackson McFarland who preceded her in death in 1936. He referred to her as 'BB', recognizing her given and maiden surnames.

Hers is an extensive resume' detailed online, all having to do primarily with elementary education.

While in the Rocky Ford District No. 4, she helped guide development of *Rocky Ford As the School Children See It*, published in 1925.

June 22, 1879, - January 5, 1966
Mrs. McFarland is interred at
Rose Hill Cemetery, York, York
County South Carolina.
Blanche Bulifant, 18, graduate of Farmville State Teachers College, Farmville, VA June 1897.

Mrs. McFarland's philosophy of education is written into the *Foreword* of the book:

"Education should prepare one to deal with the world as he finds it, to meet those situations in which he finds himself placed, to deal with the actual problems of everyday life in such manner as to get the most out of life, to reach the highest peak of good citizenship, of which he is capable. It is the business of our schools to train pupils for just this–nothing less. When the so-called 'social subjects' function as they should, they go a long way in providing for such an eventuality."

Mrs. McFarland's office, while she was principal of Lincoln School, was in the building at 601 South Eighth Street, now the Rocky Ford School District R2 Administration Building.

Among their goals, students at each school, Lincoln, Liberty, Washington and Rocky Ford High School, beginning with third grade through high school senior, wrote the history of Rocky Ford describing each category of community life from pioneer days to 1925. Their story, beginning 1870, documented the following 55 years of community social and commercial development. The result was the first, and now *rare* book, of written history of town by its younger residents.

Note: Though not part of the name of Farmville State Teachers College, the philosophical structure and curriculum with emphasis on social subjects identifies the school as being among the *Normals* in the US.

John Doll

This Rocky Ford businessman lived at 609 South Eleventh Street with wife Cornelia, daughter Colleen and sons Bert and John Jr..

Mr. Doll was a mechanic well known among townspeople, business associates, ranchers and farmers. He performed his work in the *Johnny Doll Pine Avenue Garage* on Pine Avenue between Tenth and Eleventh Streets. His building remains and until recently-2021- displayed the full name in block letters over the two bay doors. Photo from his book.

July 29, 1901-April 1985

John Doll was known to everyone as "Johnny." He had strong interest in history, especially of Rocky Ford and its pioneering citizens. He wrote many articles for local news and published a history of town.

Photo courtesy C.J. Muth

Mrs. Doll was a homemaker and a dedicated contest entrant whether through newspaper, magazine, radio or mail and was known for her many successful results with a multitude of prize awards. One friend observed that she nearly furnished her home with her success, winning numerous decor and personal items.

Unpublished papers: *Report of Interview with Horace B.U. Dye* (son of Bloomfield Usher Dye) December 26, 1933, *Inventory Data Form on Rocky Ford–The Old Crossing on the Arkansas, Beaty Brothers Manzanola, The Old Buffalo Trail (Trappers Trail), Manzanola, Fowler, The Plain Man* (George W. Swink), *The Swink Family, Cattlemen and Irrigation, Report of Interview William H. Wilson,* December 29, 1933, *Farming in the Arkansas Valley, Irrigation Trophy.*

Published: *The Story of Early Rocky Ford (Rocky Ford Colorado),* 1987, Rocky Ford Archaeological Society [now rare].

Note: William H. Wilson of Philadelphia, PA graduated from the law department of the University of Pennsylvania in 1898, served as assistant city solicitor 1900 - 1909, was member of Pennsylvania House of Representatives 1913 to 1915. He served as director of public safety in Philadelphia from 1916 to 1920. He was elected as a Republican in 1934 to the 74th United States Congress. He was an unsuccessful candidate for reelection in 1936.

Man About Town
This fellow was not mentioned at all in *Rocky Ford, Colorado–A walk Past Local Doors*, not alluded to as were others. It wasn't because his story isn't noteworthy. He was known by many and recognized in almost all of town. He knew names, events and recognized many people and what they did . His one sibling, younger brother Robert, and parents lived at 708 South Twelfth Street, very near Washington School and the playground.

He didn't often walk. Transportation for his small jobs and errands was his well-used bicycle with a basket on the handlebars. His walk was a little irregular but he had good balance on his bike. Slowly, steadily, he won the trust of people by concentrating on his course until the jobs he was asked to do were completed.

He was born June 21, 1934, the year notorious John Dillinger met his demise in Chicago. In Rocky Ford that year, American Beet Sugar Company became American Crystal Sugar Company. Details of Robert's elder brother's birth are not known but it was evident as he grew through childhood that something had occurred to affect his development. That mattered not at all to those of us who knew him and met often at Washington School. Not for classes but for play. He didn't attend school. He laughed a lot, from the belt, at almost everything.

As all of us, his pals in the neighborhood, passed through the grades, he would sometimes be on the playground alone, waiting to play ball or to play Horse, shooting some baskets. The backboard held up well among his random shots, and he was lucky, sometimes. The baseball, when we played, was eventually battered until the stitches were frazzled. He didn't run well but we often awarded his base to keep him in the game, always, quick to laugh. We laughed with him, enjoying the day and just being together.

Marbles is a game that all of us played. But Robert's brother was just fascinated and liked to watch. Knees in the dust, sometimes deep enough to cover the *dake*, would often require scraping some dirt away from the circle.

Everyone owned a marble sack, an old sock or a Bull Durham tobacco pouch, filled with a selection of glass, some steel, and other collectors of clay, ceramic, or wood. A few were larger than average size but the glass or *steelies* were used in play. Playing for keeps, or not, was decided before starting.

A large circle in the dust held each player's dake near center. With knuckles down at the ring, the thumb supplied the propulsion for the *shooter* marble, trying to hit one and knock it out of the ring. If the player knocked a marble out, that was a *keeper* for the rest of the game and the player also won another turn. If no marble was knocked out, the next player took his turn. Always, rules of the game were what the players decided before starting. Our friend watched, amused at our animated rules negotiations. A game ended when all dakes were knocked out of the ring.

People who needed someone to chore for them, whether for a pick-up at one of the Mom and Pops, or delivery for a neighbor, called him. Sometimes he would knock on doors to remind folks he could do something, anything for them. Everyone knew him and he made spending money.

When all of us were in junior high or high school in 1950 the war began in Korea. We weren't particularly concerned about this unless we had relatives or knew someone who was drafted. He was 16 while we were a couple years younger and not of Draft age. He would not register but witnessed the absence, one by one, of his buddies and friends as they left for life's next chapter.

During high school years there began a breakup of our camaraderie. In 1962, when he was 28, Marilyn Monroe died. No consequence to him, but the rest of us noted the event from our various pursuits across the state and country. In space, John H. Glenn, Jr. was the first American to orbit the earth in *Friendship* 7. Cuban and Russian governments were adding missile bases to the island. Our pal was insulated from all this.

He was 41 in 1975 when there was an assassination attempt on the life of the president, then Gerald R. Ford. A second attempt seventeen days later was also foiled. It was not news to him but to those of us out in the world, wonder and concern. He did not comprehend.

George H.W. Bush was President in 1989, the last year our friend rode his bicycle on his errands. Everyone's friend had lived to age 55, and then he left us October that year.

In retrospect, his activities were of *his* choosing and they matched his ability. Providence saw to his course. His parents, Frank and Mary McCracken, trusted him to be out in the town, on his own, without assistance. He was capable for what he wanted to do and his parents respected him for that. *Ron* achieved in large part because of their courage to allow him to succeed.

Note: A 'dake' was ante to enter the game; probably derived from '*stake*' and mispronounced in a youngster's elocution, maintained without question or correction over the years.
Horse is a shooting game. Players take shots at the hoop from different locations. If he makes his shot and the next man misses the same shot, that player gets a letter toward the word 'HORSE'. Multiple misses 'saddles' him. The last player with few or no letters wins. The name 'Horse' was given apparently without much thought to the origin.

Miles F. Porter, III came to Rocky Ford from a reporter's position in Indiana where he claimed experience with a 'large city newspaper.' He assumed editorship of the *Gazette* from editor James W. Martin, 608 S Eleventh Street in 1950.

Among the staff of the newspaper were reporter Eleanor Lacy, daughter of an early editor, Oley Romero, pressman, a print worker-laborer, an office-minder, Darcy, and about 10 newsboys. A full-time linotype operator was joined by Mr. Martin who frequently operated a second machine.

Mr. Porter could be abrasive, curt and demanding. Newsboys, having received his bossy instructions resented him, their justification to avoid him.

After several disagreeable confrontations, he was labeled Miles F, Porter the Third, replacing his hereditary number with an uncomplimentary rhyming epithet. Harsh instructions to four of them caused difficulty over a small thing such as folding papers.

Carriers folded the papers so that ends were tucked into folds making a compact package that could be thrown a long distance. Mr. Porter, watching this process one day, wanted the papers out-on-route immediately after printing and to be delivered before 5 PM each day. Folding was taking too much time. His insistence invited words and as he stood with back to the Rocky Ford Ditch his newsboys, suggested by one (R.C.), would toss Mr. Porter into the ditch. Two were much larger than he and as he backed, fell into the water. At 405 South Main in the alley he could not get out before wading upstream under the Freedom Bridge where he was able to get himself out behind Doc and Bonnie's Café.

These newsboys remained briefly, managing to avoid their boss, and vice-versa, but his humiliation, embarrassment and anger soon prompted their departure. Mr. Porter also departed not long after to an editorship in a small mountain community.   **Note**: Newsboys R.C., P.S., L.S., K.M.

Fenton Family

The Fenton's were but one of several influential and successful families in Rocky Ford. They are documented here only to add information to the text concerning their activities, especially of the elder W.E. Fenton and his association and influence in Holbrook Valley.

Physician and surgeon, W.E. Fenton was physician to many families as was later, Ward C. Fenton. Their interests also involved them significantly in the pharmaceutical retail business.

1911 Directory

Fenton, W.E. Physician and surgeon, dealer in thoroughbred Hereford cattle and Jersey Red hogs, residence 900 Swink Avenue

Fenton Drug Co. (Inc.), S.A. Masters vice-pres. & mgr.

1914-1915 Directory

Fenton, Blanche, student, residence 900 Swink Ave.

Fenton Drug Co, W.E. Fenton, President and Treas, 403 N Main, Tel. White 651

Fenton, Ward C., student, residence 900 Swink Ave.

Fenton, Dr. Ward E, Physician and Surgeon, Office 403 N Main, Hours 8 to 11, 1 to 3, Tel. White 651, home 900 Swink Ave., Tel. White 652 (Nannie A.)

1945-1948 Directory

Fenton, Dr. Ward C., Charlotte, Lawrence L. and Charlotte L., 406 South Eighth Street, ph. 666.

Note: Swink Avenue at 900 is the intersection of Swink with Ninth Street, across Ninth from Elks Club parking. Corner was homesite of the Fentons, later the Spot Café and parking. Site is currently dedicated to parking.

Editor Barkley offers this filler in the *Enterprise*, April 30, 1896.

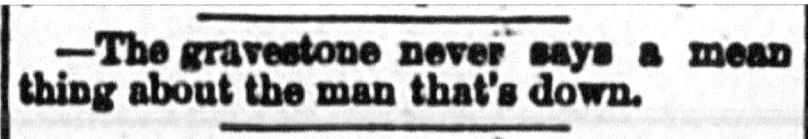
—The gravestone never says a mean thing about the man that's down.

Fenton Siding and Fenton Lake

The Fentons were prominent in Rocky Ford as early residents and landowners, with physicians and pharmacists among their family. A realty business was another interest. Some of their holdings were about three miles east of the site of the proposed new town of Shelton in the general area of Holbrook Valley called *Center*.

The town of Shelton, and news concerning, mentions Laguna three miles west of the new town, Fenton Station, Fenton Ranch and Fenton Lake three miles to the east [*2.5 mi. straight line*]. Fenton was also a rail siding about halfway between Hays and Rocky Ford. Laguna, on the track line, was named by the Arkansas Valley Railroad for the Laguna [Lake] Canal in the area. The rails were laid from the American Beet Sugar Factory in Rocky Ford north of the fairgrounds to connect to the Arkansas Valley Railroad at or near Laguna and Shelton. Rail line was abandoned after the 1912 flood and loss of the railroad bridge over the Arkansas River, bridge site undetermined.

Anticipation of the hoped-for successes of both Shelton and Holbrook Center apparently spurred the Fentons to enlarge their lake capacity to accommodate irrigation of 4000 acres in the Holbrook Valley. The lake is spoken of in the *Enterprise* January 27, 1911 as part of the Fenton ranch three miles east of Shelton. The area around the lake was not mapped for the *Enterprise*, but may be approximated by inspection of a modern map of the area.

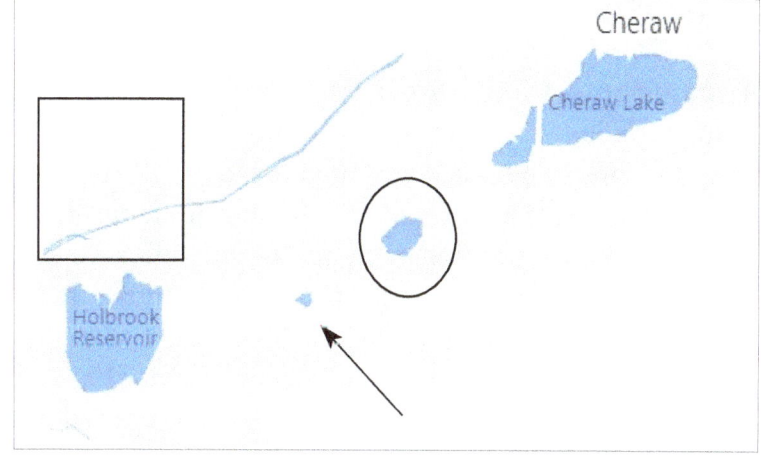

Shelton site ☐ near Holbrook Lake. Lakes to the right are Manby, Taylor, and Cheraw, all of the Holbrook Valley.
Taylor Lake-*oval*-about 3 miles from Shelton, may be the former Lake Fenton.

Manby Lake-*arrow*-is little more than a swampy pond. Taylor Lake for description of size and location appears to approximate the setting for Fenton Lake.

Cheraw Lake was known at the time by name at least five years beginning with platting of the town in 1906.

bing.com/maps

Some historians and geographers trace the ancient river bottom northeastward from about Rocky Ford or Swink eventually to enter the current riverbed between Bent's Old Fort and Las Animas. Part of this area, ranging left to right in the illustration, includes the lakes of interest.

Note: Modern farming activity in this zone is highly visible when viewed in satellite photography revealing a contiguous verdant area in a long arcing pattern north of the current river bed. Alleged ancient river channel is estimated eons before European settlement on the Arkansas River. Native populations were sole eye-witnesses to such times.
Laguna known from Laguna Canal Company prior 1900 with Henry R. Holbrook, president, then named Lake Canal.

Ethnic Groups in or near Rocky Ford - Black Americans and *The Dry-c. 1916-1930s*

President Abraham Lincoln's Emancipation Proclamation and conclusion of the War Between the States encouraged former slaves to migrate toward the West. They faced resentment and exclusion from participating in a society with laws restricting their activity. Strong incentives were the Homestead Acts that attracted many families to the Colorado plains, including those looking for alternatives to sharecropping.

A community, The Dry, attempted farming about eight miles south of Manzanola where about 50 families collectively owned around 8,500 acres. They had a school, Prairie Valley, used also as a church and community social center. It closed in 1933 as more families left. Students then were transported to Manzanola schools.

The Dry was supported by Manzanola churches, clergy and the town citizens in general. Census records show many families left the area by 1930, most due to both the Dust Bowl and the Ku Klux Klan's rise in state political power. The last house standing burned in 1998, considered by some to have been the work of an arsonist.

Nothing remains on the site but author Keck has cited Frances B. Worker as publisher of a c. 2000 paper on this community, supported with information from John Doll. Paper, if extant, was printed in Manzanola. More information of this settlement is found in *A History of The Dry* in *The Dry Archaeology* by *Michelle A. Slaughter* and in Keck, *A History of Otero and Crowley Counties Colorado (1999)*.

Hispanic Americans, *Alta Vista*

Labor supplied locally became scarce in the years of WW I while the young beet sugar industry was developing. When many men were off to war the American Beet Sugar Company sent representatives to New Mexico to hire men for laborers in the beet fields. Those who came for the work were housed, at first, in tents. Later families were induced to stay when the company built adobe housing on their beet properties. Individuals and sometimes extended families lived and worked together for the season.

A large settlement was eventually built, circa 1910s, by the ABSC on their property now the home of Rocky Ford High School just west of the golf course. There were several individual homes whose families were served by a family-run grocery on the site.

Frank R. Gandara moved his grocery to 517 North Main Street at the closing of the community. Windows, doors and frames along with any usable items were given to residents as they moved. When salvage was completed the village was razed in 1959 an event that truly and visibly demonstrated a return of the community buildings and houses to that from which they came.

Germans from Russia, *Moscow Avenue, Moscow Alley, Little Moscow*

These names reflected an area, not a Muscovite community but of Germans from Russia who lived in small neighborhoods near or on ABSC property. Natives simplified them to *Rooshians*.

Route of immigration to the United States for many of these people was through the steppes and farms along the Russian Volga River. They were emigrants from a feudal Germany in the 1700s, lured by a sympathetic Tsarina, Catherine II, herself a German by birth. Her government had in mind the agricultural and other development of the Russian Steppes and countryside.

When political and economic stabilities disintegrated under a successor to Catherine a wave of emigration to the U S began. Several families settled in the Arkansas Valley, following relatives who had preceded them in the late 1800s.

Small communities of Germans from Russia or Russian Germans, or 'Rooshians' formed on beet-raising properties, some owned by the ABSC Families worked together, as did many of the Hispanics. Concentrations of the German-speaking folk gathered at the ranches of the ABSC West, Center, and East Ranches. A few lived separately, many eventually bought and developed their own farms as they assimilated.

Almost from the beginning of their presence in the Valley natives wondered how to address them, Russians they were by citizenship sworn when they entered the Russian State, German by ethnicity guaranteed them by Tsarina Catherine while in Russia. Now, many were naturalized in the US and were American, but still *Rooshians*.

One try at explanation for reference to them came humorously by one of themselves, also a major historian of those among whom he was born and lived. Paraphrasing:

"Walking along the street in Russia you might sometime encounter the need for a public restroom or Nushnik, as the German would say. Going in you would be a Russian German, coming out you would be a German Russian, but while inside, European."

Timothy J. Kloberdanz

There were a few ethnic Germans who emigrated directly from the German State who spoke a different dialect from the *Volgadeutscher* but that was compatible in understanding. Their attraction to beet-producing areas in this country was deliberate since most were farmers who knew how to raise beets and grains in the Hesse and on the Steppes, the latter very much like our prairies. They farmed the areas near rivers and were accustomed to irrigation.

Japanese American, *Issei-first generation; Nisei-US born*

Small numbers of Japanese, *Issei*, came to the Rocky Ford area about 1905, coincident with The Russo-Japanese War fought between the Empire of Japan and the Russian Empire during 1904 and 1905. Conflict was because of rival political ambitions in Manchuria and Korea.

No doubt reasons to emigrate from Japan were to be free of conflict, conscription of young men and worsening economic times for families. Those Issei who first came to the U S worked for others on farms primarily but soon were acquiring their own farms and working for themselves. Their American-born children, *Nisei*, worked their farms, went to school, and over the years were assimilated citizens, interested in many other walks in life.

Local Japanese were not included in the population of the Amache Center in eastern Colorado where more than 7500 west coast Japanese were detained in a concentration camp, later called relocation camp. Though strong sentiment among a few valley residents existed during WW II no serious incidents were known.

Local Germans and Russian Germans during WW I and WW II and Japanese during WW II experienced some animosity. Eventually, this eased when measured against the patriotism and support for the war effort apparent when many young men from these communities fought in the conflicts wearing the uniforms of the United States.

A Letter by a First Resident

"But my friends I would say don't sell out where you are until after you come out and see our country, for it is far different than your own, and we don't want anyone dissatisfied for there are plenty of folks who know what a country we have and will settle with us. The first here will receive the greatest returns for their investments."

J. M. Hendricks

Published in the *Enterprise,* December 27, 1888

Afterword

Many authors have written Rocky Ford history, writing as contemporaries during the times, brief narratives of events or people, some of businesses, the sugar factory and small manufacturers who were vigorous and sometimes brief in existence. And, much of the farming community. Most of those authors were Rocky Ford citizens.

Stories of the 1921 Flood were written by citizen-residents in particular but also by state and some national news. Probably the most prolific of writers over the life of the city were the editors of our local newspapers, principally, the *Enterprise*. The latter chiefly because it reported on the scene for the formative years 1887 to 1950. *Enterprise* issues from the first, June 9, 1887 to the time of publication of the school children's book were available to the student writers to purview in Editor Will R. Monkman's office. Fortunately, online digital issues of August 31, 1893 to December 29, 1916 exist today.

Pioneer W.C. Steele was perhaps the first among those residents who from 1887 passed on to his contemporaries, orally and by letter, the contributions of the first settlers whom he knew personally. A large number of his experiences were drawn into the school children's 1925 book.

Published and bound works of Rocky Ford include those of school children who, guided by their teachers, recorded town history from 1870 to 1925. A centennial publication of 1987 by John Doll, along with the children's book, are now considered *rare*. The latter book, after internet search, is found in only four libraries. It is nowhere listed for sale and would be of inestimable value, if at all available. John Doll's book will cost the online shopper over one hundred dollars at one site and is unlikely to be found elsewhere for less.

Accounts of Rocky Ford in the previous *Rocky Ford, Colorado-A Walk Past Local Doors,* along with the current narrative, are not complete stories of our town but writing them has been enlightening and satisfying, hopefully also for those who want more detail. Those readers may find increased interest as a result in the stories that helped fill out this history of the town and Valley.

Finally, as an expatriate, one who lived in Rocky Ford during a significant heyday, this author notes somberly and with some nostalgia the slowly disappearing Rocky Ford Main Street. It is happening there but also on other streets where some single family houses await their final disposition.

Reasons for this are easily understood but not easy to amend. This author certainly has no wonderful remedy, only to say that somewhere in our past *possibly* we missed opportunities unrecognized after the loss of the factory and for the concerns that whelmed people then. When major businesses moved or closed, income loss for the city and the individual followed abruptly.

Cities near the mountains, thirsty for Valley water are hard to be denied. Incentive to stay here and try to be productive is dulled. Some folk leave. And so, under our feet the sewers, water delivery system, storm drains and utility lines of various services fail accompanied by crumbling street surfaces. The city is now bent on reacting to the emergent instead of anticipating and performing proactively. Even so, there is hope in the anticipation. Resignation is not the answer. Otherwise there would not now exist life in the Valley 135 years following the charter in 1887.

A Letter by a First Resident

"On a cold clear day in January, 1873, L.N. Hendricks alighted from a Kansas-Pacific train at Kit Carson and took a stage for Pueblo. He was on his way to Rye where he was to teach school.

When the stage drew up for a change of horses at a station on the north bank of the Arkansas River about 50 miles east of Pueblo, he noticed a canoe shoot out from the opposite bank and a man row swiftly across the stream. Soon above the bank appeared a tall roughly dressed man who received the mail bag from the driver and poured the contents on the ground and began sorting out the mail for his settlement. When he had finished the remainder was returned to the sack, locked and tossed up to the driver.

It was then he introduced himself as George W. Swink who was one of the partners of the store on the south side of the river."

William C. Steele

Published in the *Tribune*, 1917

Note: Barlow-Sanderson Overland Mail Company operated from about 1864 to 1868 from Fort Larned to Fort Lyon, Colorado. Route was along the north side of the Arkansas River with several Colorado stations: Sand Creek at its mouth; and Fort Lyon between Graveyard and Limestone Creeks. The stage line continued to Pueblo with several stations, including *old Rocky Ford*, along the way.

Notes of Interest

Sanborn Map of 1895 Rocky Ford

Area of town required only two cartographs.

Rocky Ford Watermelon Pickers (in Ragtime)

This tune was one of many popular jazz tunes played in ragtime. How the author, A. Garfield Wilson, came to write it isn't known but he placed it in copyright in Denver. Lyrics, if any, are not known, at least in the rendition found online.

Popularity of this music style spans 1897 to about 1920 and perhaps was popular among Rocky Ford residents. A performance of *Rocky Ford Watermelon Pickers* may be seen and heard on video: https://youtube/QcAEFr7Bdfs.

The author is identified on the internet among many musicians and authors as below. He apparently is attributed with three compositions, two of confirmed record.

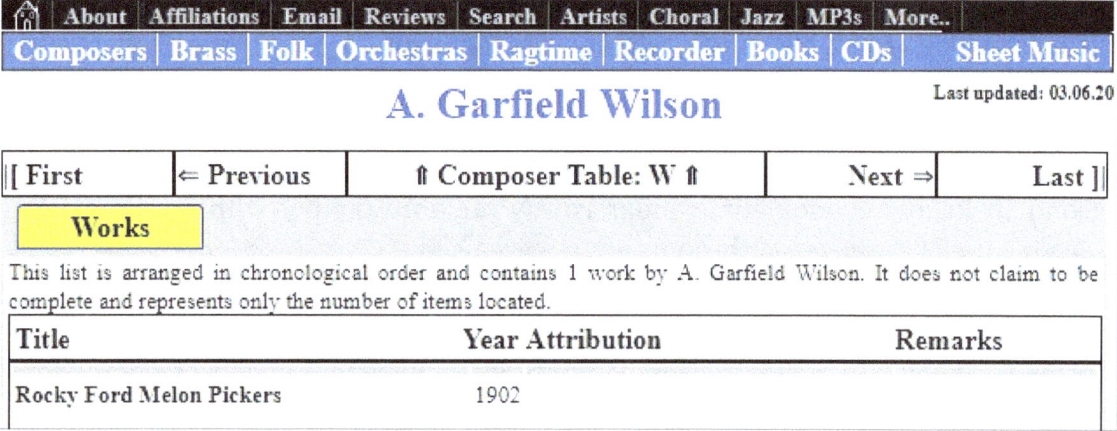

Source: grainger.de/music/composers/wilsonag.html

Another A. Garfield Wilson composition, *The Yankee Doodle Rag* of 1911 may be seen played and heard on video: https://www.youtube.com/watch?v=IIdC7tt8jkt8.

A third composition, *Wilson Rag*, was apparently only associated with the Wilson name and was popularly played by guitarist Elizabeth Cotten. Author was J. R. Rhodes.

Popular ragtime music from a famous author readily recognizable to many movie fans is the theme for *The Sting,* from 1973. It was composed by Scott Joplin, called *The Entertainer*, and was set to the film track by Marvin Hamlisch.

Note: alternate URL for *Rocky Ford Melon Pickers*: https://www.youtube.com/watch?v=QcAEFr7Bdfs

Donkey Baseball

The sport's origins are apparently from the 1930s, according to some sources. The ball-playing donkeys were provided by a small number of companies that traveled throughout the United States. One of the oldest has been in operation since 1934. The company provided services for donkey basketball, donkey racing and donkey rentals for hunting sports and packing trips.

The game was briefly popular in the Arkansas Valley and in Rocky Ford in the late 1940s and early 1950s, novel for the times but the game didn't survive. Fund-raisers benefitted from the game with its humorous antics of both players and donkeys. Many of the donkeys preferred to ignore their player's urging, some wanting to graze, others wanting to buck their rider and run off field. Donkeys often smelled bad and many were stubborn but there were some very cooperative ones, some that just wanted to idle in the sun.

The rules of donkey baseball were relatively simple. Everyone in the outfield had a donkey that was to be held by reins. Fielding a ball required taking the donkey along. Players other than the pitcher or catcher had to jump on their donkey's back to throw the ball.

If a player let go of his donkey, or forgot to mount before throwing, the opposing team got a free base. After hitting the ball, the batter had to jump on a donkey and ride it around the bases. At a second strike, batters sometimes humorously replaced the bat with something larger to ensure hitting the ball. Shovels or brooms often were used.

Another version of the game required the pitcher, catcher and batter to be on their feet; all other players were seated on donkeys.

As soon as he hit the ball, the batter jumped onto his donkey and tried to head for first base. Players could dismount to grab a ball, but had to hold onto their donkey's reins. They had to remount their donkeys to throw, all throws going to the pitcher who couldn't leave a box chalked around him but he had to throw to the necessary base. Scoring was not too important but remained part of the game. More importance was placed on the entertainment and the money raised for charity or other worthy cause.

The sport began to draw attention of animal rights organizations who claimed the donkeys were forced to do things unnatural for them. Games organizers also felt that there were more worries for the players in accidents. The cost of maintaining donkeys, their handlers, and their transportation to various sites for games eventually ended the business for all but a few.

Note: According to Old Testament prophecy, the Messiah would arrive on a donkey:

"Behold, your King is coming to you; He is just and having salvation, Lowly and riding on a donkey, A colt, the foal of a donkey!" (Zechariah 9:9).

According to the New Testament, this prophecy was fulfilled when Jesus entered Jerusalem riding on the animal (Matthew 21:4-7, John 12:14-15).

Jesus was aware of this connection (Matthew 21:1-3, John 12:14-15).
en.wikipedia.org

Sources

Books, Directories, Monographs:

Bollacker, Frances Keck, 1999, Otero Press: *History Of Otero And Crowley Counties Colorado.*
  Publisher search by author and La Junta Chamber of Commerce unproductive for permission to quote page 57.

Doll, John, 1987: Rocky Ford Archaeological Society*: The Story of Early Rocky Ford.*

Follansbee, Robert; Leon R. Sawyer, *Floods in Colorado,* US Department of the Interior, 1948.

Gilbert, Grove Karl, *1896, The Underground Water of the Arkansas Valley in Eastern Colorado.* Department of the Interior, US Geological Survey.

Ives, James, Jr., 1911: The Gazetteer Publishing Company, est. 1871: *Colorado Business Directory, Rocky Ford, Colorado, Otero County.*

McFarland, Blanche Bulifant, Ed., 1925: School District No. 4, Otero County, Rocky Ford, Colorado*: Rocky Ford As the School Children See It.*

McKinney, F.A., 1914-1915 *Rocky Ford City Directory.*

Milenski, Frank, *Papers: Water Resources Archive*, Colorado State University.

Muth, David J., 2018: Iron Gate Publishing*: Rocky Ford, Colorado–A Walk Past Local Doors.*

Parker, Willis H., c. 1921, *Pueblo's Flood in Pictures.*

Rocky Ford City Directory, c. 1945-1948, attributed to Rocky Ford *Tribune.*

Rocky Ford, Colorado in the Heart of the Great Arkansas Valley, Santa Fe Railway publication, Pueblo Litho. & Printing Co., c. June, 1902.

Sanborn Map Company, see page xiv for details.

Slaughter, Michelle A., *A History of The Dry* in *The Dry Archaeology*, Alpine Archaeological Consultants with contributions from Dores Cruz, Rebecca Goodwin, Jennifer Moon and Jessica Unger.

Spencer, D. K., *The History of the Rocky Ford, Colorado Depot, Depots, Depots Everywhere, but not one to Spare! old.atsfrr.org,* August 19, 1987.

Newspapers: issues cited on page of use: **Note**: Among several sources are red highlights from word searches.

Bent County Register, Lamar
Daily Gazette, Rocky Ford
Delta Independent, Delta
Enterprise, Rocky Ford
Leader, Las Animas
Ledger, Lamar
Record, Canon City
Tribune, Rocky Ford
New Era, Ordway
Rocky Mountain News, Denver
Tribune-Democrat, La Junta

Name Index

A

Abert, Donna L. (Burchett) 79, 164
Adams, Gov. Alva 165
Aldrich, Mr. **84**
Allen, Jack 153
Allnut, E.S. 147
Amos, Horace 16, 18, 53
Anderson (game warden) 90
   W.E. 178
Anonymous vi
Atkinson, J.W. **134**

B

Babcock, L.W. **178, 204**
Bacon. Boon **67**
Baker, Clarence, 119
Barkely, D.W. **66**, 83, **138**, 157
   D.W., Jr. 64
Barnes, Harry 118
Barney, F.L, 22
Barton, H.V. 162
   Laura 162
   Orlo M. 162, 164
Beall, R. S. **89**
Beatty, (brothers) 169
   H. S. 88
   James W. 92, **143**
   Rev. and Mrs. C.C. **107**
Beeks, Bertram 9
   Maude 9
Best, Alexander 165
   Mrs. Wallace **162**
Betterman, Mrs. 138
Beymer, Arthur S. 145, 150
   Bert **89**
Bishop, Walter **67**
Black, Charlie
   Elma 162
Boraker, Frank H. 5
   Herman 48
Bradish, Pat 61
Britt, Mr. 133
Brunstein, F.C. 146
Bryant, George 12
Buckley, H. **156**
Buis, B.R. 12
Burrell, Delavan V. 34, 64, Family **206**
Bush, (President) George H.W. 172

C

Callahan, P.L, **162-163**
Carpe, Fred A. 34
Carrier, Dr. **84**
Cartwright, Charles **66**
Catherine II, (Tsarina) 174
Chalagawtha 55

Chandler, Charles 19, 38
Chappell, Fred 109
Cheek, Fred W. 82, 204
Clark, Leo and Bill 75
   Mr. and Mrs. L.P. **75**; W.P. 41
Clute, Joyce (Bitter) 79, 164
Coffman, R.M. (mayor) 68
Cotten, Elizabeth 181
Creasy, S.W. 88
Curtis, John Bacon 138

D

Dameron, G.M. 61
Darcy, Ms. 133
Daring, George 64
Darr, Arthur 73-74
Dawley, H.A. **67**
de Lasalle, St. Jean-Baptiste 62
Denson, Mark 157-158
Dillinger, John 170
Dodd, (Pastor) Monroe E. **136**
Dodds, D.D. **136**
Doll, Mrs. Cornelia 169
   Bert 169
   Colleen 169
   John 19, 82, 106, 119, 158, **169,** 176
   John, Jr. 169
Dukes, (street supervisor) 81
Dye, B. U. 13, 28, 83-86, 88, 92-93, **134**, 169
   Mrs. B. U. **160**
   Horace B. 83-**84**, 88, 92, **143,** 169
   James K. 6

E

Ebbert, W.D. 66
Edgar, Wm. 61
Egbert, Irene 164
Elizabeth, Queen 20
Elser, Mr. and Mrs. J.J. **160**
   LeRoy 15, 53
Engle, Charles J. 10
   Maude 10
Evans, A.J. 61

F

Farmer, John S. 40
Fenlason, Leon R. 33, **99, 101**
   Blanche 172
   Charlotte L. 172
   Lawrence L. 172
   Dr. Ward C. 172
   Dr. Ward E. 172
Fielder, Naomi **102**
Follansbee, Robert 69
Ford, (President) Gerald R. 171
Frantz, George 34

G

Gallavan, George 61
Gauger, J.E. 147
Gibson, W.R. 117
Gilbert, Grove Karl **112**-113
Gilmore, Frank 157
Ging, Gee 38
Ginger, H.M. 83, 85-88, 92
Glenn, John H. Jr. 171
Gobin W.B. **66, 139, 143**
Goebel, Art **96**
Goodner, Brothers 66
Gorsuch, Lucas B., Eula, Della 74-**75**
Gracey, J.C. 88
Greear, Dr. S.J. 42
Green, Frank 81
Grenard, Gene 142
   Ruth (Muth) 79, 164
Gulch, Miss Elmira 80
Griswold, A.H. **66-67**

H

Hale, Alberta 135
Hale, (road commissioner) 119, **126**
Hall, Effie, Mrs. 4, 5
Hamilton, J.G. 86, 92
Hamlisch, Marvin 179
Hammond,George 178
Hannon, Jos. **202**
Hansborough, W.A. (Gus) 153, **156**
Happy Jack 40
Harington. Sir John, 20
Harsin, F.M. **108**-109
Hauck, Frank Y. 33
Hawley, Floyd 146, 177
Hendrick, J. M. 176
Hendrix, Thomas N. 165
Henry, Miss Edith **130**
   T. C. **156**
Herring, C.W. 135
Higgins, George 4
Hoehne, William 15
Hooper, Mary Anna, Granville **202**
Horn, Rev. J.C. **132**
Hushaw, Charles **66**

J

Jackson, A.M. 36
Jesus, The Messiah 182
John, The Chinaman, 38
Johnson Mr. (?) 70, Tom **97**
Joplin, Scott 179

K

Kane, J.E. 88
Kearby, Dr. E.W. 160
Keck, Dr. Paul P. 5, 7, 42
Keck, Frances Bollacker, 57, 174
Keith, Ray 105
Keenan, Charles E. **11**
Kennedy, Paul E. 145, 150
Kitch, Arlyn Samuel and LuLu 58
Kloberdanz, Timothy J. 175
Knaus, Frank, Fred 133

L

Lacey, Eleanor 133
Lacombe, Charles F. **143**
Lamon, Mattie (Swink) 105
Lantz, Opha, Miss **118**
Larmore, G.H. and L.W. 82, 138
Lackey, George 67
Lee, Albert 8
   Rev. W.H. **107**
Leesing, J.W. 38
Lenty, George W. **104**
Lincoln, (president)Abraham **100**, 174
Lockhart, Will **66**
Louden, R.H. 146
Lowe, James 5
Lytle, Miss (Ruth?) 16

M

Manny, Ed, 135
Manney, George **107**
Marcum, Ms. Sharon **132**
Marshall, Everett 142
Martin, A.H. **156**
   James W. 133
Mathews, S.A. 67
Matthews, William A. ix,, 139
   Mr. and Mrs, William **99, 101**
Maxwell, H.I. **84**
McCormick, Cyrus 47
McDowell, H.H. **93**
McFarland, Alfred Jackson 168
   Blanch Bulifant 56, **168**
McKinney, F.A. 54
McKracken, Frank and Mrs. Mary 170
   Robert 170
   Ronald (Ron, Ronnie) 170
Meador, George **67**
   J.D. **162**
Milenski, Eleanor (Zumbrunnen) 58
   Francis (Frank) Raymond **58**
   Victor Edward **58**
Miller, Mike 29
Mitch, John 6
Monkman, Will R. **166**, 176
Monroe, Marilyn 171
Moody, Dr, B.E. 64
   Dwight L. **107**

Morse, Harry **89**
Mossin & Marr 32
Muth C.J. 169

N
Nichols, Andy, 119, **134**
    George W. 53
Nelson, Anton 135
Noe, W.P. 19, 21

O
Old Testament Prophesy 182
Ole Peg (Peg-Leg) 40
Opothleyahola, Chief 55

P
Porter, III, Miles F. 171
    Willis H. 73
Peg-Leg (Ole Peg) 40
Pettit, Dan 61
Polhemus, Fred 135
Pollock, Dr. R.M., (Mayor) 34, **76**, 116, **118**
    Cary 64
Portus, Dr. 158
Pratt, Mrs. 73-74
Preble, G.E. **84**
Prowers, John W. 132

Q
Queen (of Sheba) **143**
Quesenberry, C.A. 146

R
Randall, G.P. 67
Recker, Charles, 22, 68, 157
Reese, Mr. **84**
Rex, J. W. 38
Ritchie, Will 162-**163**
Romero, Oley 133
Russell, Asa 28
    W.H. 4, 22

S
Sallen, Joseph, **107**
Salls, P. 19, 38
Sawyer, Leon R. 69
Scott, G.R. 146
Seeley, J. S. 19
Shelton, A.W. 143, 145, 150
    B. A. 64
Sinsheimer, S.W. 158
Smith, F.W. **66**
Snow, Cecil V. 202
Solomon (King) **143**

Spencer, D.K. 14, 44, 52-53
Stailey, J.W. 153, **155-156**
Steele, W.C. 78, 178
Stevenson, Mr, **84**
Swink, E.E. **99**
    George Washington (G.W.) 14, 18-19, 25, 29, 78, 85, 92, **100**, **102**, 105-106, (senator) 109, **143**, 145, **147-148**, 157-158, 169, **178**
    Mattie 53
Swink Family Residence **133**

T
Tecumseh 55
Tenskwatawa 55
Terry, N.W. 204
Thomas, George H. 88
Tinsley, Jack 34
Todd, Joel W. 72
Traber, Mr. 69

V
Van Buskirk, Dr. H. 66
Vroman, Ben 5

W
Warburton, Jay **132**
Weid, Karl and family **76**
    Lucille **76**
Welland, F.W. 135
Werkema, Evan 18
Whisky Jack 40
White, Mr.? 22
Whitsett, H.A. **161**
Wieland, F.W. **143**
Wiley, Mr. 145
Williams, A.J. 159
Wilson, A. Garfield **179**
    William H. 169
Winker, John 31
Wolf, J.W. 38
Worker, Frances B. 174
Wright, O.E. 135
Wykle, Mrs. Mandana 137
    W.P. 137

Y
Young, S.H. **102**

Z
Zimmerman, Earl **94-96**
Zumbrunnen, Eleanor 58

General Index

Place names and subjects are included in this section.
Page numbers with illustrations are in bold print.

A

American Beet Sugar Co. 26-27, 43, **72-73, 114, 119,** 127, 146, 162, **201**
ABSC Factory Corrals 141
American Crystal Sugar Co. 110-111, **114**, 146, 162
Aeronautics Branch, Department of Commerce 97
Agricultural Building (1898) **49**
Air Commerce Act 96
Air Navigation Ground Markings **97-98**
Alex (fire horse) 33
American Legion **76,** 94, 96
Ames Construction Co. 158
Amity Dam 71
Anderson Arroyo 70
Apishapa Creek 72
Aragon Tavern **11**
Arkansas River, Basin , Valley 69-70, 71, 85, 93-**94, 110,** 112-113, **126, 128-129**
Arkansas River Conduit 129
Arkansas Valley 143
    Dance Club 142
    Experiment Station **48**
    Valley Fair 48
    Fair Association 100
    Fair Board **49, 51**
    Gun Club 99, 101
    Railroad 143, **145**-146, 150, 152
    Seminary, Caddoa **132**
    Traction Company (Trolley) 143, 145, **147-148**
    Stock Certificate **148**
Arlington Café **202**
Artesian well, (1895), **199**
Arts Building, (1901), **50**
Aschermann Cigar and Tobacco Co. 32
Atcheson, Topeka & Santa Fe Railroad 15 , 52, **128,** 146
    Depot 14
Automobile Activity 64, **200**
    In Town 66
Author's License 80

B

Bailey's Grocery 10
Ball Games **45**
    A Game of Base Ball **46**
Barnes Park 118
Barton, New Town of **161**
Barton School (Grand Valley) 161, 164-**165**
B & A. I. E. Center 4, 7
Bath Rooms 21

Beek's Grocery **9**
Beet Dump **202**
Bent County Register **45**
Bent County School District (No. 15), 165
Benzine Buggies and Buzz Wagons 67
Best, Barton, Grand ValleySchool 164-165
Big Four Cash Grocery 38
Big Warrior 55
Bish Hardware, Lumber, Feed, Furniture 12
Boardwalk to the Country School 79, 164
Bonta Mercantile 38
Boardwalk School 164
Bridge (Saint James) **37**
Bridges Over the Arkansas **120, 130**
    After Flood 121
    Bridge Pilings, 1894 Site **124**
    Bridge Structure **125**
    Conduit over the River **127**
    First Bridge, (1888), 119, 124
    Flood Damage, (1894), 126
    Postal Card, 1908 (Rocky Ford Bridge), **130**
    Rocky Ford Bridge **73, 127, 130**
    State Hwy 71 Bridge 119-**120,**
    Satellite View (Wagon Road Bridge site), **120-121**
    State Hwy 266 Bridge 119, **123,** 126
    Wagon Road Bridge, **120-122, 125,** 127, **128**
Bruse Variety Store 138
Bryant and Johnston, Company **12**
Bullen Bridge Co. **126**
Burrell Seeds Catalog **206**
Business News 133-140
    Central Hotel 138
    Commercial Hotel 138
    C. R. Herring Garage 135
    Dodd's Commercial College **136**
    Editor Admonishes Gum-Chewers 138
    Fillers (newspaper) **137**
    George Higgins 1900 Livery 4-5, 135
    Hotel Welcome Home / Rockford Hotel 134
    Knaus Barber Shop 133
    Larmore Brick Kiln 82, 138
    Melon Field, Inc. 135
    Mexican Laborers 138
    New Method Laundry / Valley Laundries, Inc. 135
    Peanut Stand of W.P. Wykle **137**
    Rocky Ford Floral Company 135
    Rocky Ford Woman's Club 135
    T. B. Sanitarium 41, 143
    Watering Troughs 135
    Will and B.U. Dye Barn and Livery 134, 198
    Wilson Hotel 139

C

Cadillac, **64-65**
Caddoa, (Caddo) Colorado **132**
Caddos (tribe) 132
Calaboose (1895) **39**
    Amenities 40
Camp Meeting 200
Catholic Church 16, **41**
Catlin Bridge 126
    Canal 5, **128**, 153-154, 161, **163**
Cement Stone Co. 82
Central Meat Market **8**
    Park, (Railroad Park) 12, **130**
Cheraw (Ke-raw) **173**
    Lake **173**
Chewing Gum 55, **138**
Chinese Laundry 38
Chronology, events at Dye's Lake **92-93**
Cigar token 32
Circulating Library 118
City Dump (1927) **123**
City Drug 107
City Hospital 42
Clark's Food Market 75
Clettrac 90
Clubs of Rocky Ford 59-60
Colorado Agricultural College **68**
    A & M, NCAA 142
    Federation of Woman's Clubs **116**
Colorado Flight Fields 94
Colorado-Kansas Diversion Dam 71
Colorado State College 62
    State College of Education 62
    State Teachers College 62
    Traveling Library Commission **116**
Conduit over River **127**
Cottonwoods 90
Cottonwood Field 96
Country School 78, **81**, 164
    on Washington Road **81**
Cripple Creek 72, 156
Crossing the River 119
Cuban Independence 81
Culling's Hill (Reservoir Hill) 21, 34

D

Delta Independent 15
District R2 Administration Building 168
Denver and Rio Grande 70
Denver House **159**
Denver, Texas and Gulf Railroad 15

Denver Theater **159**
Department of Commerce 97- 98
    of Interior 113
Depot or Station 52
De Seeley Hotel (Seeley) 78, **198**
Dickenson & Davis Groceries and Provisions **8**
Distributive Preemption Act 100
Doc and Bonnie's Café 171
Dodd's Commercial College **136**
Doll, John, published and unpublished papers **169**
Doll, Johnny, Pine Avenue Garage **169**
Donkey Baseball **182**
Double Entendre Names 117
Dry, The 174
Dye's Lake 90, **94-95**, 109, **112**, 119, **128**, **152**
    Lake Aerial View **91**
    Lake Chronology **92-93**
    Lake Fishery 83, 85-86
    Lake Hunting **89**
    Lake Improvements 83-**84**
    Lake Transition to Dye Reservoir 92
    Reservoir Road 123

E

Earl Zimmerman Airport (1936), **94**
Earl Zimmerman Remnant (2018) **95**
East Ranch **110-111, 114**
Eighth Street Crossing **x**
Elaterite, A Fire Hazard 34
El Capital Hotel 82
Elk's Lodge **102**, 172
End of a good Business 87
Engle Grocery **10**
English Lumber Co. 34; R. W. English Lumber Co. **58**
Ersatz KKK In Rocky Ford **56**
Ethnic Groups **174**-175
    Black-American 174
    German, Germans from Russia 174-175
    Hispanic-American 174
    Japanese-American 175

F

Factory **XII**
Fads and Fashions of 1910s **138**
Failing Effort (Dye Fishery) 88
Fairground Construction and Additions **51**
Farmville State Teachers College 168
Fats, (see Leans) Team) 46
Fenton Family 172
    Drug Store 5
    Station (Siding) 173

Fenton Lake **173**
Fillers (newspaper) **137**
Fire Department (First, 1895) 34
    Big Fire (1898) 87, **205**
First Church of Christ Scientist 68, **118**
First National Bank 138
Fish Culture in Dye's Lake 85-86
Fisher Smith Hospital **41**-42
First Floods in the Arkansas Valley 69-73
    Damage, (1894) 70, **126**
    In the Wake, 74
    Near Rocky Ford, 72
    Restoration, (1921), **75**
    Satellite View, (2005) **121**
    Floods in Colorado, US Department of the Interior
      1948 Publication 69, 71
Fluke and Ritchie grocery 105
Ford Company Garage **6**, Ford Model T **6**, 63
Fort Collins Hose Cart Co. **33**
Fort Lyon 69
Frame Depot No. 1 for Branch Lines 18
Free Reading Room **116**
Funk's Confectionary 4
F.Y. Hauck Hose Cart Company **33**
    Hose Cart Action **33**

G

Garden Place 25, 81
    Hospital and Sanitarium 41
Gerbing's Slaughter House **89**
Gibson Lumber 28
    Racket Store 117
Grand Army of the Republic, (G.A.R.) 5
Grand Valley, (Best, Barton School) 161-162, 164
    Branch Line 146
    Livery 7, 42
    School District(No. 29) 165
Grape Creek 70
Great American Desert 93
    Plains (Colorado) 149
    Sand Dunes National Park 113
Green and Babcock 40

H

Hardscrabble bridge 70
Harsin Lake 90, **108**, 109, **128**
    Area Aerial View (1936) **110**
    County Site and Road Identification **108**
    Curious Water Flow 113
    Flood Interaction 113
    Historical Enigma 112
    Map View (1893 to 1895) **112**
    Mining **115**
    Natural Lake (c. 1893) **112**
    Satellite View (2020) **114**

    Satellite View (2021) **111, 114**
Hasty, Colorado 132
Hawley (Hauck Houck) 146, 162
    Store, (Meador) 161-**162**-163
Hay Palace, (1893) **47**, (1898) **48**
Herring Garage 135
Hillcrest Cemetery 5
Hoehne 16, 18
    Depot 14-**15**
    Ditch Co. 15
Holbrook Canal 85, **91**, **94**
    Center 144, 150, 152
    Irrigation District **93**
    Lake 90, 143, 152, **173**
    Lake Pavilion 142
    Holbrook Valley 119, 123, 129-130, 150-151
Holly and Swink Railroad 145, 150
Home Remedy 160
Honolulu Airplane Race 96
Horse (game) 170
Horton's Market 58
Hospitals of Rocky Ford **41**
    City Hospital 42
    Fisher Smith Hospital 41-42
    Garden Place Hospital-Sanitarium 41
    Physicians Hospital 41
    Pioneer Health Care Center 41
    Pioneer Memorial 41
    Red Cross Hospital 42
    T B Sanitarium 41
    Van Antwerp Sanitarium 41-42
Hudson's Bay Co. 69

I

Ice Blocks **27**
Ichi Ban Restaurant 138
IOOF Hall, Building (1892), **13**, **37**- 38
Iris and Isis Theaters 140

J

John Martin Reservoir 71
Johnny Doll Pine Avenue Garage **169**
June Rise 113

K

Kansas Pacific Railroad 146
KKK A personal anecdote **58**
    In the Arkansas Valley 57
Keck Veterinary Hospital **7**
Keenan Cash Produce Company **11**
Ke-raw (Cheraw) **152**
King's Arroyo Bridge 70, 139
    Ferry 139
Kit Carson Road 16, (Nichols Avenue)
    (Tenth Street) 52, 78
Kitch Feed Lot **141**

King's Crossing 74
Knight's Ferry 139
Knights of Pythias 6
Knockers, Kickers, and Croakers **166**

L
Laborers **203**
La Clinica del Valle' 5
Lake Street 25
Las Animas City (West Las Animas) **146**
Leans, see *Fats* (Team) 46
Leroy's Market **9**
Liberty School **4**-5, 82, **101, 203**
Life and Death Cycle of an Agricultural Town 149
Lincoln School 9
Little Arkansas River 113
Little Frame Box 14, 16-18
Little White Schoolhouse 5
Loaf 'N Jug 67
Long Route **128**
Longworth Hotel 38

M
Mahout 63
Main Street Crossing **12**
Man About Town 170-171
Manby Lale **173**
Marbles (game) 170
Martin General Store (Note) 138
Mayor's Proclamation **64**, Home **201**
McPherson Lumber Co. 67
Medano Creek 113; *June Rise* 113
Meador Store, (Hawley Store) **163**
Memento spoon 52
Mexico Road 53
Mitchell Wagon **13**
Municipal Reservoir, (1936) **102**
Muscogee Creek Indian Confederacy 55

N
Namesake Rocky Fords 127
Newdale Siding 101, 110-111, 163
New Madrid, Missouri 55
Newton Lumber 28
Nichols Avenue (Kit Carson Road, Tenth Street) 52
Nimrod 29
Normalites 62
    Function of the Normal School 62
    In Colorado 62
    Normalites Now 62, New Normal 62,
North La Junta 74
North Main Street at 400
N.W. Terry Brick Kiln 82, 204

O
Obelisks **43**

O'Brien Printing Company, 73
Ochre Mountain 153, Postulated **154, 156**
Ockham's razor xiii-xiv
Oil Creek 72
Oil Well **202**
Old Rocky Ford 28, 53, 72, 74, 119-**120**
Old School 164
Oldsmobile **67**
Old Stone Foundation 139
Omaha, Nebraska, Watermelon Day 35
Omar, Colorado 163
Otero Canal **154**
    County 105, 164
        Health Department 6, **118**, 157
        Inter-urban Light and Power Co. 143
        Register of Historic Places and Sites 79
        School District (No. 1), 164-165
        School District (No. 29), 164
Otero Junior College 10
    Child Development Service **165**

P
Pacific House Hotel 68, **159**
Pageant of States and Nations 35
Panic (of 1907) 151
Park Hotel 68
Patterson Hollow 139
Peanut Stand 137
Peneplane 154
Peoples Mission **107**
Philistine 46
Physicians Hospital 41
Pioneer Health Care Center 41; Memorial Hospital 41
P. Lorillard Tobacco Co. 31-32
Plants around Dye's Lake **84**
Point of Rocks 74
Polar Ice & Storage Co. **26**
Pollock Hospital, 42
Postal Card, (1908) **130**
Prairie Valley School 174
Pressure Pumping Station 34
Priorities (water) 93
Prince (fire horse) 33
Pueblo and Arkansas Valley Railroad 14, 146
Pueblo's Flood in Pictures, 73
Purgatoire River 69-72

R
Racket Store/s 117
Railroad Park, (Central Park) 12, **130**
Rails in S.E. Colorado 146
    Arkansas Valley Railway 146
    Atcheson, Topeka and Santa Fe Railway 146
    Grand Valley Branch Line 146
    Kansas Pacific Railroad 146
    Pueblo and Arkansas Valley Railroad 146

Recker's Hall **13,** 159
Red Cross Hospital 42
Red Men's Lodge **61**
Rest Room/s 116-118
    Free Reading Room 116
Reservoir Hill (Culling's Hill) 21, 34
Rhoades Food Center 140
Ribeye Feeders **141**
River flow, *June Rise* 113
Roaring Twenties 117
Roberta, Colorado 163
Rockford Hotel (Hotel Welcome Home)**134**
Rocky Ford Air Circus, (1930) **96**
    Automobile Club **66**
    Ball Club (of 1907), **45**
    Bridge (on SH 266) **73, 127, 130**
    Café **68**
    Cigar/s **31-32**
    Creamery Co. **204**
    Daily Gazette vii, 79
    Ditch (Canal) 7, 25-27, 78, **108, 128**
        141, 171
    Duck Shooting Club 99
    Dyke Road 85, **94, 123**
    Fire Wagon 33
    Gun Club **89**
    High School 10, **102, 130**
    Ice and Storage Co. 106
    Melon Boys 45
        (Rocky Ford Team, Rocky Ford Nine) 45
    Milling and Elevator Co. **200**
    School District (No. 4), 168
    School District R2 Administration 168
    Watermelon Pickers (Ragtime Tune) **181**
    Siege Gun, **35**
    State Bank 150
    Trading Co. 12
    Town and Investment Co. 39, 78
Rocky Mountain News 25-26, 31
Rollicking Twenties 117
Royal Gorge 69
Russell Cigar Factory 6

S
Safeway Store 138
Sanborn Map Company xiv
    Map of 1895 Rocky Ford **180**
Sangre de Cristo Mountains 113
Saint James Bridge 23
    Hotel 19, 21
    Bathrooms Attached 21
    Something New is Added 21
    Hotel (1892), **37**
    Water Closet 20
Saint Matthews Episcopal Mission **118**
Santa Fe bridge at Nepesta 73

Depot, Rocky Ford 14, 20, 68
    Railroad 143, 152
    Stockyards (1893, 1902) **43-44**
Santa Fe Trail 69, 155
School District (No. 1) 164
    District (No. 4), 78
    District (R2), 9
Schultz Engraving Company 73
Scorching Automobiles **63, 200**
Secret Societies 54
Shelton Afterword 151
    and Holbrook Center **173**
    At Holbrook Lake 144, 152, **173**
    Disappearance 150
    Panic of 1907
    Realty Co. **151**
Sheridan Lake **156**
Short Route **128**
Sink Box **89**
Soil Conservation Service 43
Solis Cigar Factory 31
South Dakota Agricultural College 7
South Main Street, (1905) **13, 65, 75**
Spanish-American War 81
Specimen Room 79
Spoons 36, Memento 52
Spot Café 172
Stage line (Barlow & Sanderson) vi, 178
Standard Rod and Gun Club **84**, 90
State Wildlife Area **123**
    Ryan's Ponds **123**
Stauffer's Market 140
    Packing Plant 24, 43, 105-106
Stone Quarry **128, 155**
Stoop and Green Lumber Co. 12
Studebaker **67**
Swink's Artificial Lake **24**-26, 90, 101, **103-104**
    106-107, 109, 158
    Baptism at Swink Lake 107
    Evidence for the Lake 105
    Garden Place and Swink's Artificial Lake 25
    Ice Production and Competition **27**, 105
    Plausible Location **24**
    Possible suicide 106
    Satellite View **24**
    Swink Lake in History 105
    Swink's Lake Ice Blocks **27**
    Swink Lake Postal Card **104**
    Water Sports 109
Swink Store **29, 134**
    and Holly Railroad 150
    Family Residence **133**
    Hotel **21, 37-38**
    Hotel, Sunday Dinner 19
    Lake near Fairgrounds **99, 109**
    Lake Hunting **99**
    Lake Sold **100**

Swink Milling and Grain Co. 12, **200**
Swink (Natural) Lake 99
Swink Recreation Parlor 4
Swink-Russell 1871 Adobe Store **x**
    1876 Store **28-29**, 52
        Partial Inventory **29**
Swink Timber Claim No. 1, **viii**
    Remnants (timber) **30**
    Certificate **viii**
    Trolley Line **148**

T
Target 117
Taylor Lake **173**
Teachers' Lounge 79
Tenth Street (Nichols Avenue, Kit Carson Road) 52
Texas Creek 15-16, 18
THE Clubs of Rocky Ford 59
The Rubber Hose 80
The Wizard of Oz 80
Timpas, Colorado 163
    Creek 27, 72, 82, **108**, 161
Town Characters 40
Town Not Mapped **152**
Traction Engine 106, **203**
    Coffee, (1887), 157
    in Rocky Ford History 158
Tuck-A-Batchee Club **55**
Two-Butte Creek 71
Two-story Privy 19

U
University of Northern Colorado 62
US Department of Agriculture **68**, 128, 153
    of the Interior 69, 112-113
        Geological Survey 112-113
        Post Office **201**
Union Cleaners and Pressers 75
Union Pacific Railroad 146

V
Valley Concrete 106
Van Antwerp Sanitarium 41-42
Van Buskirk Seed Company 196

W
Wagon, Mitchell, catalog 13
Wagon Road and Wagon Bridge **122, 125-126, 128**
    Aerial view **120**
    Map **128**
Walmart 117
Walgreens 117
Washington Road 78-79
    School 20, 78-82, 170
Water closet (W.C.) 23

Well head manifold **199**
White School House 5
William C. Steele Letter **178**

Y
Youmger Set **55**
    Skater 109
    Trees 105

Z
Zimmerman Airport (1936), **94**
    Remnant, airport, (2018), **95**
Zone (modern farming) **173**

Previous volume by author.

Rocky Ford, Colorado—A Walk Past Local Doors:

Businesses and Residences from the Fairgrounds to Reservoir Hill, US 50 Curve to Curve

by David J. Math

Van Buskirk Seed Company

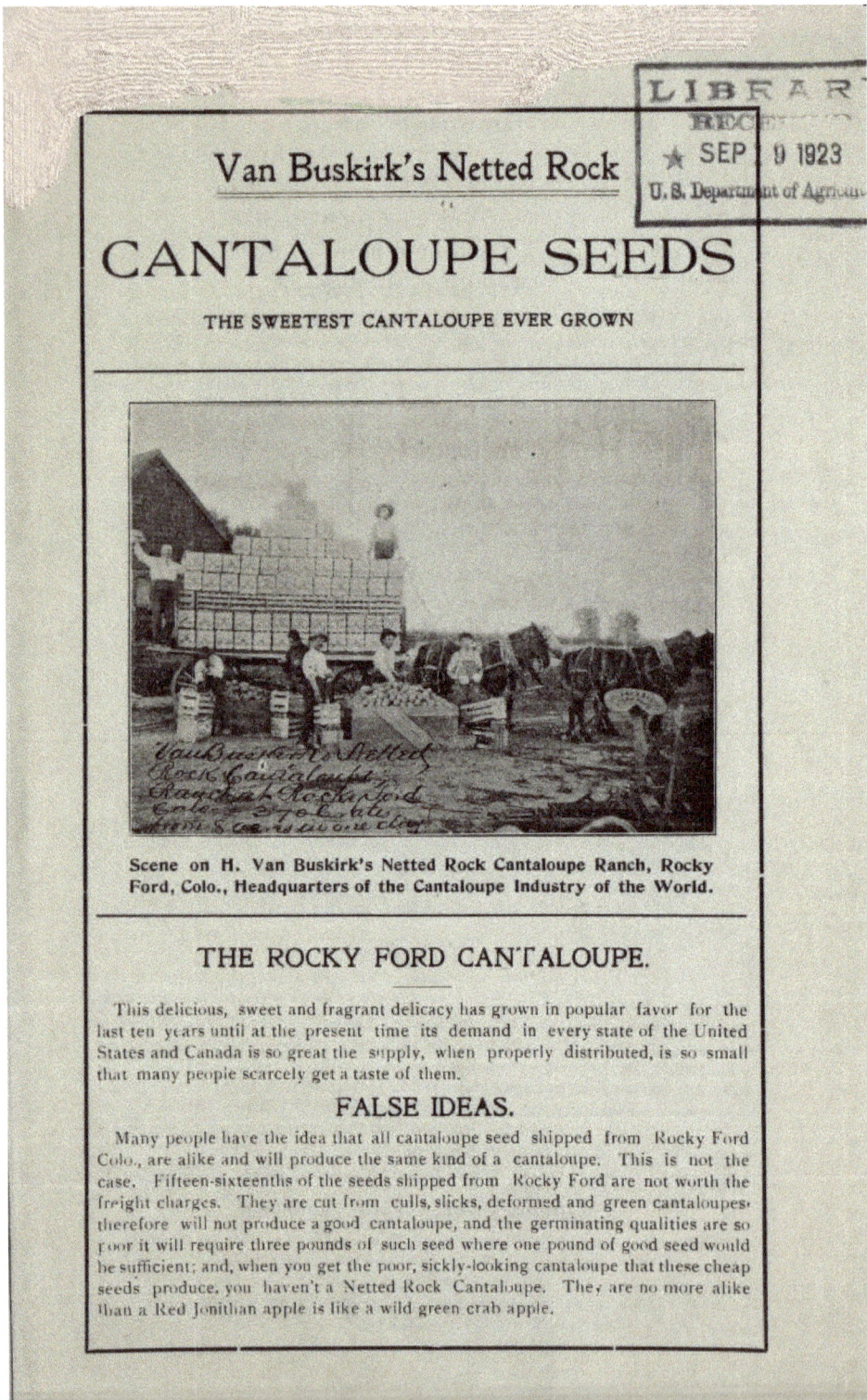

Handwritten notation at bottom of photo:

Van Buskirk Netted Rock Cantaloupes Raised at Rocky Ford, Colo.-370 crates from 8 acres in one day.

Individuals in the photo are not identified.

Courtesy *worthpoint*

Several seed company catalogs were printed over many years in Rocky Ford. This vintage copy survived from H. Van Buskirk who was also mayor of Rocky Ford 1909-1911.

Addendum

Continuing research after pages are ready to publish frequently discovers items which should be included. Such comprise this section.

First Business Block in Rocky Ford, c. 1886

Photo courtesy of Rocky Ford Public Library

Blacksmith and Repair Shop facade at far right in this photo is enlarged in the small photo c. 1890s. Signs advertise *Horseshoe Tobacco* and *Diamond Soap*. Apparatus at left bottom is built to hold wagon wheels horizontally for repair. *Rocky Ford, Colorado-A Walk Past Local Doors* reveals business of other shops in the large photo.

Frequently, vintage photos such as these corroborate one another. Both were from separate photographers, in time as well as years. They photographed lively businesses on Rocky Ford's original Main Street.

So few photos exist of town before the turn of 1900 they are much valued for historical preservation. The large photo has been identified with publication dates of 1881, 1884, and 1886. The smaller one listed as circa 1890s may well have been taken during one of those years. Signs, although indistinct, indicate advertising, improvements or possibly change of ownership, frequent in some businesses.

Hotel De Seeley anchored the block as businesses carried on trade for a few years before the town re-plat in 1887, after the failure of the 1876 start. That encouraged moves from this original Main Street to other locations. By 1894 the city was again re-platted. Possibly by then all but the two-story adobe livery of Will and B.U. Dye, not pictured, stood at the corner of the intersection of Eleventh Street and the former Main Street, now Railroad Avenue.

Archives and Special Collections, Colorado State University Libraries, Colorado State University

198

First Artesian Well, 1895

Photo courtesy *worthpoint.com*

September 7, 1911, a Thursday and Watermelon Day. At this morning hour few people or vehicles are seen. The near intersection is North Main and Railroad Avenue with Rocky Ford National Bank behind the trees.

Tent awning at left advertises *Information Bureau* and *Public Comfort Headquarters* next to undetermined vendor kiosks and their offers.

Photo enlargement reveals a type of wellhead manifold set in the concrete sidewalk. Black image at right suggests several ports for gage, valve or hose attachments. The manifold marks the 1895 artesian well, first in town. The location is today extant, covered with a simple iron cover identified as *Water,* the well long ago piped into the city delivery system at Reservoir Hill..

Black image from
thumbs.dreamstime.com

Some trees remain on Main Street although their removal was coincident with addition of sidewalks, storm drains and in fourteen more years Main Street paving.

Photos in Another Perspective

Cartwright Building 421 North Main Street. Charles Cartwright offered the REO automobile and later Gene Shelton the Buick at this location.

North Main Street from near tracks. No horses or mules in 1930. Only the *Tin Lizzie* and those *Scorching Automobiles*.

Swink *Factory* 100 South Twelfth Street where Swink Grain, Flour Mill and Elevator stood near tracks.

The first Camp Meeting was held here in 1879 preceding the factory construction.

Photos courtesy *worthpoint.com*

Addendum

Photos in Another Perspective

Whatever they did in the factory in 1910, they were busily at it.

Home of the Mayor April 3, 1910, the Honorable H. Van Buskirk.

US Post Office was at this time in the south store front of the Knights of Pythius building, 401 North Main Street, center, c. 1902.

Photos courtesy *worthpoint.com*

Photos in Another Perspective

Arlington Café was open all night, made possible because the staff lived in rooms on second story.

Proprietors Mary Anna and Granville Hooper stand at their 308 South Main Street entrance.

Cook Cecil V. Snow and dishwasher Jos. Hannon roomed upstairs.

Waiting at a beet dump near town in 1910. We dump this load and go home for another.

Drilling for oil near Rocky Ford in 1910. Searching for water was a better deal.

Photos courtesy *worthpoint.com*

Addendum

Photos in Another Perspective

Traction engine or steam engine at stationary position working a cable and reel in tandem with another at right, out of photo, by alternately pulling five-bottom plow across field near Rocky Ford.

Another view of Liberty School at 401 North Tenth Street as it would have appeared after 1899-1900 before removal of the peaked third story and modification of the roof.

This field receives attention of pickers pausing for this photo. Cucumbers or possibly cantaloupe are waiting for picking and sorting for market.

An orchard appears in background.

Photos courtesy *worthpoint.com*

Rocky Ford Creamery Company

A small frame building at Thirteenth Street and Walnut Avenue preceded this large brick one. This brick building was in operation in 1897, about two years after the first Sanborn Map of 1895 Rocky Ford was drawn.

The preceding small frame building housed a cream separator and was powered by a liquid propane boiler-(LP BLR)-according to map notes. It had a composition roof, not conducive to fire prevention or reduction.

If L.W. Babcock was the proprietor at Thirteenth and Walnut Avenue he most of all was eager to have larger, safer facilities. His new brick creamery building, built by Contractor Fred Cheek beginning January 27, 1897 was completed and operational that year.

Mr. Cheek used the locally-produced brick from N.W. Terry's kiln at the east end of Maple Avenue. Transportation of the brick involved a short haul from the kiln, across the tracks to Thirteenth Street, crossing Elm Avenue to 1300 Elm on the future corner.

From *Rocky Ford, Colorado in the Heart of the Great Arkansas Valley*, Pueblo Litho & Prtg Co. Pueblo, CO c. June 1902.

Streets were rudimentary but the creamery was established on the future US 50-Elm Avenue, proving an advantageous business location with access for local farmers and their milk deliveries.

Note: N.W. Terry brick Yard began firing brick October 1894 when Fred Cheek was Yard Manager. Mr. Terry sold the yard to Fred W. Cheek and Sons, contractors, soon after completion of the sugar factory in 1900.

Before the 1898 Fire

Courtesy Rocky Ford Public Museum

Fair week during September 8, 1898 the even numbered addresses of the 200 block on the east side of Main Street burned. Fire started in the drug store and spread in both directions. Paints among the drug store merchandise were involved. All buildings were lost until complete rebuilding by 1900. New construction was all brick, seen below as photographed in 1909. Of course, the trees suffered in the conflagration.

After, fire was a terrible memory.

Courtesy *worthpoint.com*

D. V. Burrell and our "All-America" Selections Winner, Burrell's Yellow Valencia Onion.

Burrell's Better Seeds FOR 1941 — We Invite the Planting of These Seed in Comparison with Those Obtained from Any Other Source.

SEED MAN of Rocky Ford

Delevan V. Burrell stands in one of his many productive experimental crop fields.

D.V. Burrell, as he was known, was involved in constant research that brought to fruition the best seed that his plants could provide in the environments the fields around Rocky Ford and the Arkansas Valley could support.

The entire family from
D.V. Burrell, Sr. and Maude,
to
D.V. and Mabel, Dennis R., John H.,
to
J.H. and Amelia, Bernita Maude, William E.,
and
Jimmie and Helen with their family Mary Lois, and Joyce Ann worked as seedsmen and women among their several other life pursuits.

Since 1900 to now the Burrell legacy continues under *Burrell Seed Growers, LLC* at 405 North Main Street guided by Greg Smith.

Courtesy *worthpoint.com*

The Burrell business motto: *AS GOOD AS GROW FOR YOU TO SOW*